Pirandello: *Six Characters in Search of an Author*

Since its explosive premiere in Rome in 1921, *Six Characters in Search of an Author* has gained worldwide recognition. Pirandello's challenge to the very notion of stage representation was taken up by the leading directors of the time. The playwright incorporated details from the early performances into his revised text, which he directed himself in 1925. Jennifer Lorch examines the two texts in the context of different theatrical traditions and traces Pirandello's growing awareness of the development of advanced theatrical facilities outside Italy. She also offers an analysis of selected productions of the play in Italy, England, France, the USA, Germany and Russia in both commercial and avant-garde theatres. This comprehensive study includes a production chronology, bibliography and illustrations from major productions.

PLAYS IN PRODUCTION

Series editor: Michael Robinson

PUBLISHED VOLUMES

Ibsen: *A Doll's House* by Egli Törnqvist
Miller: *Death of a Salesman* by Brenda Murphy
Molière: *Don Juan* by David Whitton
Wilde: *Salome* by William Tydeman and Steven Price
Brecht: *Mother Courage and Her Children* by Peter Thomson
Williams: *A Streetcar Named Desire* by Philip C. Kolin
O'Neill: *Long Day's Journey into Night* by Brenda Murphy
Albee: *Who's Afraid of Virginia Woolf?* by Stephen J. Bottoms
Beckett: *Waiting for Godot* by David Bradby
Pirandello: *Six Characters in Search of an Author* by Jennifer Lorch

PIRANDELLO
Six Characters in Search of an Author

*

JENNIFER LORCH
University of Warwick

CAMBRIDGE
UNIVERSITY PRESS

PUBLISHED BY THE PRESS SYNDICATE OF THE UNIVERSITY OF CAMBRIDGE
The Pitt Building, Trumpington Street, Cambridge, United Kingdom

CAMBRIDGE UNIVERSITY PRESS
The Edinburgh Building, Cambridge, CB2 2RU, UK
40 West 20th Street, New York, NY 10011–4211, USA
477 Williamstown Road, Port Melbourne, VIC 3207, Australia
Ruiz de Alarcón 13, 28014 Madrid, Spain
Dock House, The Waterfront, Cape Town 8001, South Africa

http://www.cambridge.org

First published 2005

Printed in the United Kingdom at the University Press, Cambridge

Typeface Adobe Garamond 10.75/14 pt.   *System* LaTeX 2$_\varepsilon$ [TB]

A catalogue record for this book is available from the British Library

Library of Congress Cataloguing in Publication data
Lorch, Jennifer.
Pirandello: *Six characters in search of an author* / Jennifer Lorch.
p.   cm. – (Plays in production)
Includes bibliographical references and index.
ISBN 0 521 64151 9 (hardback) – ISBN 0 521 64618 9 (paperback)
1. Pirandello, Luigi, 1867–1936. *Sei personaggi in cerca d'autore.*   2. Pirandello, Luigi,
1867–1936 – Dramatic production.   3. Pirandello, Luigi, 1867–1936 – Stage history.
I. Title.   II. Series.
PQ4835.I7S4348   2004
852′.912 – dc22   2004045817

ISBN 0 521 64151 9 hardback
ISBN 0 521 64618 9 paperback

CONTENTS

ILLUSTRATIONS

Note: Every effort has been made to trace the copyright holders of the illustrations included in this volume. Any queries concerning copyright should be directed to Cambridge University Press, The Edinburgh Building, Cambridge CB2 2RU.

GENERAL PREFACE

Volumes in the series Plays in Production take major dramatic texts and examine their transposition, firstly on to the stage and, secondly, where appropriate, into other media. Each book includes concise but informed studies of individual dramatic texts, focusing on the original theatrical and historical context of a play in relation to its initial performance and reception followed by subsequent major interpretations on stage, both under the impact of changing social, political and cultural values, and in response to developments in the theatre generally.

Many of the plays also have been transposed into other media – film, opera, television, ballet – which may well be the form in which they are first encountered by a contemporary audience. Thus, a substantial study of the play-text and the issues it raises for theatrical realization is supplemented by an assessment of such adaptations as well as the production history, where the emphasis is on the development of a performance tradition for each work, including staging and acting styles, rather than simply the archaeological reconstruction of past performances.

Plays included in the series are all likely to receive regular performance and individual volumes will be of interest to the informed reader as well as to students of theatre history and literature. Each book also contains an annotated production chronology as well as numerous photographs from key performances.

Michael Robinson
University of East Anglia

ACKNOWLEDGEMENTS

I have been much helped in the writing of this book by friends, colleagues and institutions. My thanks go first of all to the many Pirandello specialists, theatre scholars and practitioners who have been so generous with their time and materials; in particular, Clive Barker, Birgit Beumers, Guy Callan, Orazio Costa, Alessandro d'Amico, Felicity Firth, Anna Frabetti, Richard Jones, Anna Laura Lepschy, Dick McCaw, Mario Missiroli, François Orsini, Domenico Pietropaolo, Sacha Pitoëff, Michael Rössner, Alessandro Tinteri and Anatoli Vasiliev.

My visits to libraries and archive collections have been much enhanced by staff who have gone out of their way to help in my work: Joël Huthwohl of the Bibliothèque of the Comédie française, Annette Fern of the Houghton Library of the Harvard College Library, Olga Khramtsova of the Moscow School of Dramatic Art, Louise Ray of the National Theatre Archives, London, Gian Domenico Ricaldone of the Biblioteca dell'Attore, Genoa, and staff of the British Library and the New York Library for the Performing Arts, Lincoln Centre.

As any one who has attempted to do this knows, the acquisition of illustrations can be both time-consuming and frustrating. I have been most fortunate in my dealings with Birgit Beumers of the University of Bristol, Annette Fern of the Houghton Library of the Harvard College Library, James McDougall of Group Three Photography, Mélanie Petetin of the Comédie française and Gian Domenico Ricaldone of the Biblioteca dell'Attore, Genoa. That I have not always used the photographs provided in no way diminishes my appreciation of their assistance.

The research materials for this book exceeded my linguistic competence. It is with much gratitude, therefore, that I thank two translators, who translated material from German referring to Klaus Michael Grüber and Anatoli Vasiliev: Andrea Klaus and Richard Lorch.

I wish also to record my gratitude to the British Academy whose award of a Small Research Grant enabled me to spend some time in Rome and Genoa researching the Italian productions included in this volume.

I am grateful, too, to Michael Robinson, the series editor, and Vicki Cooper of Cambridge University Press who have waited with patient forbearance for the completion of this volume, and to Libby Willis, the copy editor, whose efficient and courteous attention to detail has much improved the text. (Any remaining errors are, of course, mine.)

And, finally, a heartfelt 'thank you' to those who have given me support and encouragement along the way: in particular, to members of the Society for Pirandello Studies and of the Department of Italian at the University of Warwick, and to a longstanding friend from undergraduate days, Patricia West. I have much appreciated the support of colleagues, friends and family. Unfortunately, the person to whom I owe most can no longer receive my thanks: Meg Stacey died while this book was in production. My debt to her is immeasurable.

Jennifer Lorch

INTRODUCTION

Six Characters in Search of an Author is now recognised as a classic of modernism; many would echo Felicity Firth's words, asserting that it is 'the major single subversive moment in the history of modern theatre'.[1] In 1921 its story of family strife and sexual horror, set within the philosophical context of relativism, and its self-conscious form provided a double-pronged challenge: to bourgeois social values, and to the accepted mode of naturalist theatre-making. *Six Characters* is a deeply disturbing play as well as an intensely exciting one. It was also very influential. Written and presented in Italy long before the word 'director' became part of the Italian vocabulary, it gained its early European and American reputation through the work of particular directors: Theodore Komisarjevsky, Brock Pemberton, Georges Pitoëff and Max Reinhardt. Georges Pitoëff's production in Paris in April 1923 was to be recognised as a major force in shaping subsequent French theatre. In other countries the influence is perhaps less distinct, and becomes blurred with that of other Pirandello plays. Certainly, Alan Ayckbourn, Samuel Beckett, Nigel Dennis, Michael Frayn, Harold Pinter, N. F. Simpson and Tom Stoppard in the UK bear affinities with Pirandello, as do Thornton Wilder and Edward Albee in the USA.

The man who wrote this European classic was born in a house called 'Caos' on the southern coast of Sicily near Agrigento in 1867, the second child (but first son) of six children. His father owned a sulphur mine, one of the few thriving industries in a declining island economy. Although he spent his working life outside Sicily, Pirandello never forgot his Sicilian origins nor the symbolism inherent in the name of his birthplace. After secondary education in the island's capital, Palermo, he enrolled in the city's university, then transferred to the University of Rome in 1887, and moved again in 1889 to the University of Bonn, where he graduated with a thesis on the dialect of his native Agrigento. In Palermo there had been an erotic attachment to a cousin, Lina Pirandello; in Bonn he had fallen in love with a young German woman, Jenny Schulz-Lander, but in 1893, two years after his return from Germany, his family arranged his marriage to Antonietta Portulano, daughter of a business associate of his father's. The marriage took place in the following year. Three children were born: Stefano in 1895, Lietta in 1897 and Fausto in 1899.

After his marriage Pirandello settled in Rome, and in 1897 he took the post of professor at the Istituto Superiore di Magistero (a teacher-training institute) to supplement his father's allowance. Six years later disaster struck the family. Flooding in the sulphur mine led to the loss of Pirandello's father's capital and his wife's dowry, both of which had been invested in the mine. This disaster was a major turning point in Pirandello's life: his wife became mentally ill, developing persecution mania fed by obsessive jealousy, and financial concerns became acute. He had already embarked on a literary career but now, with a sick wife and three children to support, turned to writing with a frenzied earnestness. His first major work of this period was *Il fu Mattia Pascal* (*The Late Matthias Pascal*, 1904), considered a major example of European modernism. Between 1903 and 1915 nine volumes of short stories appeared and three further novels. In 1908, with a collection of critical essays that included the important and seminal 'L'umorismo' ('On Humour'), Pirandello won the competition for a permanent post at the Magistero.

Pirandello's outlook on life, which he refined in his essays, remained constant throughout his life and was formulated early.[2] It was already clear in a letter written to his elder sister in 1886 when he was a nineteen-year-old student in Palermo. He described meditation as 'the black abyss, inhabited by black phantasms and guarded by the most wretched despair, where no light penetrates but where the desire for light throws you into an even deeper darkness'. Human beings were 'a nobler type' of spider, snail or mollusc who cling, not to their webs or shells, but to their ideals, occupations, habits and feelings: protection mechanisms against an overwhelming sense of futility. Without these 'you are as a traveller with no home, a bird without a nest'. 'I write, and study,' Pirandello confided to his sister, 'to forget myself, to distract myself from despair.'[3] Seven years later, while he was in Rome setting up the matrimonial home, he told his fiancée, in his first letter to her, that he saw life as 'an immense labyrinth surrounded by an impenetrable mystery'. He wrote that it was impossible to know anything for certain, that human beings can never have a precise notion of life, but 'only a feeling, therefore continually changing and varied', nothing absolute. In this state of shipwreck, Art was his only rock of safety and he clung to it desperately.[4]

It is interesting to note that Pirandello expressed the same ideas, and with even the same language, in both his personal letters and his public writing. The phrases used in this letter had appeared three months earlier in the essay 'Arte e coscienza d'oggi' ('Art and Consciousness Today'), and the notion that we can have no knowledge of life, only a feeling, recurred in a number of his writings. Pirandello's fictional and dramatic works, most of which are set in his own time, carry a vast range of persons; beneath the articulate ratiocination of many of his characters lies this personally felt cry of anguish concerning the purpose of human suffering and, indeed, the purpose of life.

At the heart of Pirandello's pessimism lies a tragic paradoxical tension between life and form. Form gives a lasting quality to aspects of life but in so doing arrests its essential movement and spontaneity; thus art, which is form, and life are fundamentally opposed. Pirandello's ideas concerning identity and knowledge are closely related to this opposition, and are central to his writing. For him identity is a collection of masks, forms imposed upon the life within us by ourselves and by others. A contemporary dramatist, Luigi Chiarelli, called his best-known play *La maschera e il volto* (*The Mask and the Face*), but for Pirandello there was no face behind the series of masks. The overall title he gave to his collection of plays was the sinister and terrifying phrase *Maschere nude* (*Naked Masks*). The title of his last novel, *Uno, nessuno e centomila* (*One, No-one and a Hundred Thousand*), finally completed and published in 1926, states this theme succinctly: we are one physical body, we have no self, and we comprise a multiplicity of *personae*, depending on the situations in which we find ourselves. Like identity, knowledge is relative. The *raisonneur* character, Lamberto Laudisi, in *Così è (se vi pare)* (*Right You Are! [If You Think So]*) – another emblematic title – can recognise himself as brother to his sister but cannot say who he is. It is the expression of the pain that derives from these two areas of identity and knowledge that distinguishes Pirandello's approach – the 'pena di vivere così' (the pain of living like this), as the title of another story expresses it.

Pirandello considered this revolution in the perception of identity and knowledge as devastating as the Copernican discovery of the place of the earth in the cosmos. One of his major achievements, however, is to make comic creations from such a profoundly pessimistic vision. Humour comes from situation; in the short story 'Il capretto nero' ('The Little Black Kid') of 1913, the young English lady who visits Sicily discovers that the little goat with which she has fallen in love is a hairy monster by the time it reaches her in London. Humour also comes from characters. Pirandello is master of the grotesque caricature; for instance, the two inquisitive ladies in *Right You Are!* (*If You Think So*), or Dr Gennoni, the psychiatrist in *Enrico IV* (*Henry IV*); and he has a fine line in grumbling housekeepers and landladies. But his humour is blended with compassion, as the poetics of the long essay on humour maintain that it must be. To be aware of discrepancy and incongruity provides material for the comic; to reflect on them and feel them leads to the humorist's vision. The example given in the essay is of an elderly lady (one of his many caricatures), overdressed and heavily made-up. The effect is incongruous and therefore laughable; but think of her possible situation – trying to please a young man friend, or to deceive herself in the face of encroaching death – and the laughter becomes suffused with compassion.

Distinct from his dark unchanging vision of the universe, Pirandello's attitude to theatre changed and developed over the years.

Letters home during his student days in Palermo and Rome testify to his intense interest and hopes for the performance of his texts. His first student attempt at playwriting, *Gli uccelli dell'alto* (*The Birds on High*) ended up with several others in the incinerator. He then composed two plays for Eleonora Duse, who went to Palermo in April 1887. Newly arrived in Rome in the autumn of that year, he wrote home to his family that he might not be returning to Sicily for Christmas as his new play *La gente allegra* (*The Happy People*) would be staged at the Valle Theatre at the end of December. In the following January he wrote *Le popolane* (*The Women of the People*) for Cesare Rossi's company. None of these ambitious attempts bore fruit, however, and Pirandello's first published work in 1889 was a volume of poetry.

There is no doubting, though, the almost hallucinatory compulsion the theatre held for the young writer. In early December 1887, two months after taking up residence in Rome, he wrote to his family about his enthusiasm.

> Oh the theatre! I will succeed in it. I cannot go inside a theatre without experiencing an intense emotion and a strange sensation, without the blood rushing through my veins. That heavy atmosphere you breathe in there, laden with the smell of gas and paint, inebriates me; and half way through a show I always feel taken over as if by a fever and I'm on fire. It's that old passion that gets hold of me, and I'm never there alone, but always accompanied by the phantasms of my mind, persons that agitate in a centre of action, not yet stilled, men and women of dramas and comedies, alive in my brain, and who want to leap straightaway onto the stage. Often I don't see or listen to what is really happening on the stage because I am seeing and listening to the scenes that are occurring in my own head.[5]

After an eighteen-month respite from the theatre when he transferred his philological studies to Bonn, Pirandello's return to Rome saw the old enthusiasm return, but again none of his various attempts to stage his plays resulted in performance.

By 1899, at the age of thirty-two, he had published four volumes of poetry and a collection of short stories and completed two novels. His theatrical phase was over, it seemed, except for a few reviews and short articles. Advised by Luigi Capuana to concentrate on prose, it looked as if Pirandello was set to become a writer of fiction. And during the next decade he wrote and published an impressive number of short stories and novels, particularly after the family disaster of 1903. Pirandello was anxious at this time to turn his hand to any form of writing that would pay, and it was in that spirit that he accepted a commission to refurbish some short theatrical pieces for Nino Martoglio, a fellow Sicilian. Martoglio had established a theatrical company in Rome – Teatro Minimo a Sezioni – that offered each evening a selection of one-act plays – hence the title *a sezioni* (in sections). Both Pirandello's *La Morsa* (*The Vice*) and *Lumie di Sicilia* (*Sicilian Limes*) were presented in December 1910. Three years later Lucio d'Ambra and Achille Vitti presented another one-acter, *Il dovere del medico* (*The Doctor's Duty*), in Rome.

But success continued to elude him. Encouraged by Marco Praga, a well-known dramatist, critic and theatrical company manager, his first full-length play, *Se non cosí* (*If Not Like This*) was staged in April 1915 at the prestigious Manzoni Theatre in Milan. It was a resounding failure, leaving Pirandello with a large advance to pay back to the Italian Authors' Society. Disappointed but undaunted, Pirandello continued to persevere in the world of theatre. From mid-1915 to mid-1916 Angelo Musco, the talented Sicilian dialect actor and theatre company manager, presented four plays in Sicilian dialect by Pirandello during his company's visit to Rome. Pirandello, who had hitherto shown little interest in the theatrical presentation of his plays, attending until then, it seems, no rehearsals or performance, was present at the first night of *Sicilian Limes*.

From then onwards Pirandello was to write plays with an impressive speed and engage himself fully in the process of seeing his plays on to the stage. The Italian version of *Pensaci, Giacomino!* (*Think About It, Giacomino!*), first presented in Sicilian the previous year, was ready in early 1917. By April 1917 he had completed *Right You Are!* (*If You Think So*), his first play set on the mainland since *If Not Like This*, which was staged in the following June by no less a theatre manager than Virgilio Talli. Pirandello had hoped that the much-respected actor and theatre company manager Ruggero Ruggeri would take it on, but instead Ruggeri's first Pirandellian role was to be Baldovino in *Il piacere dell'onestà* (*The Pleasures of Respectability*) in November of the same year. Pirandello was to write and have successfully staged eight further plays in Italian before *Six Characters in Search of an Author* in May 1921.

By 1924, after the presentation of yet eight more plays, including *Henry IV* in 1922, so intense had his renewed interest in drama become, that Pirandello agreed to head a group of people who were preparing to launch an art theatre in Rome. Though initially there were no plans to privilege Pirandello's own plays, requests from abroad to stage them (from C. B. Cochran in London in the first instance) meant that a number of the Teatro d'Arte's most memorable productions were of Pirandello's plays. In 1928, however, government funding lapsed and the company was forced to disperse, without achieving in full the reform of Italian theatre that had been its aim. Pirandello had long inveighed against the prompter for colluding with the laziness of actors in relation to their scripts, but he himself was forced to employ one. He had complained bitterly about the competition for playing places and lack of funding, and fell foul of both issues. Nevertheless, the achievements of the Teatro d'Arte over its three and a half years of life were impressive: a varied and ambitious repertoire (fifteen world premieres and nine Italian premieres of foreign plays); the fostering of new talent among his actors and stage designers, in particular Marta Abba and Guido Salvini; the introduction of innovatory lighting, and a high standard of acting based on careful attention to the text.[6] From 1928 until his death, Pirandello continued to write plays and follow their fortunes in his self-imposed exile in Berlin and Paris. When he died, in Rome in December 1936 during one of his intermittent stays in Italy, he left an unfinished play, *I giganti della montagna* (*The Mountain Giants*).

Nearly forty years earlier, at the turn of the twentieth century when he had temporarily stopped writing plays, Pirandello published some essays on theatre. In the first of these, 'L'azione parlata' ('Spoken Action', 1899), he quoted for the first time from Heine's poem 'Geoffrey Rudel and Melisande von Tripoli'.[7] Each evening the figures in the tapestry illustrating the legend leave the tapestry; the troubadour and his lady stir their ghostly limbs from sleep, come down from the wall and move around the room. 'Through the miracle of art', Pirandello wrote in that early essay, 'characters should step out from the written pages of the play, alive in their own right, just as the Lord of Blaye and the Countess of Tripoli stepped down from that ancient tapestry.'[8] Pirandello's concern in this essay is with playwriting. It is his first explicit statement about character autonomy. Dialogue should not be assigned to characters; rather, the character's language should be born with the character. Characters, Pirandello stated, are central to the concept of the play. 'The play does not make people; people make the play. And therefore one must have people before anything else, living, free and active. In them and through them comes the idea of the play.'[9]

In his later essay of 1908, 'Illustratori, attori e traduttori' ('Illustrators, Actors and Translators'), Pirandello uses the same quotation from Heine's poem, not only to prescribe how each character's language should be unique and born with the character, but also to focus on the unsatisfactory nature of illustration, acting and translating. On dramatic art he had this to say:

> Unfortunately, there always has to be a third, unavoidable element that intrudes between the dramatic author and his creation in the material being of the performance: the actor. As is well known, this is an unavoidable limitation for dramatic art. Just as the author has to merge with his character in order to make it live, to the point of feeling as it feels, desiring as it desires, so also to no lesser degree, if that can be accomplished, must the actor.
>
> But even when one finds a great actor who can strip himself completely of his own individuality and enter into that of the character that he is playing, a total, full incarnation is often hindered by unavoidable facts: for example, by the actor's own appearance. This inconvenience can be improved slightly by the use of make-up. But we still have what is more an adaptation, a mask, than a true incarnation.[10]

An actor gives material reality to a character, but in so doing makes that character less true. The actor, by the very nature of his art, removes the abiding truth from the character 'because he is translating him into the fictitious, conventional reality of the stage'.

> [T]he actor gives an artificial consistency, in an illusory, artificial environment, to persons and actions that have already received an expression of life superior to material contingencies and which are already alive in the essentially ideal characteristics of poetry, that is, in a superior kind of reality.[11]

Here, in 1908, is one of the seeds of *Six Characters in Search of an Author*, the play that took European theatre by storm by insinuating that theatre was an 'impossible art'. These ideas could be seen as the bitter notions of a man frustrated by his lack of success in the theatre. However, unbeknownst to Pirandello at the time, those very ideas were to be at the heart of theatrical debate in Europe, finding echoes in Strindberg, Craig and the French Symbolists, and were to challenge the prevailing mode of naturalism. Mallarmé, Maeterlinck, Lugné-Poe and Jarry all made statements indicating that for them theatre held within itself an insoluble contradiction.[12]

Pirandello's notion of the actor doomed to failure because no human being can produce exactly the image of the character sprung from the author's mind is a naturalistic concept and recalls the French theatre practitioner André Antoine's quip that the dramatic action is interrupted each time the actor is visible behind the character. For all Pirandello's utterances about the uniqueness of the character, however, it is clear from his working practices that he wrote plays for specific actors, notably Ruggero Ruggeri and Marta Abba, 'borrowed' speeches from characters of previous plays and interchanged speeches between the characters in individual plays. Pirandello's method of creating characters left visible the process of construction: a form of montage, a collection of parts that could be put together or dismantled at will. Though he clung to his provocative ideas about the impossibility of true mimesis, repeating them in an interview published in

1925 in Paris when his company was performing there,[13] his experience as a playwright and man of the theatre prompted different
approaches to his work. These were also influenced by the presence
in the Teatro d'Arte of Marta Abba, who took the leading roles and for
whom Pirandello wrote a number of plays. In Marta Abba, Pirandello
found the actor best able to produce on stage the effects he wanted:
the impression of a suffering puppet, a being of passionate intensity whose actions and speech delivery were fragmented and staccato.
Claudio Vicentini posits that at this stage of his thinking and theatrical practice, Pirandello thought actors should not aim to represent the character, nor try to be the character; rather, they should
make themselves available to the character, attracting the character to
themselves.[14]

A hint of this is caught in *Six Characters in Search of an Author*,
when the Stepdaughter encourages the Mother to scream, but is best
seen in Sampognetta's 'death scene' in *Questa sera si recita a soggetto*
(*Tonight We Improvise*), the third play in Pirandello's theatre trilogy
(the second was *Ciascuno a suo modo* (*Each in His Own Way*). During
an 'improvisation' (fully scripted by Pirandello), the Comic Actor,
given the role of Sampognetta, finds himself unable to act out a good
death scene. He cannot get the mood right, no one responded to his
cue, and as a comic actor, he has no training to do a death from cold.
So why don't they cut the build-up to his death? He lies down on
the sofa and declares, 'I'm dead!' The Director interposes; the Comic
Actor begins to justify himself, describing how he had constructed
the scene, explaining his character and his reactions to members of
his family and to the director, working himself into the situation to
the extent that he defends himself as if he were being contradicted;
inserting the actions, smearing blood on his face from his wounds,
trying out his last fluttering whistle (for which he was known), and
finally, with one arm round the Singer's neck and the other round
that of the Client, he lets his head drop and falls on the ground.
The Singer cries out 'Oh God, he's dead, he's dead!' and his daughter
throws herself on to her father crying 'Daddy, daddy, oh my daddy'

and bursts into real tears. The character has taken possession of the actor, who makes himself available by creating space within himself for the character's presence.

During the last decade of Pirandello's life, European theatre itself suffered an identity crisis. The rise of the director as the most important figure in the theatre created tension between writers and directors. In Germany, in particular, where Pirandello began his self-imposed exile, there was considerable debate concerning the terms 'production' and 'reproduction'. Was it the director's task to reproduce what the writer had written, or was it to produce a work of art inspired by the writer's text? In his *Der Régisseur* (*The Director*), Leopold Jessner claimed that what the writer had written ('produced') was the director's material in the same way that reality was the writer's material. The stage had its own laws that were determining factors of the director's work. The director had to unravel the writer's text into parts that would constitute the stage work. It was this process of unravelling and analysis that comprised both the director's freedom and his work. It was how the director transformed the written play into a stage performance.[15] Part of that process was to use the new equipment available: new lighting systems with high-power bulbs, revolves and electrically powered lifts. It was Pirandello's view that technique, carried to its maximum effect and unrelated to the text, was beginning to destroy theatre. His play *Tonight We Improvise*, presented in Germany (at Königsberg and then Berlin in 1930), addressed the theme head on. The director within the text, Hinkfuss, was not a direct satire of Reinhardt, as the Berlin audiences mistakenly thought, but the play was, at least in part, a satire against what Pirandello saw as the excesses of German theatre direction.

A second destabilising factor for theatre in the late 1920s was the invention of the talking film. Pirandello saw the first, *The Jazz Singer* (1927) in the spring of 1929 when he was in London to discuss the possibility of a film of *Six Characters in Search of an Author*. By the autumn of that year he had completed his essay 'Se il film parlante abolirà il teatro' ('Will the talkies abolish theatre?'). Pirandello, who had taken a keen interest in the development of this new art since 1896, responded positively in 1924 to Marcel L'Herbier's film version of *The Late Matthias Pascal*. Film, Pirandello said in an interview for *Les Nouvelles Littéraires*, had special qualities that differentiated it from any art form. The cinema could more easily and more completely than any other artistic means of expression make thought visible. It made no sense to remain aloof from a means of expression that offered the possibility of doing things that neither narrative nor theatre could do, that is, put into images dream, memory, hallucination, madness and the doubling of personality.[16] In 1929, coining the word 'cinemelografia', Pirandello developed these ideas to describe film as an evocative art that explores the intermingling of image and music. Film should not try to ape theatre. Both linear narrative and the talking character belonged to other art forms. In attempting to imitate theatre with characters who use dialogue, film could only produce a mechanical copy of something that is living and vibrant. A film character was but an image with a disembodied voice. And theatre was also wrong to appropriate cinematic techniques because this led to a repertoire that emphasised visual effects over and above dramatic power and had led some directors to aim to provide 'a spectacle for the eyes'.[17] The economic advantage of the production of film over theatre had also not escaped Pirandello.

What Pirandello had to say in his essay on the relationship between film and theatre seems a far remove from the ideas expressed in 'Illustrators, Actors and Translators' in 1908 and seventeen years later in 'In confidence'. Theatre was no longer an 'impossible art', it was a fragile and precarious art. Along with other practitioners throughout Europe, Pirandello refrained from provocative utterances concerning theatre, concentrating on theatre as unique, and theatre as an undying cultural heritage.[18] Two of his last essays, his opening speech to the Volta conference in Rome in 1934 and the introduction to Silvio d'Amico's history of Italian theatre (1936), concentrate on these themes. In the second paragraph of his address at the Volta conference, Pirandello referred to the theatre as a 'patient' and continues:

Though I should, of course, add that all the doctors who have come here with advice to offer have come to give the patient hope for life rather than death, since they are all certain that the patient cannot die.

The theatre cannot die.

It is a form of life itself and we are all actors in it. If theatres were abandoned and left to rot, then theatre would continue in life, it could not be suppressed, and the very nature of things would always be spectacle.[19]

From the early 1920s Pirandello had been involved with others in trying to establish a national theatre, a repertory theatre based in Rome and state funded. The government, however, had other ideas. Though the Fascist government gave more financial support to theatrical companies than it is often given credit for, its interest was, in the main, in mass theatre. The *carri di Tesbi* (Thespian carts) initiative, begun in 1929 but continuing into the early 1940s, took entertainment, sometimes of a high quality, to the furthest reaches of the country, to people unlikely 'to go to the theatre'.[20] Such an initiative sat uneasily with Pirandello's hopes of an Italian high art theatre, comparable to that in Paris and Berlin. In his last years Pirandello felt out of sympathy with a government of which earlier in his life he had held high hopes.

Six Characters in Search of an Author holds a special place both in the history of European theatre and in the development of its author's career. By 1921, when the play had its controversial premiere in Rome, Pirandello was, as we have seen, an Italian dramatist of some standing in his own country. He had fourteen Italian plays to his name (including some in his native Sicilian), eight volumes of poetry (including a translation of Goethe's Roman elegies), fourteen volumes of short stories and six novels. Interested in theatre from an early age – there is a photograph of him performing in amateur dramatics with friends at his home near Agrigento – it was not until the First World War, when he was in his late forties, that he returned compulsively to writing for the theatre. Narrative was insufficiently direct, he said at the time, to express his feelings (he had a son at the front, and a mentally sick wife at home who accused him of liaisons with his students and incest with their daughter). 'My taste for the narrative form had vanished. I could no longer limit myself to story telling, while there was action all around me . . . The words would not remain on the written page: they had to explode into the air, to be spoken or cried out.'[21]

It was after the production of *Six Characters*, which was quickly followed in 1922 by *Henry IV*, that Pirandello received his first invitation overseas, to Paris and New York in the first instance, and subsequently with his own theatre company, the Teatro d'Arte, to London and further afield. His publisher, Bemporad, reissued his works in Italy; the American publisher, Dutton, began a series of translations; and in Paris, Pirandello mania was in full swing from the spring of 1923. Writing from Paris to his daughter Lietta in April of that year on the occasion of Pitoëff's production of *Six Characters in Search of an Author*, Pirandello announced excitedly, 'I've truly arrived at the peak of my literary career.'[22]

CHAPTER I

SIX CHARACTERS IN SEARCH OF AN AUTHOR – THE PLAY (1921)

From the initial stage directions, Pirandello presented *Six Characters in Search of an Author* as a challenge to the audience.[1] As the spectators come into the theatre, they find the curtain raised: the prompter's box is placed to one side, the Director's chair has its back to the audience, two tables are positioned on either side of the stage with chairs placed round them. The whole gives an impression of a stage ready for a rehearsal, rather than performance. The first piece of action comprises an unscripted scene involving the entrance of members of the company who are to rehearse an earlier play by Pirandello, *Il giuoco delle parti* (*The Rules of the Game*). With the entry of the Director, Pirandello's script maps out the beginning of the rehearsal. The Prompter reads out the stage directions, the Director decides on a few details concerning the set, an Actor queries his costume, and the Director complains that they have to stage Pirandello because there are no more new good French plays. Just as the Director is dealing with yet another interruption, this time from the Prompter, the Theatre Usher creeps round the stage, doffs his cap and tells him that there are some people asking to speak with him. At the back of the stage stand six people, the Characters, bathed in a strange faint light, which seems to irradiate from them. The older man in the group (the Father) explains that they are looking for an author.

Told in spurts of narrative interlaced with quarrels and the Father's ideas on life and art, the story reveals a dysfunctional family. The story begins some twenty-three years ago with the marriage of the Father and the Mother and is set on its tragic trajectory after the birth of their Son. Wanting him to have a good start in life, the Father gave him to be nurtured to a wet nurse. Some three years later, aware that his wife and secretary had a mutual understanding, he sent his wife from home. The Mother and secretary set up house together and over the following years the Mother had three further children: the Stepdaughter, the Boy and the Little Girl. After her second partner died, the Mother fell on hard times and took on sewing for a certain Mme Pace, who used dressmaking and millinery as a cover for her less respectable establishment. Mme Pace lured the Stepdaughter on to her staff by telling her that she needed to compensate for her mother's poor sewing. It was here that the Father was a regular client. After the Mother interrupted an encounter between the Father and Stepdaughter, the Father decided to take her and her second family home with him.

The fragmented tale conveys the individual pain experienced by each family member as they recount the experience from their own viewpoint. The Son was confronted by a woman whom he was told was his mother, and saw equivocal scenes between his Father and the Stepdaughter. She in turn had no respect for the Father, hated the legitimate Son, and despised the Boy. The Mother, deprived of her son soon after his birth, yearned to know him; and the Father could see all the pain that came from his actions. The Mother's attention was deflected from her young children by her desire to speak with her firstborn. The Little Girl, the Stepdaughter's only solace, drowned while playing on her own near the garden pond and the Boy shot himself as he saw his sister floating in the water. The Stepdaughter ran away, leaving the three members of the original family physically together but isolated from each other.

The interfamilial conflicts reveal what Pirandello described in his 1925 preface to the play as 'the fierce sources of suffering' that racked his spirit for years: 'the delusion of reciprocal understanding hopelessly based on the hollow abstraction of words' and 'the multiple nature of every human personality, given all the possible ways of being inherent in each of us'.[2] The Father, in discussion with the Director, articulates these themes in two speeches. One concerns the failure of words to communicate understanding between people. Each person inflects the words they use with a personal understanding: the consequence is that 'we think we understand each other, but in fact we never do'. The second concerns multiple personality, the theme at the centre of the novel *One, No-one and a Hundred Thousand*, which Pirandello broke off from writing in order to concentrate on this play. We see ourselves as one person, whereas in fact we are many. The Stepdaughter, the Father claims, has caught him in a reality he should never have had for her and is trying to fix that reality as his only identity.

By the end of the first part of the play, the Director and the Actors (and the audience) will know some parts of the Characters' stories but will have had little opportunity to piece them together into a narrative whole. The story the Characters bring appears so much more exciting than the play he is struggling to rehearse that by the end of part 1 the hard-pressed Director is flattered into accepting the role of author. He takes the Characters off stage with him to work out how their story might be staged. This break constitutes the interval.

After the break tensions increase: between the Characters, between the Actors, between the Actors and Characters, the Director and Actors and the Director and Characters. The second part begins with two discrete scenes, one between the Stepdaughter and the two children, the other between the Mother and the Son. The Stepdaughter, first on stage, accompanied by the Little Girl and, following at a distance, by the Boy, shouts back to the dressing room a rejection of the Father and Director as she realises that the Father is succeeding in impressing his viewpoint on the Director. She explains to Rosetta, the Little Girl, that they are on a stage, that everything is false, made of paper. She recalls that Rosetta will try to catch at one of the ducks in the pond. While trying to restrain the child, she catches sight of the Boy mooching around the garden and, wrenching his hand from his pocket, discovers the gleam of a revolver. She is called back to the dressing room by the Father and Director, which allows space for the scene between the Son and Mother.

The Son comes on stage first, followed by the Mother. Unable to attract his attention, she sits, the two children draw close to her, and she voices her feelings of shame at having their lives exposed. The Son echoes her objections, but without addressing her, and expands on his particular shame: to experience his parents as man and woman rather than only as mother and father.

The theatrical company now return from the dressing rooms and the Director begins to set the scene for the first part of the rehearsal. The Prompter, whose moment of glory derives from his knowledge of shorthand, is sent off to get paper, so that he can take down the words. Uneasiness prevails. The Actors fear they will have to improvise and the Characters, knowing they are the Characters, cannot understand why the Actors are needed at all. The Father and Stepdaughter cannot see themselves in the Leading Man and Leading Lady and they, in turn, see it as their task to enhance the Characters as they are presented to them. And then, just as they are about to start, they realise that a character is missing: Mme Pace is not with them. The Father evokes the missing Madame, conjuring her by assembling on stage associations with her millinery shop, the hats and coats of the Actors. The scene between her and the Stepdaughter is inaudible because they are talking of matters others should not hear. The Director asserts some of the rules and conventions of theatre, such as audibility and respect for the audience. The Father and Stepdaughter then play out the scene in the little room in Mme Pace's establishment. It is clear from the stage directions that this is no mere replay or repetition but life as it happened.

The two Actors then take over. In a stage direction Pirandello indicates that this attempt should appear as something quite other from the experience as played out by the Father and Stepdaughter, but should not come across as a parody. The Father and Stepdaughter react with amazement and horror: to them the whole enactment is an appalling travesty of their lives. The Director explains that a play has to be selective. One character cannot be allowed to dominate the others; it must be organised so that all the characters are contained in 'one harmonious picture', and only what can be represented to the public be staged. The task of the playwright is to reveal what is necessary in relation to the other characters and at the same time to give an impression of what is going on inside each individual character. The Stepdaughter persists; she is determined to live the moment in Mme Pace's shop. The Mother objects and explains to the baffled Director that, far from being a moment in the past, the action is happening in the continuous present. The Stepdaughter buries her head in the Father's chest as she had done on that fateful day and the Mother screams as she did then. The Director is delighted and shouts 'Curtain!', and the Stagehand thinks he really wants the curtain lowered. The curtain comes down and the second part ends with the Director and Father on the audience side of the curtain, the Father overcome by the reality of his life, the Director delighted at this climax to the scene.

The raising of the curtain on the short third part reveals that the Stagehands have been busy. Gone is the semblance of Mme Pace's shop and on stage now is the bare outline of a garden: cutouts of two or three trees and a fountain can be glimpsed between them. The Characters are on one side of the stage, the Actors and Actresses on the other, with the Director centre stage. During a discussion of where to set the scene, the Leading Actress uses the word 'illusion', a word the Father finds extremely painful, since what is illusion to the Actors is his only life, what is the pretence of their art his only reality. The Father challenges the Director: his reality is consistent and continuous, while that of human beings is fleeting and changing. He demands that the pain of his position be understood, and in reply to being told that he reasons too much (for drama is action not philosophy) the Father explains that he reasons because he is human. Animals suffer without reasoning; human beings want to know the cause of their suffering. The Director has a sneaking feeling that the Father talks like the author of the play he has been trying to rehearse, an author he particularly dislikes, and thinks he and his Actors have fallen out of the frying pan into the fire. He turns to the Father and asks him if he has ever heard a character discussing his position in the way he is doing. The Father explains that they are characters who have been given no life, for the author has not put them in a work of art. In a moment of unity, he and the Stepdaughter recall the Characters pleading with the author for life as they tried to tempt him in his study.

The Director finally manages to continue his rehearsal, and he decides to play everything in the garden. It is necessary to combine and group characters in a tight and cohesive action, so the Boy will mooch in the garden, not the house, and be hidden behind a tree; the Mother will follow the Son into the garden, not his room. The Stepdaughter challenges the recalcitrant Son to leave them, but he cannot leave. The Second Actress and the Juvenile Lead pay special attention to the Mother and Son, much to the latter's annoyance. The Father grapples with the Son, insisting that he participate. He refuses to act out a scene but is persuaded to tell what happened: how he left his room when his mother approached, and went out into the garden. As he was going through the garden, he saw the Little Girl in the water and ran to fish her out but suddenly stopped short, for he could see the Boy staring at his little sister with madness in his eyes. The Son moved towards the Boy. At this moment a shot rings out from behind the trees where the Boy is hidden. The Mother screams, Actors and Actresses are confused – some think the Boy is really dead, others that it is pretence. The Father insists that it is real, while the Director has the last words, complaining that he has wasted a day.

Six Characters in Search of an Author had a long gestation. One of its major themes – the reality of the character – is present as early as 1902 in the short story 'Quando ero matto' ('When I was mad'). Two years later, in a letter to a friend, Pirandello described the pressure of his creative imagination in images similar to those he was later to use about the six characters:

> If material and social commitments did not distract me, I believe I would remain from morn to night in my study, at the beck and call of the characters of my narratives, who throng around me. Each of them wants to come to life before the others. They all have a particular wretchedness they want made known. I have sympathy for them all.[3]

There is a strong connection between Pirandello's narrative and his drama. A number of his short stories form the bases of the plots of his plays. The narrative connection here is with the novel. In a letter of 23 July 1917 to his son Stefano, Pirandello wrote that his head was bursting with new ideas:

> Lots of short stories . . . and a strange piece, which is sad, so very sad: Six Characters in Search of an Author: novel in the making. Perhaps you'll understand. Six characters, caught in a terrible drama, who approach me asking to be put into a novel, it's an obsession, and I don't want to have anything to do with them, and I tell them it's useless, I'm not interested in them, I'm not interested in anything, and here they are showing me all their wounds and here I am sending them away . . . and so in the end the novel in the making will emerge complete.[4]

Of that initial project one episode remains: part of the story of the Father's visit to Mme Pace's establishment, on the upper floor of 'a five-storey building in one of the busier new streets of the city'. It is an account sympathetic to the Father's shame and self-consciousness. 'He could see with a brutal, savage nakedness that which was still undeniably young in him moving down that street, hidden by the serious, outer form of the ageing man.'[5]

It is not known precisely when Pirandello decided that *Six Characters* should become a play – rather than a novel – in the making, but the seeds of the play are clearly here in this extract: sympathy for the Father, who becomes the bearer of some of Pirandello's ideas, distancing from the Stepdaughter, seen as feminine Other, and the awareness of the characters' autonomy. The characters, Pirandello notes in the final paragraphs, which come across as notes to himself, are leaving him and beginning to 'act out the scenes of the novel amongst themselves'.

> They performed in front of me, but as though I were not there, as though they did not depend on me, as though I could not stop them at all.
>
> The girl more than anyone. I see her come in . . . She is a perfect reality created by me, but who simply cannot involve me, even though I can feel the deep pity she arouses. What about the mother? Do you think about her? Her shame before her legitimate son: not being able to look him in the face, because in order to look at him she would have to cancel out the lives of her other children, the children of her pain and her shame, from another life of hers that he can never share.[6]

When the text became a play, it retained a strong narrative element. It is, as we have seen, a linear presentation of the attempt to create a play: a rehearsal is interrupted by six people who announce themselves as characters and insist that their family drama be put on the stage. Different members tell their story of the dysfunctional family, and the first part of the play is largely narrative, if fragmented narrative. As the play progresses it reflects psychoanalytic and narratological observations concerning the importance of narrative in shaping our lives – as Philippe Sollers has indicated, we are our story.[7] The Son's speech, describing his walk through the garden at the end of the play, reveals the moment when narrated memory explodes into drama.

Echoes of Pirandello's critical writing are also present in the text of the play. The Director's speeches on the harmonious whole, combining and grouping, his insistence that the way a character is presented must allow for a glimpse of the totality of the character's life, are present in 'Spoken Action' of 1899 and 'Illustrators, Actors and Translators' of 1908. This latter essay can also be seen as a source of a major theme of the play: the impossibility of the actor, despite costume and make-up, to present the character who is an autonomous being.[8]

Another inspiration for the play came from nineteenth-century spiritualism. Pirandello had become interested in this phenomenon quite early some two years after he had returned from Bonn, through his friend and mentor Luigi Capuana whose studies on the subject were published as *Spiritismo* (1884) and *La scienza della letteratura* (1902). As Ann Caesar points out, this latter work includes 'an account of the analogies that can be drawn between communications with the spirits and the process of artistic creation'.[9] The Characters, doomed for ever to existence without life, are outsiders yearning to cross the threshold into theatrical life.

Not only did the play take time to mature in Pirandello's mind, it is also the most radically revised of all his plays and the one that ran into the most editions. Though the 1933 edition is defined as definitive by Alessandro d'Amico in his Mondadori edition, since that text had received the author's last emendations, the two texts that are most important from a theatrical viewpoint are the first (1921) and the fourth (1925). Dario Niccodemi presented the first in the Teatro Valle in Rome in May 1921; Pirandello himself directed the fourth with his own company, the Teatro d'Arte, at the Teatro Odescalchi, also in Rome, in April 1925.[10] This text differs substantially in a number of places from the 1921 play, differences that will be described in chapter 6 of this book.

Six Characters in Search of an Author was first presented at a time of great ferment in the theatre. Naturalism, as conceived by the French theatre practitioner André Antoine as a means of addressing burning contemporary issues in the theatre in a direct and physical way, was being challenged by Symbolism, which threw doubts on the validity of physical representation – the best plays are perhaps those we conjure in our minds rather than those we see on the stage. Gordon Craig, working in Italy, saw theatre as closer to music and poetry than to the bodily representation of characters and even mooted the elimination of the human actor. Adolphe Appia, the Swiss theatre designer, was working in a similar direction in Germany. In Italy, Filippo Tommaso Marinetti had challenged the *pièce bien faite* (the well-made play) from a different perspective but one that also concentrated on the nonverbal aspects of theatre-making. He claimed that his *sintesi* ('syntheses') carried as much meaningful substance as full-length plays. In *Simultaneità* (*Simultaneity*) he presents a family after supper on one side of the stage (The Mother and Daughter sewing, the Father reading a newspaper, and the two Sons doing their homework) and a *cocotte* attending to her toilette in her boudoir on the other. This synthesis is a *compenetrazione* (reciprocal penetration), as Marinetti explains in one of his long stage directions: 'the *cocotte* is not a symbol, but a synthesis of feelings of luxury, disorder, adventure, and waste which live with anguish, desire or regret in the nerves of all the people sitting round the peaceful family table'. Marinetti claimed to obtain 'an absolute dynamism of time and space, with the simultaneous reciprocal penetration of two different environments and two very different times'.[11]

Placed within this context, *Six Characters in Search of an Author* is Janus-faced. The unlikely and highly emotive plot of the Characters' story looks back to nineteenth-century melodrama and the well-made play with its emphases on the secret to be revealed, plot complications and climactic curtains and swift closure. The fragmentation of the plot's presentation, on the other hand, with the continuous intertwining of time levels and the challenges to representation, make of it an avant-garde play. It did in the 1920s what Beckett's *Waiting for Godot* was to do thirty years later: in David Bradby's words they both turn 'the conventions of theatre upon themselves and reveal their inner contradictions'.[12]

A major challenge to the theatre in this play is the representation of time. European theatregoers had already been made aware of the way the past meets the present in Ibsen's immaculately plotted plays. Pirandello, however, takes this double movement of time, the unravelling of the past as current time moves inexorably forward towards its explosive meeting with the past, into uncharted territory. He further complicates this two-way temporal process by introducing Characters into the quotidian reality of the stage, beings of a different time dimension. They are timeless beings who nevertheless have a history within their own dimension, a past that is continually present.

Pirandello appears to ignore the audience in his opening stage directions: nevertheless, the outer frame of the play, the rehearsal, is set in the morning while the spectatators, of course, are there in the theatre in the evening (or afternoon). There is a temporal divide between the play on stage and the audience parallel to, in 1921 at least, the physical divide between the stage and the auditorium; no action takes place in audience space. Apart from that, stage time and audience time run more or less parallel; there is little or no 'temporal perspective', a condensing of time to fit the required playing time.[13] The interval is the period when the Director and Characters go off stage to plan the play and, though the text falls into the three conventional parts, these are not referred to as acts. Within the play there is the simple chronological period of the rehearsal, but even this, what we might call the Actors' time, is not as simple as it looks since it carries with it the articulated awareness of the history of stage presentation and its conventions. Challenged to represent the life of the Characters as it happened, the Director claims the modernity of his approach: he will combine and group the separate scenes into one composite whole and not resort to the medieval practices of putting up signs to indicate when and where we are in the plot. Such practices, he and his actors indicate, are associated with naïveté and lack of sophistication. The company is seen in terms of evolving theatrical practice.

The Characters participate in the running time of the play; they discuss and argue their case with the Director and Actors. They also bring with them the story of their lives, a chronological story as all stories are, which is complete. Since they are characters, all moments of their lives conceived in the author's mind are also potentially present, ready to be called upon and rendered actual. Their lives belong to a continuous present. As Pirandello explained in the preface to the 1925 edition, characters are ready 'to be' as soon as we open a page of a book and read a passage; as the Father explains, characters who become famous will live for ever. However, though they haunted the writer's imagination, he decided against giving them artistic form; instead, he wrote a play about rejected characters seeking fulfilment in the form they were refused.

The intertwining of these times is present throughout the play, as the Mother explains to the Director in one of the most emotive and lyrical moments of the play.

> No, it's happening now, it's happening all the time! My torment isn't over. I am alive and constantly present at every moment of my agony, which keeps coming back, alive and constantly present. Those two children there, have you heard them speak? They can no longer speak. They still cling to me all the time, to keep my pain alive and present. But they, for themselves, are no longer alive. And she (*indicating the Stepdaughter*) has run away; she has run away from me, and now she's gone, forever. And if I see her standing here before me now, it's just for this, just for this, to renew forever and all time, to keep alive and constantly present the pain I have suffered on her account as well.[14]

Key sections of the play show the time levels interacting with each other. One of these is 'the scene', the presentation of the incident when the Father meets the Stepdaughter in Mme Pace's establishment. The Father and Stepdaughter 'are' at this moment as they 'were' and always 'will be'. The Father is described as 'wholly engrossed now in the reality of his created life'. (The Characters, of course, cannot be asked to repeat the scene for the benefit of the Actors as no human action can be repeated exactly as it happened.) During this scene the Mother, with her three other children, is on the opposite side of the stage from the Actors, her face registering 'pain, outrage, anxiety and horror'. When the Father asks if he may take off the Stepdaughter's hat, she moans, 'Oh God! Oh my God!' At this the Father is jolted forward out of the time of the action into the time of remorse; but he then reverts to the time of the encounter in Mme Pace's shop and offers the Stepdaughter a hat. At this point the Young Actress, following what she understands to be the dramatised narrative, interrupts to remind the Father that those hats are not his to offer and shatters momentarily the Characters' time, bringing both Actors and Characters into the stage time. Another such moment of 'time clusters' occurs at the end of part 2, when the Stepdaughter, frustrated that the scene will not be presented as it happened for her, focuses on the cry the Mother uttered on seeing the Father and her daughter together. She conjures the Mother's cry by positioning herself in an embrace with the Father and urges the Mother to scream. Through the following speech the Stepdaughter remembers the scream, addresses the Director on stage, and through memory and association evokes the scream.

> That scream is still ringing in my ears. That scream sent me out of my mind! Oh, you can represent me as you like, it doesn't matter. Even with my clothes on, if you like. As long as my arms are bare – just my arms – because, you see, standing like this . . . (*She goes up to the Father and places her head on his chest.*) . . . with my head placed here like this, and my arms like this around his neck, I could see a vein throbbing here in my arm. And then, as if just that vein filled me with disgust, I screwed up my eyes like this . . . like this . . . and buried my head in his chest.

Scream, Mum, scream! (*She buries her head in the Father's chest, and with her shoulders tensed as if to prevent herself from hearing the scream, she adds in tones of muffled anguish*) Scream as you screamed then!

The end of the play in the first version provides the last 'time cluster'. As the Director draws the story from the Son, the Mother begins to tremble and moan, her gaze intent upon the pond, where the Stepdaughter has already placed the Little Girl in simulation of her death. Pressed by the Director, the Son explains that he rushed over to the Little Girl, but then something caught his eye that made his blood run cold:

The boy, the boy was standing there, motionless, with the eyes of a madman, staring at his drowned sister in the pond (*the Stepdaughter, bent over the pond to hide the Little Girl, sobs*). I started to draw nearer; and then . . .
(*From behind the trees where the Boy is hidden, a revolver shot rings out.*)

At the end of part 2, the Characters' reality impresses the Director and his company but he is not totally persuaded of it. Now the Characters' reality takes over. Not only the Mother believes that the Boy is dead, but some of the Actors do as well and pandemonium follows, the Father insisting that this is reality, some actors denying it.

In *Six Characters in Search of an Author,* the first of what he will later call his theatre trilogy,[15] Pirandello challenges theatre to present reality but theatre fails to meet the challenge. The failure is on a number of levels: for instance, stage and social conventions do not allow the encounter between the Father and the Stepdaughter to be presented in its fullness, and the particular theatre company has not the means to reproduce Mme Pace's room, having only a few sets at its disposal. But the core of the problem is that theatre, even given a change in conventions and greater financial resources, cannot represent reality: the actor playing the Father will never 'be' the Father; the pond, whatever the attempts at naturalistic presentation, can only approximate the one imagined by the author; dramatic dialogue and action, formerly considered an adequate expression of being, are, in Peter Szondi's words, 'an illicit and injurious limitation on the endless multiplicity of internal life'.[16] Given Pirandello's ideas on personality and reality, theatre is not merely a flawed art, it is an impossible art.

Yet Pirandello wrote *Six Characters in Search of an Author* as a play, not as a novel, as he had first conceived it. As early as 1917 he had rejected the characters and their 'terrible drama' and later explained in his preface to the play (1925) that this was because he could find no 'universal significance' for them. Simple portrayal was an insignificant motivation: 'I cannot just tell a story for the sake of telling it or describe a landscape simply as a creative exercise.'[17] The Father (who speaks in part for the author) explains that Pirandello was perhaps 'technically' unable to bring them 'to birth in Art'. Nevertheless, the drama of their rejection, as differentiated from their 'terrible drama', was, Pirandello realised some time after 1917, better suited to the stage than the page. That decision had consequences. Theatre may be an impossible art, but it was his chosen medium for his expression of that notion. He had written to his son in 1917 that 'in the end the novel in the making will emerge complete'.[18] By 1921 the work had emerged – but as a play 'the perfectly clear, straightforward and orderly' presentation of 'natural organic chaos', as Pirandello was to describe it in 1925.[19]

Critics have focused on different aspects of this play. For instance, some have seen it as a debate between reality and illusion; others have dwelt on the Freudian (and biographical) implications of the family scene, drawing on theories of repetition; others have concentrated on it as an exploration of the creative process; yet others have drawn out the gender implications of the extended family. For directors, however, the major challenge is how to render the play's ideas theatrically. This also became a major concern for Pirandello and formed the basis of his 1925 revisions. As will become clearer in chapter 6 with the analysis of the 1925 version of the text, productions by other directors in better-equipped theatres than those to which he was accustomed in Italy helped Pirandello to refine his theatrical imagery. In 1921 he depended much more on verbal expression for communication than he would do four years later. But even at this stage in his development as a playwright, he was well aware of the deictic quality of the theatrical image.

Drama is an art form that 'shows' as well as 'tells'. It is able to communicate ideas to an audience differently from how this is done in narrative. So one of the main themes of *Six Characters in Search of an Author*, the impossibility of communication, is shown by the way the Characters and Actors are grouped on stage. A tableau of this theme comes after the rise of the curtain on the third part of the play. The Characters are on one side of the stage, the Mother flanked by her two younger children, the Son with the Mother but apart from her, and the Father and Stepdaughter together down front. On the other side of the stage, the Actors are sitting in a group. In the middle of the stage, between them, stands the Director, whose self-appointed task it is to mediate between the two groups, his clenched fist over his mouth in pensive pose.

In the preface to the 1925 edition of the text, Pirandello inveighed against 'symbolic art' in which 'representation is reduced to mechanistic allegory'. His own stage imagery makes use of a multiple and dynamic symbolism. The two younger children stay close to their Mother and do not speak because, on one level, they are the Mother's guilty thoughts from which she cannot escape. The Little Girl, Rosetta, can also be seen as the Stepdaughter's lost innocence. Throughout the play the Son stands separate from his Mother and says little, as an expression of his painful aloofness. In a manner that records Marinetti's 'syntheses' and notion of 'reciprocal penetration', different time levels are presented simultaneously on stage. The audience experiences the Mother's distress after the discovery of the quasi-incestuous encounter between her husband and daughter at the same time as the Stepdaughter and Father present their 'scene'. Likewise the Stepdaughter's expression of her grief at the death of her sister is communicated by her huddling over the fountain, sobbing uncontrollably, while the Son tells of his walk through the garden at the end of the play and the gunshot explodes. As Pirandello was later to say, the catastrophe that explodes 'needs no human words'. Indeed, many of the moments of the play convey simultaneously within their presentation the different times levels within which Pirandello articulates his ideas. Between 1921 and 1925 Pirandello will explore other theatrical means to convey his meaning. For instance, the Stepdaughter will be described as 'abstracted' to indicate that she is no longer with the family; the Son's aloofness will be given a more definite stage presence, and the nuclear family will be presented as a stage image at the end of the play rather than evoked in words earlier in the text.

Six Characters in Search of an Author has become a classic because it offers a cluster of human situations that strike chords of sympathy and can raise deep emotion, food for philosophical debate, and an arresting critique of the theatre's resources to deliver representation. Its challenge to theatre came from within the established tradition: *Six Characters in Search of an Author* was not first presented, as was the later icon of avant-garde drama, *Waiting for Godot*, in a small experimental theatre, but in a mainstream Roman playhouse. But it did ask of its early twentieth-century audiences responses to which they were not accustomed. Catharsis comes not after an orderly unfolding of events, but after a (meticulously orchestrated) rollercoaster experience of what Pirandello called his 'hotchpotch of tragedy, comedy, fantasy, and realism' set in 'a completely original, extraordinarily complex humoristic situation'.[20]

THE FIRST PRODUCTION: TEATRO VALLE, ROME, 9 MAY 1921, DIRECTED BY DARIO NICCODEMI

The reaction to the first night of *Six Characters in Search of an Author* has made of it a theatrical legend: vociferous defenders and detractors of the play, scuffles in the theatre and a hasty exit by Pirandello and his daughter by the stage door thence to be bundled into a taxi by friends. The event was described as a 'battle', the most violent and noisy ever experienced in the Teatro Valle. Outside in the street angry encounters continued into the night.[1] And as the play gained its place in the Italian and international repertoires, so the memories of that first night became more prolific. In 1936, just after Pirandello's death, Orio Vergani, journalist and playwright and brother to the actress Vera Vergani, who took the part of the Stepdaughter, recalled the evening in vivid detail.[2] And when Orio Vergani died in April 1960, Lucio Ridenti, the current editor of *Il Dramma*, which Vergani had founded in 1925, commemorated Vergani's role in the first-night drama, describing an impetuous young man, rushing up and down the street, punching into the air, and stammering out his abuse of 'Cowards!'[3]

Claqueurs were not unknown in Italian theatres. In this case evidence suggests that the uproar in the theatre had been encouraged by young supporters of the avant-garde known as *sciacalli* ('jackals'), who were opposed by the *parrucconi* ('old fogies').[4] The leader of the 'jackals' was the same Orio Vergani, and among them was Galeazzo Ciano, a future Fascist party official. In any case, Teatro Valle audiences were accustomed to tumultuous first nights, both successes, such as Pietro Cossa's *Cleopatra* and *Cecilia*, and disasters, such as

Giaocosa's *Tristi amori* (*Sad Loves*) and D'Annunzio's *Sogno di un mattino di primavera* (*Dream of a Spring Morning*). Furthermore, Pirandello liked to present himself as one who fostered an antagonistic relationship with his audiences, as he explained in correspondence with Virgilio Talli, whose company had presented the premiere of *Right You Are!* (*If You Think So*):

> For my part I have made my public expect from me all kinds of outrageous things. I have always gone out to offend my public and the public knows it. It is my delight and pleasure. All my work has always been and always will be like that: a challenge to the opinions of the public and above all a challenge to its moral – or immoral – peace.[5]

Given these circumstances, it is difficult to tease out which aspects of the play would have disturbed the audience if spectators has been left to make up their own minds. One point *can* be clarified. The audience could not have been disturbed by Pirandello's use of theatre space, as has sometimes been supposed: it was not until the fourth edition of the play text, and his own 1925 production, that Pirandello introduced the use of the auditorium as part of the performance space. Until then the play was contained within the proscenium arch.

As it happens, more is known – or imagined – about the reception of the play on that first night than about the performance. *Six Characters in Search of an Author* had been well advertised; there was a full house on the first night, 1,040 seats sold in advance, in addition to the press and the expected gatecrashers:[6] a situation ripe for excitement. From the reviews it would appear that there was unanimous and enthusiastic approval of the first act, some interruptions to the second (particularly at the appearance of Mme Pace) and third, followed by uproar at the end. Anyone trying to reconstruct the performance of *Six Characters in Search of an Author* is confronted with a frustrating dearth of documentation. There are no photographs of the play in action, no prompt copy, no director's script, no programmes, not even a cast list belonging to the period. As Alessandro d'Amico, who, as son of the theatre critic Silvio d'Amico, and husband to Pirandello's

granddaughter is the person who knows most about Pirandello's theatre, has put it, we know 'almost everything' about the skirmishes
both inside and outside the Valle Theatre but virtually nothing about
what happened on stage on that memorable evening.[7]

It is possible, however, to piece together information about the
preparations for the performance. On discovering that his favourite
actor-manager, Ruggero Ruggeri, who had already taken leading roles
in some of Pirandello's plays and was to star in *Henry IV*, was not available for his new play, Pirandello sent the script to Dario Niccodemi.
With this choice Pirandello showed himself to be a shrewd theatre
operator. Niccodemi had recently established his first theatrical company in 1921, with much panache and amid a blaze of publicity
(Rome had not seen theatre hoardings as huge as his before). The company, Compagnia Niccodemi-Vergani-Cimarosa-Almirante-Borghesi
(shortened by some to Nvcab) comprised some thirty members.
Niccodemi had taken over the Teatro Valle and was proposing to
stage an art theatre repertoire of classics, plays by new writers, and
specifically new Italian writers, in high-quality productions and then
to take the company on tour in Italy with the repertoire.

Dario Niccodemi (1874–1934), originally from Livorno, had spent
his childhood and youth in Buenos Aires, where he had developed
a lively interest in theatre, and written a couple of plays in Spanish.
There he met the French actress Réjane when she visited the city on
tour. She invited him to work for her in France where Niccodemi
spent many productive years as her secretary, making a name for
himself as a playwright in French and associating with the leading
French dramatists of the time, Henry Bataille and Henry Bernstein.
He moved back to Italy during the First World War, settling first in
Milan, where he wrote a number of well-received plays in Italian.
By the time Pirandello came to know him, Niccodemi was a cos-
mopolitan man of the theatre, with a number of successful plays to
his credit that showed him to be a sharp observer of society and a
sensitive creator of character. There was no other company in Rome
at the time that could promise so much in terms of both quality and

box-office returns. Furthermore, Niccodemi was at the time President of the Italian Authors' Society, an organisation established in 1893 that helped to promote the rights of dramatic authors.

Six Characters in Search of an Author was Niccodemi's third production at the Teatro Valle. His first two, appreciated by the audiences, give some indication of his tastes and style, and of the expectations of his Roman audience. *Romeo and Juliet* had its first night on 5 March 1921. Whereas many companies provided their own versions of Shakespeare's texts that bore little relation to the English original, Niccodemi made only a few cuts; his scene designer, Bruno Angoletta, provided a magical set, and the production showed an impressive attention to detail. The dreamlike, almost Maeterlinckian quality did not please every one, nor did the delicate, softly spoken Luigi Cimara ('a romantic hero, uncertain and weak, a little Hamlet in love' according to Silvio d'Amico) convince as the hot-blooded Romeo.[8] These qualities showed, however, that Niccodemi had new ideas concerning the play and was able to sustain them throughout the performance. Vera Vergani was a popular Juliet and Luigi Almirante's Mercutio was also very well received.

While *Romeo and Juliet* gained the approval of its audience, it was Niccodemi's second offering, a new text by a contemporary author, Fausto Maria Martini, *Il fiore sotto gli occhi* (*The Flower under Scrutiny*), that really inspired both audience and critics. This time Silvio d'Amico declared that he had rarely witnessed such a success and such a warm reception from the public.[9] *The Flower under Scrutiny* is the story of a marriage. Silvio Aroca has a beautiful wife, Giovanna, who is the 'flower' of the title. Silvio, a grammar school teacher, fears that his marriage will wither in the boring routine of teaching. So he conceives the idea of escaping his mundane life to live with his wife as her lover in a hotel. The second act takes place in a hotel, where the couple have separate rooms and Silvio is a passionate admirer of Giovanna, who is now Signora Vinci. However, the atmosphere of the hotel seems to affect his beautiful, pure wife who, Silvio discovers from a friend, is beginning to see Silvio as just one of her admirers. Silvio breaks the illusion of exciting adultery and, in front of all the astonished hotel guests, claims Giovanna as his wife, and signals his claim by kissing her passionately on stage. The third act sees the couple back home. Silvio has thrown a little party for friends, teachers and their families to mark their return while Giovanna feels suffocated by their old life. During the party a school pupil comes to ask the professor's indulgence for flouting the rules of an examination answer: he had rendered his essay in verse rather than prose, contrary to the rubric. Silvio lectures the boy passionately about our desire to flout the rules of life, to take the wrong path, and the remorse that follows. The boy is taken aback by the professor's response, but Giovanna understands her husband's pain, indicating that they have both come to accept their life as it is.

It is easy to see why this play pleased the audience so much. Like other new postwar plays linked loosely under the term 'theatre of the grotesque', *The Flower under Scrutiny* is a play about illusion and reality and the relationship of the individual to society; but unlike Luigi Chiarelli, Luigi Antonelli, Rosso di San Secondo and Pirandello himself, some of whose plays written before *Six Characters* are included in this genre, the ethos that pervades Martini's play is one of quiet acceptance, rather than savage and bitter rejection of conservative values. There is finally no anger in *The Flower under Scrutiny*. And Martini's deft dramatisation, allowing for pleasant sets and ensemble work, assured the audience of an entertaining and morally edifying night out. Well-used theatrical devices, such as the soliloquy and the use of confidantes to convey vital information, did not detract from the freshness of the dialogue. The whole, according to the reviews of the time, was acted magnificently, from the 'perfect' Giovanna (played by Vera Vergani) to the small parts of the teachers at the reception. And this time Luigi Cimara, the quietly spoken Romeo, pleased Silvio d'Amico with his bursts of passion and quiet pathos as the teacher, Silvio.[10]

It is understandable that the Valle audiences, which had so appreciated *The Flower under Scrutiny*, should have had difficulty with

Six Characters in Search of an Author. Indeed, it was no less of a shock for both the director and the actors. After Niccodemi had read it, he wrote in his diary: 'I've read Pirandello's new play, *Six Characters in Search of an Author*, and I am stunned by it, as much by the truly noble greatness of its theme as by the strangeness of its form. I'll read it again. Perhaps everything will become clear in rehearsals.'[11] The custom at the time was for the author of a new work to read the whole play to the assembled company. Pirandello's reading was an intense, breathless eruption of words. Niccodemi tersely records, 'admiration began as understanding faded – and that happened after the first few words'. 'All of us were caught up, gasping and transfixed, in that rush of words. The actors were deeply and utterly convinced and burst out with their unanimous and enthusiastic applause. But nobody had understood a thing. We were, all of us, stunned, completely at sea.'[12]

Pirandello, who attended most of the rehearsals, as was also the custom with a new play, was insistent that his words were understood, not merely spoken, and spent time explaining the ideas in the play to the bewildered actors. He also horrified the company by speaking vehemently against the role of the prompter. Niccodemi recorded that Pirandello would become increasingly excited as he warmed to his theme 'and the actors would stand around him, stunned and amazed by the radical revision of all their convictions, which were invariably founded in the importance of having a good prompter'.[13] Something of Niccodemi's appreciation and irritation with the work can be caught in a diary entry that refers to the 'tangle of cerebral oddities of this powerful work'.[14] In his memoir he was more expansive, showing his sympathy for his surely tried actors:

> The actors were quiet, deferential, and attentive, held in that religious respect which lack of understanding can always inspire. They let themselves be guided along the intricate paths of that weighty and entangled creation, so full of dazzling mental fireworks, imaginative leaps and solutions, all suffused by an atmosphere as enticing as sin. The layers of mist slowly thinned out and the first rays of light appeared, flickered,

and then shone more brightly. A moment of clarity was achieved. We all sighed happily, satisfied, as if to say 'We won't let that go.' But the actors were still somewhat lost. They were unable to form an opinion about what they were saying. And this just cannot be. An actor without an opinion about the work he's performing in is like a lamp that has gone out or a rowing boat with no oars or a motor with no piston. On stage it is essential to have an opinion about the work one's acting in – whether good or bad is irrelevant.[15]

Compared to *The Flower under Scrutiny*, this was hard work indeed. For the actors the difficulty was in the understanding of the text, in coming to terms with the ideas, and being able to speak those ideas as if they were natural to the actor/character. When acting, Pirandello had told them, 'they must no longer be actors but the very characters of the play they are performing in'.[16]

And who were these actors? The structure of professional Italian theatrical companies was a hierarchical one based on the concept of 'role'. Each company comprised a leading man (*primo attore*), leading lady (*prima attrice*), a second actress (*seconda donna*), juvenile lead (*primo attore giovane*) and young female lead (*prima attrice giovane*), a comic actor (*brillante*), a character actor and character actress (*caratterista*), mother (*madre*), actors able to play various parts (*promiscui*), several bit-part players (*generici*) and some non-speaking actors (*comparse*). The most sought-after roles were leading man and leading lady, and even here there was room for distinction: a leading man and leading lady could claim to be *primo attore assoluto* and *prima attrice assoluta*, which meant that a leading actor of this status could define his/her terms with relation to the company's repertoire. Any self-respecting company would have a team of backstage staff: stage manager, property man or mistress, a treasurer, a secretary and stagehands. The prompter requires special mention. He held a particular power within the company. Only he and the director held the whole script; the actors tended to be given only their parts. Perhaps as a hangover from an oral culture, many actors learnt their parts by listening to the prompter, who spoke the whole play even during the public performances. At the head of each company was an actor-manager (*capocomico*). As the Italian name implies, this person was often the *primo attore* or *prima attrice*, and usually lent their name to the company. The role of director was slow to be recognised in Italy. Frequently at this time the *capocomico* took responsibility for mounting the production as well as taking the main part.

Niccodemi's company was less hierarchical than some, as is clear from its cumbersome title, based on the names of the important actors, actresses and administrator within it. It also comprised comparatively young actors, the oldest being Alfonso Magheri, the character actor, who took the part of the *capocomico* in *Six Characters in Search of an Author*. The distribution of parts will have been partly influenced by the youth of the company, but also by Niccodemi's and Pirandello's ideas of the play and its characters. The company's thirty-year-old leading man, Luigi Cimara, took the part not of the Father but of the Son, while the company's thirty-five-year-old comic actor, Luigi (Gigetti) Almirante, took the main male role of the Father. This is in line with other castings of Pirandello's plays. It had been expected, for instance, that the famous *brillante*, Antonio Gaudusio, would take the role of Lamberto Laudisi in the first performance of *Right You Are! (If You Think So)*, but a nervous breakdown prevented this. It is also indicative of how Pirandello saw the delivery of thought in his plays – light and quick-witted. The distinguished second actress and *madre*, Jone Frigerio, took the role of the Mother, the company's character actress Margherita Donadoni was Mme Pace and, of course, Vera Vergani, the company's leading lady, took the part of the Stepdaughter. The company's actual stage manager, property master and chief stagehand played those parts in the play.

A characteristic of Italian reviews was that they concentrated mainly on the text, particularly if a play was new, so little is to be expected from them in terms of description or evaluation of performance. Niccodemi's diary entry for 9 May has a brief comment on the first night:

Evening of battle. Performance which it is not exaggerated to call impec-
cable. Vera revealed her simple and very human capacity for drama with
wonderful vigour. The public, confronted with a beautiful revelation,
applauded with enthusiasm. Almirante was truly extraordinary for his
clarity and intelligence. At certain moments, however, he was slightly
mannered, but this has to be attributed to the falseness of certain long
speeches that have nothing of the theatre about them, rather than to
the actor. Magheri was absolutely perfect. He knew how to make the
actor disappear and gave his part a most effective truth and colour. All
the others were attentive, serious and composed. The public made great
efforts to come to grips with the tangled mass of strange ideas of this
powerful work and held out for two acts. But with the third act, as
if what was happening on stage went beyond their understanding and
their patience, it rebelled. And there was a battle. Very few times have I
seen greater passion of conflict in a theatre.[17]

Apart from Arnaldo Frateili, who substituted for Silvio d'Amico of
the *Idea Nazionale*, and wrote a totally favourable review, the critics
had ambivalent responses to the new play. They were conscious of having seen the work of a great mind, which had tackled a theme of powerful originality and daring, but taken in its entirety they thought the
work had failed. There was general consensus that the first act worked,
and different reasons were put forward to account for what they saw as
the failure of the second, and particularly the third act. Fausto Maria
Martini (a theatre critic as well as dramatist) thought that the fundamental concept of the play was undermined by the dominance of
the Characters in the third act. Adriano Tilgher, whose strictures and
clarifications are said to have influenced Pirandello's revisions of the
play, found a regrettable lack of order in the last act, and insufficient
development of its theme.[18] Niccodemi was profoundly disappointed
by these reviews. Rather than educating the public, which he saw as
their role, the critics were submitting to its opinion, he confided to
his diary. He recalled that at the public dress rehearsal critics had said
things – presumably complimentary – that perhaps no director had
ever heard before, but in their reviews these same critics could muster

only a few compliments for Vera Vergani, Luigi Almirante and Alfonso Magheri.[19] These in effect were quite lavish. Fausto Maria Martini praised both Niccodemi and the actors. Niccodemi had directed the piece with a 'clarifying intelligence' and taken 'exquisite care over every detail'. Both Almirante and Magheri were appreciated, the latter particularly for being able to live a part that many another actor would have been only able to act.[20] But the most heartfelt praise from Martini and the other critics was for Vera Vergani, who was deemed to have reached a new maturity with this role.[21] However, despite praise for the execution, the reviews, and presumably, word of mouth, had a negative effect on the box office: on the second night there were only 367 spectators, by the fourth only 225. On 13 May the play was withdrawn and Sem Benelli's *Tignola* presented instead. *Tignola* had been premiered in 1908 and its treatment of reality and illusion constituted less of a challenge for its audiences than Pirandello's play. And in Florence, on the first leg of their tour, Niccodemi decided not to play *Six Characters*, informing Pirandello that Almirante's voice had given out. The company's administrator, Angelo Borghesi, renamed the play *Six Characters in Search of Box Office Takings*.[22] Nevertheless, Niccodemi kept *Six Characters* in repertoire until 1927 and took it to South America (Montevideo and Buenos Aires) and Spain (Madrid).

Five months after the premiere in Rome, the text of the play was published, the first of a number of editions. It is significant that Pirandello tended to publish all his plays before their premieres after the reception of *Six Characters* in Rome and that the first really favourable reception of this play was in Milan on 27 September, the first presentation after the text's publication. Pirandello was also delighted with the lively response of the Venetians in December of the following year, confirming for him the power of his play. As in Rome, but even more so, Vergani's interpretation of the Stepdaughter received ample praise. She was 'shameless, brazen, impudent, and immodest'; 'she created perfectly the complex character of the Stepdaughter: part sorrowful, part bitter, part yearning, part despairing, weighed down with a kind of cynicism willingly superimposed on her proud feeling of primordial woman and young girl; magnificently mixed with the human and the bestial'; 'Vera Vergani . . . knew how to portray a character who was only half real, that is, she managed to remain in that state of incompleteness, of restlessness, of painful inconstancy, as required by the imperfect nature with which the author has endowed her. She sustained, without a moment's tiredness, one of the most difficult parts of the contemporary repertoire'.[23]

Despite the lack of documentation and visual evidence, it is possible to see in this first production some of the parameters for the future. The studio portrait thought to be of Vera Vergani as the Stepdaughter (see fig. 1), shows, both in her costume and in her stance, some of the characteristics to be repeated in some future productions: the décolleté black dress, cut to reveal her figure, with the light accentuating the nakedness of arms and neck, the challenging seriousness of the direct gaze, the flaunting of the body, the erotic twist of the ankle.[24] Luigi Almirante's Father is also the first of a particular interpretation of the character. As a *brillante*, Almirante had a light delivery, with a distinctive, and sometimes, hoarse tone.[25] He looked for the theatrical in the part. From Niccodemi's comments on the first night, it is clear that he had some doubts about the theatrical effectiveness of some of the long speeches in the Father's part. On several occasions in later life, Luigi Almirante, in conversation with Alessandro d'Amico, indicated that the Father's part was 'lightened', because whenever the Father opened his mouth 'the action *piétinait sur place*'.[26] It seems likely therefore that some of the changes to the text that are evident in later editions were already in place in the performances from Milan onwards, and instigated by the actor and director. Almirante explained later that the part was not a difficult one for him because as a Sicilian, like Pirandello, he understood the Italian text to be Sicilian translated into Italian. He also recorded (as have many others) that Pirandello was a brilliant actor and acted the part 'in a wonderful way',[27] and that he, Almirante, was able to catch Pirandello's inflections. The most insightful comment on Almirante's performance came from the theatre historian and critic Mario

1. Vera Vergani as the Stepdaughter in the first production, directed by Dario Niccodemi, Teatro Valle, Rome, 1921. (Photo: Museo dell'Attore, Genoa.)

Apollonio, who saw the performance at Brescia in the autumn of 1921:

> He knew how to rediscover behind the tradition of nineteenth-century Italian actor the salient characteristics of the seventeenth century actor [i.e., of the old commedia dell'arte companies in their heyday], who bent the skill of acting to the service of elementary characterisation. The Father came across as gently mad in his insistence on justifying himself, innocently hypocritical in rushing to demand pity, with an insolence full of charm when he exhibited his good will and philanthropy, and the mask of his ever increasing good intentions in the manner of Molière of *L'école des Femmes*.[28]

CHAPTER 3

TWO EARLY PRODUCTIONS IN
LONDON AND NEW YORK (1922)

Six Characters in Search of an Author had an immediate impact on international theatre. Between 1921 and 1925 there were productions in Austria, Denmark, England, France, Germany, Greece, Japan, the Netherlands, Poland, Romania, Spain, Sweden, the USA and Yugoslavia. The best remembered are Theodore Komisarjevsky's at the Kingsway Theatre, London, in February 1922; Brock Pemberton's on Broadway, New York, at the Princess Theater, from 30 October 1922; George Pitoëff's at the Champs-Elysées Theatre, Paris, from 10 April 1923; and Max Reinhardt's at Die komödie, Berlin, from 30 December 1924.

KINGSWAY THEATRE, LONDON,
26–7 FEBRUARY 1922, DIRECTED
BY THEODORE KOMISARJEVSKY

First off the mark was the Stage Society, which mounted a greenroom production of the play in a translation by Nancy Green. The Lord Chamberlain, who until 1968 exercised the right to permit, amend or forbid stage productions, had refused *Six Characters in Search of an Author* a licence so a public performance was not possible. The Stage Society, which succeeded J. T. Grein's Independent Theatre in 1899, was founded expressly to perform in greenroom conditions on a Sunday evening and Monday afternoon plays of distinction that were either banned by the Lord Chamberlain or were refused production by ordinary managements. The Society survived the First World War and continued until 1940. Before the war it had presented the early works of Shaw, Granville Barker and Somerset Maugham as well as introducing Ibsen and Chekhov to its discerning audiences. After the war the programmes included a number of innovative foreign plays, such as Kaiser's *From Morn to Midnight* (1914), Elmer Rice's *The Adding Machine* (1924), and Ernst Toller's *The Machine Wreckers* (1923) and *Masses and the Man* (1924).

Six Characters in Search of an Author was brought to the attention of the Stage Society Committee by Allan Wade after he had read about its premiere in Rome in the *Observer*.[1] It was directed by Theodore Komisarjevsky (as Fyodor Fyodorovich Komissarzhevsky, half-brother of the famous Russian actress Vera Komissarzhevskaya, called himself in England after he emigrated to Western Europe in 1919). He also directed Wilhelm von Scholz's *The Race with the Shadow*, Chekhov's *Uncle Vanya*, Knut Hamsun's *At the Gates of the Kingdom* and Arnold Bennett's *The Bright Island* for the Stage Society, but he is probably better remembered for his productions at the Barnes Theatre. In 1947 Norman Marshall wrote warmly of these productions, saying he had seen 'nothing more lovely in the theatre than the stage pictures Komisarjevsky created on that cramped little stage at Barnes'. His productions were 'as satisfying to the ear as they were to the eye'. Marshall also commented on Komisarjevsky's 'subtle variations of tempo, modulation of tone and delicately timed pauses', which he deemed 'far in advance of anything in the English theatre of that time'.[2] Both John Gielgud, who was directed several times by Komisarjevsky (or Komis as he was known by his actors), and Marshall recall not only Komisarjevsky's talents in theatre design and lighting but also his impressive gifts as a director: his concentration on ensemble work, his attention to the script as to a musical score, and his method of gently guiding an actor rather than imposing his own conception of the role.

Komisarjevsky himself described his approach to actors: 'I think a producer should know how to make expressions come to life in an actor's mind and not to force intonations, and movements upon him, which have been invented in the producer's study before rehearsals.'[3] He also had firm views on the relationship of the text to the design. Psychological credibility was more important than pictorial effect. A director, or producer as he was then called, should first of all conceive 'a broad conception of the production', then visualise and hear each character, putting 'all of them into rhythmical movement'. Only after this important work has been completed should he think about 'the environment best suited for the expression of the movement' and begin to design sets, ground and lighting plans. Komisarjevsky believed firmly that the sets and stage furniture should 'suit the acting and not vice versa'. Putting characters first and creating sets and lighting plans to support them would enable the director 'to create what is called an atmosphere and to make the sets seem "alive"'.[4] John Gielgud was generous in his praise for Komisarjevsky's talents as a director.[5]

Both Marshall and Komisarjevsky have left testimony as to the difficulties of mounting a Stage Society production. It was seldom possible to get all the actors together, or to hold a rehearsal on a stage, with or without the set, which on some occasions was erected just before (or even during) a performance.[6] Komisarjevsky's conditions were, in fact, worse than those of the fictional director in *Six Characters in Search of an Author*, who at least had sets of different colours to choose from. In his Stage Society productions, he was forced by the economic conditions to use one convertible set, which he had designed himself, for every production, and then to construct 'ten different interiors and exteriors out of it'.[7] Despite these problems, actors rose to the challenge of these productions, and Komisarjevsky enjoyed excellent relations with both cast and stagehands. (One of them called him 'Come and Seduce Me', which amused him considerably.)

There is little extant information about the production of *Six Characters in Search of an Author*. It is known, however, that the performance was well received. Muriel Pratt was the Stepdaughter, Franklin Dyall the Father and Alfred Clark the Producer (as the role was then called). Desmond McCarthy was impressed. He had not seen Muriel Pratt 'act so well before', 'Mr Dyall's performance was of the first excellence' and 'No one can act better than Mr Clark that frame of mind which is expressed by the simple words, "Well I'm blowed."'[8]

PRINCESS THEATER, NEW YORK, 30 OCTOBER 1922, DIRECTED BY BROCK PEMBERTON

One of the two performances of the Stage Society's production was attended by the American theatre manager and director, Brock Pemberton. He sat in the same row as George Bernard Shaw, who 'roared at the cracks at authors, particularly at the thrusts at playwrights'.[9] So enthusiastic were the two men about the play that Pemberton put off his appointment with the director of the Victoria and Albert Museum, with whom he was due to have a meeting about a possible exhibition of stage design, and stayed to watch the rest of the play.

Laughter shared with Shaw was not the only link between the London and New York productions. The note in the Princess Theater programme was identical (apart from changes to American English) to that of the Stage Society programme, and carried the same initials, A.W., identified by Frederick May as possibly those of Alfred Wareing, a founder member of the Stage Society.[10] The two dominant themes of the note concern the theatre's inadequacy to fulfil the author's intentions and the question whether characters are any less real than actors and members of the audience. It ends 'lest we should apply ourselves to them [the questions] with overmuch seriousness, he [Pirandello] has taken care to season his work with irony and humor'.

Satire, comedy and irony were the main burdens of the New York reviews.[11] The reviewer in *Theatre Magazine* called it 'a rare and often amusing satire' while the *New York Evening World* saw it as 'an exciting jumble of everything theatrical with the whole mass burned to a cinder by irony about as gentle as the flame from a Bunsen burner'.[12] The emphasis on satire, comedy and irony probably stems, at least in the first instance, from the common misconception that the Italian word *commedia* translates as 'comedy' whereas its main meaning is 'play'. The translator, Edward Storer, also did not spot this 'false

2. The first American production, directed by Brock Pemberton, Princess Theater, New York, 1922. (Photo: New York Public Library.)

friend' and translated Pirandello's descriptive phrase *commedia da fare*, as 'comedy-in-the-making' rather than 'play-in-the-making'. Not all reviewers were impervious to the tragic elements of the play, however. Charles Darnton in the *New York Evening World* suggested that 'Luigi Pirandello's so-called "comedy-in-the-making"' was 'a tragedy in the breaking'.[13] And in the most impressive review of the production, Stark Young concludes that the greatest achievement of Pirandello's play 'is that the sum of it is moving'. 'It gives the sense of spiritual solitude. Under this fantasy and comedy and brilliant mockery and pity, it releases a poignant vitality, a pressure of life. It moves you with the tragic sense of a passionate hunger for reality and pause among the flux of things.'[14]

The play, the first Pirandello to be staged in the USA and the one that made Pirandello's reputation there, was, in the main, well received. The number of reviews of the production in New York alone is impressive. The New York presentation of *Six Characters in Search of an Author* was a major cultural event and as such it received the attention of the city's intelligentsia and was the butt of the wit of less enthusiastic society journalists. Kenneth Macgowan claimed the production 'easily the best exercise in town' and the reviewer in *Theatre Magazine* described it as 'an extraordinary piece with a brilliant idea'.[15] In the following month the same reviewer boasted that though the USA is known internationally as a 'materialistic nation', there is 'no country that welcomes intellectual novelties as eagerly as the United States'. To appreciate Pirandello 'presupposes an agility in mental acrobatics. Surely upon that basis alone Pirandello should become a fad, if not a pleasure.'[16] Margaret Rowe, writing for the *NEA Service Cleveland*, includes a witty piece in rhyming verse. The first verse reads:

> Luigi Pirandello
> Our hats are off to you
> You're such a clever fellow
> Satirical and new
> The Highbrows dote on you
> And the morons think they do.

Pirandello is all the talk in New York but, as she informs her Cleveland readers no doubt eager to hear satire at the expense of New Yorkers, while they sip their drinks it is clear that they do not know whether he's a new show, a new drink, 'oil of citronella' or 'a disease that will kill a fella'.[17] The Stepdaughter's costume figured in fashion magazines and news concerning the production was relayed in the press. New Yorkers were puzzled that productions were banned in the UK and asserted their superiority in having a less restrictive censorship. During the run, however, the mayor's office issued a demand that all juveniles under the age of ten be withdrawn from public performance. Brock Pemberton complied with the order and trained up another Little Girl.[18]

Pemberton was a lively director with independent views. (He was also a shrewd businessman: he announced in the press before the opening night that the play 'would be presented for an engagement of four weeks only and all morons would be denied admission', thus ensuring a longer run.)[19] The Characters' entrance was modest but efficacious: led by the Father, they appeared from behind a stack of scenery. Pemberton achieved differentiation from the Actors by heavy, pale make-up, as Pitoëff was also to do; and by two distinct acting styles. Two reviews called attention to the startling pallor of the Characters' faces, and one to the acting style, 'the fiercely sincere manner, exactly opposite to the cynical professionalism of the Actors, in which they develop their theme'.[20] At the end of the play, Pemberton has the Mother carry out the body of her dead son[21] (the 1921 script followed by Storer indicates that the child is carried out but does not say by whom). And in addition to sending the Actors home after a frustrating day, the Manager (Director) tells them that they will rehearse another play, *The Bride's Revenge*, 'for that is what the public wants'.[22] From other reviews there is evidence that the name of the play changed with alterations in Pemberton's repertoire over the three-month run.

The cast included established American actors and some impressive young talent. Six of the cast had played in Pemberton's production of *The Plot Thickens* (translated from *Quello che non t'aspetti* by Luigi

Barzini and Arnaldo Fraccaroli), with the consequence that members of the cast were used to working with each other: Fred House, Dwight Frye (the Son), Jack Amory, Russel Morrison and John Saunders. The cast was large: the six Characters, Mme Pace, the Manager and twelve named actors and stage staff; plus unspecified Stagehands – the cast even ran to a fourth actor and fifth actress. Moffat Johnston was praised for his performance as the Father. Stark Young thought he caught 'the essential quality, which was a strange mixture of analytical and physical passion and of boldness and fear, candour and shame',[23] though two reviewers thought he spoke the longer speeches with too great an insistence. One referred to it as 'a ranting part' and wondered whether the blame for this should be assigned to Johnston or to Pirandello; the other asserted that 'a steady and unrelieved roaring dulls the eardrums and finally the wits'.[24] Stark Young expanded on his enthusiasm for the twenty-one-year-old Florence Eldridge's interpretation of the Stepdaughter:

> As the daughter her work was astonishingly good; it was impetuous, flickering, sometimes crude, sometimes leaping up, sometimes darkened from within. She achieves the ebullience and the tragedy of the character, the necessity for living and speaking out, the tears, animation and mind. Against the more stolid and upright bodies of the director's own company of actors, Miss Eldridge created something strangely real and unreal and irrepressible. There were moments when she seemed to be a flame; behind her eyes and brow there seemed to shine the light of some youthful urgent and extremely fixed reality, about her movement the force of some haunting vitality and enthusiasm.[25]

It is clear that some of the productions that took place between 1921 and 1925 provided details to Pirandello for the revised version of 1925. The opening part of the play was considerably reworked in Pirandello's own production of the play and was one of the areas also much enhanced by both Pitoëff and Reinhardt. The 1921 Italian text begins with a page of stage directions, which include the opportunity for some invention and improvisation on the part of the company, as it makes its way on to the stage for the rehearsal of *The Rules of the Game*. Pitoëff enlarged this section, Reinhardt even more so: his opening scene runs to ten pages of scripted dialogue.

Reviews of Pemberton's 1922 production indicate that he, too, enhanced the opening scene. The reviewer for the *New York Owl* mentions the bare stage, the empty space, the few chairs, flats leaning against the side walls. The Props Man saunters on to the stage, whistling, the Actors begin to assemble. 'The Manager, burly, genial comes striding down the house, climbs on to the stage; the leading lady, of course, is late; her entrance is spectacular, also through what is supposed to be a blank theatre.'[26] The *Daily Hotel* reporter confirms the innovation: the Leading Lady 'arrives a second after the Manager, running up the centre aisle only to be given a dressing down for coming through the front of house'.[27] As far as printed texts of the play are concerned, it is not until 1925 that Pirandello includes the details of the Director and Leading Lady arriving through the auditorium (the latter carrying a little dog); the 1921 text, which Storer translated, has all the action behind the proscenium arch; and neither Pitoëff nor Reinhardt in their reworking of this scene altered the entrances of the Director and Leading Lady. Pirandello did not see Pemberton's 1922 production until 6 February 1924, in a special revival with the original cast (in the main) during his stay in New York for the season of his plays mounted by Brock Pemberton at the Fulton Theater.[28] This means that he had already seen Pitoëff's Parisian production (April 1923), which offered much material for reflection, providing ideas that Pirandello was to incorporate into his revised version. The innovations in the opening scene, suggested by Pemberton's production, were therefore fairly late additions to the reworked text.

The 1922–3 New York theatrical season was an impressive one. The Moscow Art Theatre visited New York for the first time and other new foreign plays were presented: *The Plot Thickens*, Karel Capek's *RUR*, Joseph and Karel Capek's *The World We Live In* (an adaptation of *The Insect Comedy*), George Kaiser's *From Morn to Midnight* and John Galsworthy's *Loyalties*. There were also five productions of

Shakespeare. *Six Characters* was not voted one of the 'best plays of the year' but it and Pirandello benefited from the considerable amount of media attention.[29] Pemberton's *Six Characters in Search of an Author* sparked an enthusiasm for Pirandello that continued for several years. Other productions of the play quickly followed.[30] The Dutton collection of three plays by Pirandello (including the Storer translation of *Six Characters*) was extensively reviewed: a full page in both the *Christian Science Monitor* and in the *New York Times Book Review*.[31] In late 1923 Pemberton mounted a Pirandello season at the Fulton Theater (renamed the Pirandello Theater for the duration). Journalists travelled to Italy to interview the playwright in his Roman home.[32] By 1931, when *Six Characters* was revived at the Bijou Theater, the fervour had died down. John Hutchens of *Theatre Arts Monthly* found fault with Pirandello's 'incessant use of the same theme in later and poorer plays'.[33] *Six Characters in Search of an Author*, however, has remained a staple of university drama societies and club theatres in the USA,[34] and has enjoyed some outstanding later productions.

CHAPTER 4

PITOËFF'S PRODUCTION IN PARIS (1923)

COMÉDIE DES CHAMPS-ELYSÉES, PARIS, 10 APRIL 1923, DIRECTED BY GEORGES PITOËFF

The production of *Six Characters in Search of an Author* that contributed most to rendering the play a European and world classic
was staged in Paris in 1923 by the Russian director Georges Pitoëff.
Through this production, as a French critic has put it, Pirandello was
'suddenly hoisted up from plain Italian notoriety to universal fame'.[1]
Pitoëff's production gained legendary status as a presentation that
would have a lasting influence on future French theatre.

> Without Pirandello and without the Pitoëffs (for one can no longer
> separate them, the genius of the Pitoëffs having given its form to that of
> Pirandello), we would not have had Salacrou, nor Anouilh, nor Ionesco,
> nor . . . but here I stop, this enumeration would be endless. All the theatre
> of an epoch has emerged from the belly of this play, *Six Characters in
> Search of an Author*.[2]

It caused an enormous stir at the time. The theatre critic Paul Brisson
went to see a play by Sardou and *Six Characters* over two consecutive
evenings and felt that he had 'crossed a distance of fifty years in twenty-
four hours'. On the one side, he concluded, 'there is the theatre as
conceived by our grandparents; on the other here is the most new and
courageous of contemporary works'.[3]

Georges Pitoëff (1884–1939) had come to Paris with his wife,
the actress Ludmilla Pitoëff, in January 1922, at the invitation

of the enterprising theatre manager Jacques Hébertot. It was Hébertot's intention to create an international theatrical centre at the Champs-Elysées Theatre and he saw the Pitoëffs as making a major contribution to that dream. Georges Pitoëff was a man of some international theatrical experience before his stay at the Champs-Elysées Theatre. He had trained in Russia with Stanislavsky and Nemirovitch-Danchenko at the Moscow Art Theatre (1902–5), and lived in Paris as a student. In 1908 Vera Komissarjevskaya persuaded him back to her theatre in St Petersburg, where he worked from 1908 to 1910. He followed Jacques-Dalcroze's courses in Hellerau in 1911, toured with a theatre company through much of Russia and directed his own company in Geneva from 1915. His repertoire had included Shaw, Lenormand, Chekhov, Andreev and Björnson. It was Pitoëff's passion for the new and the foreign as well as his outstanding talent as actor, stage designer and director that led Jacques Hébertot to offer him the contract.

As a director, Pitoëff, like Komisarjevsky, preferred to provide an artistic environment (in terms of conception of the play and design plans) in which the actors could interpret their roles rather than tell them what to do. There is no doubt, however, where Pitoëff stood in the early twentieth-century debate concerning the role of the director. It is the director (*le metteur en scène*) who is the 'absolute master' (*maître absolu*), the 'absolute autocrat' (*autocrate absolu*) when it comes to staging a play.

> The written text exists by itself in the book, one reads it, and each reader will assimilate it according to his imagination. But when it comes to the stage, the writer's mission is finished, it is by another that the text will be transformed into spectacle. I do not diminish the role of the author, I merely defend the absolute independence of the scenic art.[4]

This assertion was in direct contrast to Pirandello's views at the time. Pirandello believed firmly in the supremacy of the author as maker of the text. In Pitoëff's personal experience authors more often than not had no idea of how to present their plays correctly. Chekhov, he wrote, never knew how his plays should be staged; it was Stanislavsky who showed him. Pirandello, who had objected to the use of the stage lift in Pitoëff's production, was to adopt, Pitoëff claimed, 'all my staging of his play when he put it on in Rome'.[5] This exaggerated claim holds more than a grain of truth: Pirandello's 1925 production was influenced by Pitoëff's, and Pirandello's views on the balance of power in the theatre changed over time. He used Pitoëff's words on the relationship between the text (for the reader) and the script (for the stage production) almost verbatim – and without attribution – some thirteen years later when introducing Silvio d'Amico's book on the history of Italian theatre.[6]

The history of Pirandello's play, and indeed of subsequent French theatre, might have taken a different course, for Pitoëff was not the first to consider presenting *Six Characters in Search of an Author* in Paris. Jules Romains, one of the theatre director Jacques Copeau's readers at the time, had passed the text to him earlier in 1922 for consideration. Copeau rejected the play, adding that 'if it had been by a young French author' rather than a 'foreigner in his fifties', his response might have been different.[7]

It was during the summer of 1922, after a successful first season that established him and his company as leaders on the Parisian theatrical scene in the views of discerning critics and theatre practitioners, that Pitoëff conceived the idea of staging *Six Characters in Search of an Author*. At the beginning of the enterprise, he and his wife were the only people who had faith in the play. The initial reading of the script to all the personnel of the theatre was a complete fiasco, and it was only friendship that prompted Jacques Hébertot to concede 3,000 francs to Pitoëff to mount the production.[8] It had been Pitoëff's intention to be the first to stage a Pirandello play in Paris and open the new season with this play, but a motor accident in which Ludmilla, who was to play the Stepdaughter, broke her leg, prevented this. The production was postponed to April of the following year. This delay meant that Paris audiences already had some experience of a Pirandello play, in the form of Charles Dullin's presentation of *The Pleasures of Respectability* in Camille Mallarmé's translation, *La volupté de l'honneur*, a play that has remained one of Pirandello's most performed texts in France. Dullin's production stimulated a number of articles and lectures on Pirandello, which meant that by the spring of 1923 Pirandello was no longer a mere 'foreigner in his fifties' to the intelligentsia of Paris.

Pitoëff worked from Benjamin Crémieux's translation of the 1921 text. A man of letters of some repute, Crémieux was to become Pirandello's chief French translator and only in the latter part of the twentieth century were his translations superseded. Crémieux had already written an article on Pirandello for the *Revue de France* in 1922 and was later to publish a book, *Henri IV et la dramaturgie de Luigi Pirandello*. In his preparation for the production, Pitoëff appears not to have referred back to the Italian text of *Six Characters in Search of an Author*, for errors made by Crémieux remain in his script. These include translating 'water' (*acqua*) as 'water jug' (*cruche*) and 'mixing bowl' (*ciotola*) as 'chocolate' (*cioccolata*). Pitoëff did, however, make amendments and, in a few instances, some quite substantial alterations. Most of these were not included in Crémieux's published versions, but a number of the alterations appear to have been picked up by Pirandello, for they are included in his 1925 version.

Pitoëff altered the Pirandello/Crémieux text by running some speeches together, changing a few words in some speeches, cutting some interchanges completely and rewriting the passage in the 'garden scene' where the Director arranges how the scene is to be played. Pitoëff cuts the following passages:

(a) the interchange between the Father and the Stepdaughter in which she challenges his assumptions of 'a certain moral healthiness' if he visits establishments such as Mme Pace's shop;

(b) a long speech in the first part in which the Father describes the present situation of the Father, Mother and Son living together after the death of the other two children and the Stepdaughter's escape;

(c) the Son's speech at the beginning of part 2 when he describes a child's problem when forced to recognise his parents as fully human;

(d) the Ingénue's interruption to 'the scene' in part 2, when she objects to the actresses' hats being used;

(e) an interchange between the Director and the Father in part 3 during which the Father expressed himself with words similar to those used by Pirandello in his Afterword to *The Late Mathias Pascal* – 'it's beasts who suffer without reasoning';

(f) the Stepdaughter's speech in part 3 in which she remembers her little sister playing in the garden and bringing her flowers.[9]

The removal of some of the Father's speeches is in line with Giorgio Almirante's inclination to lighten the Father's discourse when the play went on tour (see p. 41) and is confirmed in later printed editions of the play. Both (a) and (b) are dropped in the Italian 1923/4 version, (c) is shortened in 1923/4 and entirely cut in 1925, and (e), a passage of more than two pages, is also cut in 1923/4. Pirandello also removed a further section of the third part in 1923/4, another discussion between the Father and the Director during which the Director explains that theatre is action and not philosophy and accuses the Father of confusing the issue.

All these alterations show a tendency to make the play more theatrical, to tighten the structure, and to lessen or lighten those parts where thought is expressed in words rather than in visual image or action. A section where Pitoëff clearly showed his theatrical command of the text is in the 'garden scene' in part 3. The Director's speech, during which he sets the scene, is rewritten by Pitoëff, perhaps with the collaboration of the actor who took the part of the Director, Michel Simon. In the script Crémieux's translation is crossed through and on the facing page (p. 111) a typed substitute has been pasted in. Here are the two versions in English translation: Crémieux's version (from Pirandello's 1921 text)

DIRECTOR: Listen. You'll have your garden. You'll have your garden, we'll put all the scenes in the garden. (*He calls a stagehand by name.*) Hey! A few trees straightaway and a fountain basin. (*Turning round to look at the back of the stage.*) Ah, you've fixed it up. Good! (*To the Stepdaughter.*) This is just to give an idea, of course. Your little brother, instead of hiding behind the doors, will wander about here in the garden, hiding behind the trees. But it won't be easy to find a little girl to play that scene with you and the flowers. (*Turning to the Boy.*) Come forward a little, will you please? Let's see what we can do. (*The Boy does not move.*) Now, come forward, come on. We've got a problem here, with this boy. What's the matter with him? All the same, he'll have to say something.

Pitoëff's substituted version

DIRECTOR: All right. You will have your garden. You'll have your garden, we'll put all the scenes in the garden. Blanc? Are you there? Give me some trees and a fountain. (*To the stagehands.*) Take away those chairs. (*To the actors.*) Clear the stage, please. (*The actors retire to the side of the stage. The stagehands go to look for some trees. The Characters remain in the middle of the stage. To the Stepdaughter.*) You see, just to get an idea. Instead of hiding behind the doors, your little brother can hide behind trees. (*The stagehands place the trees.*) Look out! (*To the Mother.*) Madam, come this way please. (*The Mother goes to the left with her children. She sits down. The Son breaks away to the right down by the proscenium. The Father stands in the middle of the stage, the Stepdaughter between the Mother and the Director. To the stagehands.*) That's good. Now give me some kind of a backcloth. The sky. (*To the Stepdaughter.*) But it won't be easy to find a little girl to play that scene with you and the flowers. (*The stagehands light the backcloth.*) Good, very good. (*To the Boy.*) Come forward, yes, you. Let's see what we can do. (*To the electrician.*) Dim the light a little. (*The stagehands put the fountain in place.*) Good, that's right. (*To the Boy.*) Now, come forward, come on. We've a problem here, with this boy. What's the matter with him? All the same, he'll have to say something.[10]

Pitoëff's script builds on Pirandello's original text, rendering the episode more theatrical. He makes the Director aware of all the people he has on stage, the Actors as a group, and each of the Characters, not only the Stepdaughter, Boy and Little Girl but also the Mother, the Son and the Father. Pitoëff is visually aware of the positions of each, and of the spectacle he is creating with what is, in effect, the Director's moment of creativity. The major innovations he contributes are the introduction of the backcloth and the use of lighting, neither of which is mentioned in Pirandello's 1921 version and both of which are present in the 1925 edition. The white backcloth enhanced the stark outlines of the trees and the black costumes of the Characters. The dimming of the lighting helped to create a dreamlike atmosphere redolent of Symbolist drama.

Finding a way to present the Characters is one of the major areas of interest for a director of *Six Characters in Search of an Author*. Pirandello opens the second paragraph of his 1925 stage directions, which differ quite considerably from the 1921 directions, with a phrase that could sound strange to a theatre director: 'Anyone wanting to attempt a stage production of this play . . .' In these few words we glimpse not only the narrative origins of the play, but also the struggle to find a means, a theatrical 'objective correlative' to convey Pirandello's epiphanic experience. In 1921 the Characters used the same entrance as the Actors: they came in from the stage door at the back of the stage. A barely perceptible, very faint light appeared around them, as if irradiating from them, 'the light breath of their fantastic reality'. How is the audience to understand that this 'barely perceptible' light is to convey that this new set of actors is comprised of characters? In 1921 this is done gradually through words, in the main through the Father's explanations and discussions with the Director. In 1925 Pirandello cut some of the speeches that reiterate the theme of the difference between characters and mortals and emphasised the theatrical presentation. The second paragraph of the stage direction goes on to insist that anyone wanting to stage the play should use 'every means to obtain the effect that the Six Characters are not confused with the

Actors of the Company'. Pirandello suggests the use of stage space by separating the Characters from the Actors, and coloured lighting, but considered the most effective means to be masks. He provided quite detailed information about these masks: 'special masks . . . of some material solid enough not to go limp with sweat, but light enough for the Actors to wear them comfortably, and so designed that the eye, nostrils and mouth are left free' and fixed the motif of the mask of each Character.[11]

Unlike Dullin, who had conceived of Pirandello's theatre as theatre of action, grounded in social satire and essentially comic, Pitoëff approached the play as theatre of ideas. And for him the central idea of *Six Characters in Search of an Author* was the conflict between two kinds of reality: Pitoëff took the Father's statement that 'Nature's highest instrument in the creative process is the human imagination' as the pivotal idea of the play. As human beings, we see the Characters as fiction, he wrote, but for the Characters the opposite is true: it is they who are 'unchanging and eternal in their shadowy reality while human beings can touch and breathe only a reality destined to perpetual change: a fleeting and transitory reality', an illusion of reality in the empty comedy of existence.[12] Pitoëff had also understood that the presentation of the different reality of the Characters needed scenic solutions, not verbal explanations.[13] In a stroke of genius, he devised an entrance that differentiated the Characters strikingly from the Actors, shook the audience, and at the same time revealed the aspirations of the Characters to fulfil themselves as characters for the stage: he brought the Characters in by the stage lift, bathed in a green light. Like gods from on high, six strange, disturbed beings, dressed in black (with the exception of the Little Girl who wore a white dress) descended on to the stage. It was a moment that deeply impressed those who saw it. Something of the effect can be seen in this account: 'All of a sudden, right in the middle of these marionettes, there comes down from behind the borders, by means of the stage hoist, an extraordinary family, a band of ghosts or drowning people. Figures from another world, deathly pale [*blafardes*], dressed in black, suspicious, agitated.'[14] Antonin Artaud, who was to take the part of the Prompter in the revival of Pitoëff's production the following year, wrote of the Characters emerging from the lift as 'a family in mourning, their faces completely white, as if hardly awake from a dream'.[15]

In order to accommodate this new entrance, Pitoëff made some alterations to the end of the play. Though these alterations are not written into his director's script, reviews provide the evidence that the Characters returned whence they came, by the stage lift. The 1921 Italian text (and therefore Crémieux's) ends with some actors believing what has happened and crying out 'Reality, reality' while others think it is all a pretence. Exasperated, the Director sends the Actors home, complaining that the Characters have made him waste a day. In Pitoëff's presentation it seems that all the Actors believe the deaths to be real and are overcome by what has happened.

> [The actors] rush back on stage crying repeatedly 'It's the truth' while all the six characters, including the two dead children, take their place again in the lift and are lost in the flies. Has this end no other purpose than to disconcert us? Or is the intention to demonstrate the invincible force of the illusion of art since the actors, who are the most resistant to it, have allowed themselves to be persuaded?[16]

In Pitoëff's production, then, the Characters' difference was set from the start. The audience was stunned into awareness. Pitoëff also enhanced the opening scenes, building up to the impact of the Characters' difference. To the stage itself, in addition to the objects mentioned by Pirandello, such as the Director's chair with its back to the audience and the little tables and chairs about the stage, Pitoëff added a stepladder, frames and lights. In other words, Pitoëff transformed Pirandello's rehearsal space into a more total representation of a theatre at work, a space that includes technicians and backstage staff. The Actors wore bright clothes. Pirandello's improvised scene of the entrance of the Actors with the minor climax of the Director's entrance is given greater build-up than in the 1921 text with the introduction of a piano, not mentioned in the 1921 stage directions, but introduced in 1925. As an anonymous reviewer recorded: 'There is a piano in a corner. One of them sits at it and plays a foxtrot. A few couples dance. Suddenly a cry goes up "The Director". Everything returns to order. Everyone gets into place.'[17]

Pitoeff is careful throughout to keep the Characters separated from the Actors. The moves during the first part of the play show the Characters gradually taking over the stage, pushing the Actors to outer positions. For instance, at the point when the Stepdaughter accuses the Son of denying the family hospitality, Pitoëff had the Son downstage left, the Director downstage on the opposite side, the Mother centre stage with her two children just in front of her, the Father (right) and the Stepdaughter (left) behind her with the Actors positioned at the back of the stage. Only the Director, in his distinctive light suit, was allowed to bridge the groups, which were three at times, as Pitoëff was careful to include moves for a third group, the Stagehands. Pitoëff excluded even those points of contact included in the Italian 1921 text. When the Mother intervenes in part 1 and is about to faint, in Crémieux's translation the Father and all the Actors rush to her aid and one goes for a chair. Pitoëff kept the stage direction about the chair but cut those referring to Actors crowding round and supporting the Mother.[18]

In addition to the black costumes, appropriate for a family in mourning, Pitoëff also differentiated the Characters from the Actors by make-up. Photographs indicate that the make-up for the Characters was deliberately white, heavy and stylised, a form of mask, anticipating Pirandello's 1925 stage directions. Significantly, too, though there is no evidence that the auditorium as such was used as stage space, photographs show that Pitoëff had deepened the shallow Champs-Elysées stage by placing three steps in front of it. This gave Pitoëff a further possibility to centre the Characters on the stage and bring the Director, and, at times, the Actors of the company out on to the steps. This was particularly felicitous in part 2 when the Father and Stepdaughter present their 'scene'. At this point the Characters had the stage to themselves, and the Actors were grouped to the side on the steps. In his 1937 revival of the play, Pitoëff placed the Actors in the front row of the auditorium for this scene.[19]

As we have seen, Pitoëff's interpretation of the play took as its centre the tragic reality of the Characters. He himself took the role of the Father, his wife, Ludmilla, the Stepdaughter. Photographic evidence suggests that her interpretation was markedly different from Vera Vergani's and Marta Abba's (in 1925). In a long, unrevealing black dress reaching down nearly to her ankles, leaving only the left arm and hand bare, white (rosary?) beads at her waist, a black headcovering banded in white low on her forehead, here is a slight young woman in deep mourning. Looking forward with big eyes in a deathly pale oval face, she avoids contact with her client, the Father (see fig. 3). Another image, probably a studio portrait, shows her looking out and up to the camera, the flesh of her left arm and hand startling in its whiteness. She is posed casually on the chair, sitting sideways on. The exposed foregrounded arm with its elbow on the chair's back and hand supporting her head, coupled with the delicate but firm, unsmiling mouth in the pale perfectly shaped face give a sense of both weary but steady acceptance and challenging clear-sightedness.[20] Each illustration has a stillness about it, so different from the provocative and febrile movements associated with the role of the Stepdaughter. Marie Kalff as the Mother was also impressive in her simplicity. But the reviewers concentrated most on Pitoëff's presentation of the Father. Pitoëff varied the tempo of his performance considerably, at times showing him highly intelligent and frenetic with an intensity of gesticulation, and at others showing him gently and sweetly sad.[21] It was Antonin Artaud who differentiated most strikingly Georges Pitoëff's acting from the rest of the cast and saw in him a revelation:

> The character of the play is Georges Pitoëff who gives to the central character a mask and visionary gestures. There's one thing to say, just one thing to say about him, and that is it. Ludmilla Pitoëff and Kalff were very beautiful but still remained human, I mean of flesh and blood, I mean actresses in a word. The one ingénue, the other 'mother', very intense, but nevertheless of this life, not of the spirit.[22]

3. The first production in France, directed by Georges Pitoëff, Comédie des Champs-Elysées, Paris, 1923. (Photo: Nicholas Treatt.)

Charles Dullin was concerned that Pitoëff might overemphasise the tragic element of the play: as he was a Russian, he wrote, he was perhaps not suited to 'stage a work from a Latin writer. He will most certainly emphasise the strangeness of the work to the detriment of its overall sense and gaiety'.[23] That Pitoëff was well able to perceive and deploy the comic elements of the play is clear in his casting. Though Michel Simon was first cast in the role of the Father, it became clear during rehearsals that he would be better suited to the role of the Director. Jean Hort, a member of Pitoëff's original Geneva company and who played the Props Man in this production, remembered Michel Simon's performance with admiration and affection. The part, he said, required a gift for improvisation, which Michel Simon clearly had. 'Michel Simon's rendering of the Director was physically impressive, for his gestures, for the sobriety of his humour and the flashes of wit he aptly improvised throughout the performance.'[24]

Pitoëff's production of *Six Characters in Search of an Author* was a great success, both financially and artistically. During the 1921–2 season in Paris, no Pirandello play took as much as 2,000 francs a night at the box office; the sum increased the following season to an average of about 3,000 for each performance, while *Six Characters in Search of an Author* took an average of about 10,000 francs a night over thirty-nine performances. (During the previous season no production by Pitoëff had taken more than 3,000 francs a night.)[25] Bearing in mind the Parisian concern for the purity of the French language, that the audiences were so enthusiastic about the production is all the more impressive. The cast of the play was dominated by actors who were not French: Georges and Ludmilla Pitoëff (Russian), Marie Kalff (Dutch), Alfred Penay (Swiss – he played the Son), and among the Actors, Eugene Ponti, Henri Schimeck and Jean Hort were all Swiss.

It is interesting to note the differences in reception in Italy and Paris. Both Italian and French reviewers concentrated on the newness, originality and surprising qualities of the text, but it was in France that 'dreams' and 'hallucinations' dominated the prose. This is perhaps best caught in L. Gillet's appreciation of the production:

These supernatural creatures release a moving power of phantasmagoria and hallucination . . . In the middle of their quarrel, darkness invades the stage; in violent light one can see only these six spectres that thresh about and grieve, like more than human figures of love, pain and hate. Suddenly a gunshot rings out. Daylight returns. The vision has disappeared. Nevertheless there is blood. One no longer knows where one is. Where does illusion begin? Where does nature finish? The players come back on stage, perplexed, uncertain, troubled, not knowing whether they are the playthings of a dream, and what the frontiers are between Life and Dream.[26]

This concentration on the fantastic, oneiric and hallucinatory quality of Pirandello's play reflected the new tendencies of French culture, soon to be identified with Freudian psychoanalysis and surrealism.[27]

Acclaimed in its own right, Pitoëff's production was compared with Pirandello's own when it came to Paris in 1925. The contrast between two acting styles was immediately apparent, and became dubbed the 'northern' and 'southern', Pitoëff's being associated with Ibsen and tragedy, while the Italian style, lighter and more animated, was less obviously tragic. Characteristics of Pitoëff's cultural and theatrical make-up (his Russian background and his experience in a variety of theatrical environments), combined with a deep sensitivity, enabled him to discover the theatrical 'objective correlative' that expresses mystery. As Lenormand expressed it, in Pitoëff's theatre 'the constant interrogation of forces which dominate the human marionette become perceptible'.[28] It was Pitoëff's production that first explored beyond the surface of the text, and revealed dimensions unrealised hitherto on the stage. Despite differences in approach, Pirandello is said to have been delighted with the production when he saw it at the press night and to have told Pitoëff that it was he who had taught Italian actors how to perform his play.[29]

CHAPTER 5

REINHARDT'S PRODUCTION IN BERLIN (1924)

DIE KOMÖDIE, BERLIN, 30 DECEMBER 1924, DIRECTED BY MAX REINHARDT

By the time Max Reinhardt came to present *Six Characters in Search of an Author* at the Berlin Komödie, there had already been several German productions of the play, including one in Vienna (the first); and two productions of *Right You Are!* (*If You Think So*), one of which was presented in Berlin. *Six Characters in Search of an Author* proved to be Pirandello's most popular play in Germany with more than a hundred different productions over the two theatrical seasons from 1924 to 1926.

The reception of Pirandello's plays was more complex in Germany than in France. This was due in the main to three factors: the accelerated development of German theatre thanks to the economic boom, a particular attitude to the avant-garde from the early 1920s, and Pirandello's failure to comprehend the specific situation of German theatre. These factors resulted in a discrepancy in the reception of his plays. Pirandello was respected by theatre practitioners, who appreciated the theatrical nature of his plays; he was continuously in the public eye – indeed, hardly a newspaper or magazine omitted to write about him, and cartoons of Pirandello and his characters were numerous in the mid 1920s; but he was not, on the whole, well received by critics.[1]

From being a country with a short theatrical history, Germany's Weimar Republic became, during the first quarter of the twentieth century, the major centre for theatrical exploration and innovation. The economic boom of the 1920s, due to the stabilisation of the

German mark, which in turn led to investment, had its effect on theatre as well as other walks of life. There were new theatrical buildings
and, most notably, impressive improvements to the theatre apparatus
in existing theatres. The growing success of the two major electrical
firms, Siemens and AEG, had its spin-off in the refurbishment of
theatre lighting systems. The incandescent carbon filament made it
possible to provide a steady light source that could be dimmed gradually and without flickering. As Michael Patterson has pointed out, the
introduction of the tungsten filament in 1910 and of the powerful
three-kilowatt bulbs in the 1920s made it possible to set light at a
required level of intensity, to direct individual beams on the set or
actor and to project colour on to the stage. Such technical possibilities
allowed for both convincing illusionistic naturalistic effects and for a
range of experimentation with mood and symbolic lighting. With the
invention of the 'Rundhorizont' or white cyclorama in 1869 and For-
tuny's sky-dome (or 'Kuppelhorizont' as it was known in Germany),
it became possible to create a scene with lighting rather than with a
backdrop. Starlit skies, the sun rising, the moon setting could all be
created through this new technology. Scenery could also be projected
on to the backcloth, a method used by Linnebach in Dresden and
later by Piscator.[2]

Innovative lighting played a large part in the refurbishment of the
Odescalchi Theatre in Rome, the home of the Teatro d'Arte for a
brief period. Struggling as he was to impress upon his own government the importance of theatre, Pirandello would have appreciated
the new German republic's attitude. This German perspective, however, was not modernist in any formalist sense. The arts in Germany
in the 1920s were not art for art's sake, and practitioners did not
separate themselves from the people in a privileged position. Theatre,
along with the other arts, was seen not as a luxury or entertainment,
but as part of the process of self-improvement and therefore social
improvement.[3] The Bauhaus epitomised this approach to the arts,
its philosophy encapsulated in the slogan 'Art and Technology, the
new Unity'. From the perspective of theatre, technical innovations

were not simply mechanisms with which to create effects or modify the ways a stage could be organised; they were expressions of theatre's entry into history, of its ability to adapt to new social forces in the integration of the new products and new technologies.[4] As Stephen Lamb has emphasised, the concept of avant-garde was redefined in the 1920s to remove the conventional distinction between formal experimentation on the one hand and politically committed realist or representational art on the other.

> The best politically committed German theatre produced during the short-lived democracy experimented with new techniques and devised new ways of looking at reality not in order to express the disturbed emotional state of the artistic mind, so often the primary concern of the self-preoccupied avant-garde, but in order to illuminate the more rational domain of social, political and economic processes.[5]

Pirandello, it seems, did not understand the ideology that accompanied this progress. Likewise, German intellectuals and theatre critics sympathetic to this approach did not appreciate, as their counterparts in France had, Pirandello's fundamental questioning of theatre itself. They saw in Pirandello a modernist, one who believed in *l'art pour l'art*, a formalist who enjoyed playing with ideas, who posited the work of art as autonomous. Siegfried Jacobsohn dismissed the Pirandello of *Six Characters in Search of an Author* as 'not the right one for us' (or 'not our sort of chap'). 'Playing with plays', as he defined the play, fitted Reinhardt's style, but Reinhardt himself was *passé*, and, according to Jacobsohn, unable to engage with the burning political and social challenges that confronted the Weimar Republic.[6] Two other major critics of the time, Herbert Jhering and Bernard Diebold, saw Pirandello as providing variations on petit-bourgeois themes, dressed up as philosophy.[7] Even Rudolph Pechel, a critic sympathetic to *Six Characters in Search of an Author* – he thought Pirandello's fantasy 'superb and shatteringly enigmatic' – attributed the success of the first night of the play to Reinhardt, not Pirandello. 'The more one reflects on it, the clearer it becomes that it was Max Reinhardt rather than Pirandello who was the poet of this performance of a play in the making.'[8]

In terms of technical and directorial innovation, much of the development of Germany's theatre in the first quarter of the twentieth century can be attributed to Reinhardt. The great moment of his early career was his production of *A Midsummer Night's Dream*. The first memorable use of Europe's new revolving stage was in this production, presented in the Deutsches Theater in Berlin in 1905. Reinhardt's designer, Gustav Knina, constructed a forest with three-dimensional trees and apparently authentic grass (made of raffia). As the stage revolved a magical scene was revealed of trees, hillocks and lake with elves and sprites gambolling through the greenery. Actors were no longer set against a backdrop but became 'an integral part of a complete stage picture'.[9]

By 1924 Reinhardt's domination of theatre in Berlin was over. Disenchanted with the city, having handed over artistic direction of all his theatres to Felix Hollaender, he left Berlin in 1920, to return to his native Austria. Over the next nine years, however, he returned to Berlin intermittently as a guest director. It was in this capacity that he directed *Six Characters in Search of an Author*. The play was presented, therefore, when Reinhardt was very well known to Berlin's audiences and critics and when theatrical approaches different from his stylised realism were in vogue.

Six Characters in Search of an Author was a play that suited Reinhardt's views on theatre well and one to which he returned more than once in subsequent life. Despite some reservations about the production, Pirandello held Reinhardt in considerable respect and dedicated *Tonight We Improvise* to him. Nevertheless, there were differences in their approach to the theatre. Pirandello's directorial approach, at least in 1925, echoed his views on theatre representation as expressed in earlier essays, 'Spoken Action' and 'Illustrators, Actors and Translators': the focus of his concern was the writer's text. Reinhardt's approach centred on the actor. He said in 1901 that he believed in 'a theatre that belongs to the actor'. No longer would literary points of view predominate as they had in the past. 'The theatre owes the actor his right to show himself from all sides, to be active in many directions, to display his joy in playfulness, in the magic of transformation.'[10] Martin Esslin, who worked as a student actor with Reinhardt many years later, testified how this approach was still operative in 1937. 'Being a superb character actor, Reinhardt was able to show an actor not how he, Reinhardt, would act the part, but how that particular actor or actress would do it in order to give full expression to his or her essential individuality.'[11] Another difference in approach between Pirandello and Reinhardt concerns the audience. Pirandello liked to challenge his audience. Reinhardt's attitude to the audience was more benign. Like Pirandello, he was well aware of the audience – 'the contribution of the audience is almost as important as that of the cast'[12] – but his aim was to immerse the spectators in a total theatrical experience, rather than to disconcert them. He wanted the impact of the performance to enhance the audience's experience. Sometimes this would be through vast spectacle, such as performances with immaculately rehearsed crowd scenes. At other times it would be in intimate theatre. As he explained to his biographer, it had been an obsession of his to 'bring together actors and audience – squeezed together as tight as possible'.[13]

Reinhardt emphasised the theatrical potential of *Six Characters in Search of an Author,* and amended the text to suit this purpose. The script shows firm interventions in the fairly free translation by Hans Feist. These included cuts to the Father's discursive speeches, an additional scene towards the end of the second part after the Mother's cry, and the beginnings of a scene between the Mother and the Son in the third part. It altered the Characters' yearning to include a desire to know the end of their story. The end of the play was also changed: in Berlin the play finished with the Director turning to the audience asking for applause in the old manner.[14] This change is symptomatic of the direction of Reinhardt's approach to the play. Consonant with his interest in Hofmannsthal and Calderón, it became a play about theatre. Its main character was the Director, not the Father, who as one of the Characters became the symbolic representation of existence.[15]

The enhancement of the theatricality of the text was particularly evident in the opening scene. Entering from the richly decorated foyer with its Bordeaux-red lounge chairs and Impressionist decorations by Hans Meid, the audience found an auditorium in semi-darkness with a low ceiling, which seemed to suck its spectators into the gloom rather than inviting them to a show.[16] At the far end the open stage, no wings and flies visible, appeared cluttered with scenery and props from various productions. Hermann Krehan's sketches show Greek pillars leaning against each other on stage left, the façade of a modern building with 'RAUCHEN VERBOTEN' in large letters above the door with a ladder against it, centre stage back. A cleaning woman with a mop is about to clean the floor right of centre; left of centre is a man dressed in a hat and coat, standing with his hands behind his back in front of a table and chair. To his right, left of centre, stands a large upended flat. Dominating the scene, stage right, is a tall ladder at the top of which is a technician attending to a spot on the main batten, which is slightly lowered, crossing the stage horizontally.[17] The stage is presented as a theatre workshop (initially there are no actors) and as a place of tension and competition. Here technicians from lighting and properties, and later actors, compete with each other for time and space, and actors concern themselves with the size of their roles. By 1923, in the second edition, Pirandello had added the Stage Manager to his cast list; otherwise the opening stage directions were the same as in the first edition. These describe a company of actors coming on to the stage to rehearse *The Rules of the Game*. Reinhardt amplified this single page of directions, which allow for an improvised scene, into ten pages of dialogue.

Significantly, in this opening scene, it is the lighting that dominates. Technicians, one placed in the lighting box in the auditorium, another on stage, try out the colours and test each spot and communicate with one another, speaking in technicians' shorthand and communicating with other stagehands on stage and in the auditorium.

Spots placed in the auditorium light up the stage, flashing on and off. In an apparently unintentional way, the lighting test allows a spot to rest momentarily on one of the technicians or, later, the Prompter. In a carefully orchestrated scene, Reinhardt at one and the same time shows a theatre at work, deconstructs the magic of theatre and provides an entertaining light-show for the audience. The Actors (the first to arrive is the Leading Man) are presented sympathetically, with only a little satire at the expense of the Second Actor who is upset that his part is so small. In an interchange between the Stage Manager and the Leading Man, Reinhardt in fact stipulated that it was to be played 'realistically, without parody'.[18]

In Reinhardt's reworking of this initial scene, the Leading Lady arrives late, though a little earlier than the rest of the cast (and not accompanied by the little dog Pirandello will give her in 1925 and not subject to the ridicule of that version). At the same time as the rest of the Actors come on to the stage, some stagehands bring on a small piano and chairs. The Actors gather round as one of them begins playing a banana foxtrot. Someone sings, others hum, two couples dance, an actor sits at the director's desk and reads the paper, the Leading Man goes over his part, the lighting technicians flood the stage with red, yellow, blue, moonlight, sunset, green . . . Then the theatre bell sounds loud and clear and the Stage Manager rushes on stage shouting, 'The Director's coming!'

The Director does not make a grand entrance as he will do in Pirandello's revised version of 1925 but slips in absorbed in his own thoughts and would get down to work straight away if his cast were all present. As they are not, he complains (his oft-used word is 'Outrageous') and retires to his office with his post, which he has already begun to open and answer via his secretary. Reinhardt avoided the temptation of taking the part of the Director himself, as both Rudolf Beer had done in the premiere in Vienna and Richard Weichert had done in Frankfurt, and cast Max Pallenberg in this role. One of the functions of the extended introduction was to establish the role of the Director. He is described as 'quick, nervous, distracted but intelligent and gifted, showing a measured, but sometimes explosive, interest and an amazing gift for acting'. Reinhardt lifted a concept from the third part of the play, about the need for organisation in a play's structure, and makes of it one of the Director's longer speeches in this opening scene, highlighting, at an early stage, the Director's competence. The Director is at this point talking with the discontented Second Actor who claims that it is unjust that he should have a part that is merely that of a gentleman with four words to say. The Director takes up the word 'unjust', says life is unjust and that the actor's viewpoint is unjust, and continues: 'Obviously not every one can have the main parts. You have to agree on that, damn it! Theatre can only give an outline. It has to concentrate, cut, stop, condense, possibly few words . . . This is one of the principal conditions . . . [. . .] Three words can signify a world.'[19] The only speech that is recognisably from the original *Six Characters in Search of an Author* is the one in which the Director says he is reduced to putting on plays by Pirandello because there are no longer any good plays coming from France. This, of course, assumed rather a different meaning in Berlin from the auto-irony of the Italian production.

As might be expected from a director who had done so much to develop lighting techniques in the theatre, the entrance of the six Characters was effected not through a mechanical device but by lighting. The stage darkened and six 'wax statues in a panopticum'[20] appeared on the stage, intense and spectral, the lights catching the whiteness of their hands and faces, the Stepdaughter's décolleté, the top of the men's shirts and the Little Girl's dress. The Characters crowd round the Director, who, seated at his desk, appears startled and alarmed, his body flinching into a hunch, his left arm raised in self-protection as if to shield his eyes. This is a nightmare image: beings from another place have come to haunt the sensitive Director, already put out by the lateness of his cast and the difficulties of the play he has to stage.

It would be a mistake to think that all Reinhardt's efforts were concentrated on the stage effects of this play. As indicated above, actors were at the centre of Reinhardt's concept of the theatre. In this production they were not only distinguished, they all had experience of Reinhardt's production methods, even those who were substituted during the run of the play. Pallenberg had been trained in the comic Viennese tradition but he was well able to bring out the potential tragic dimensions of his part, keeping a balance between bitter farce and the tragedy of impotence.[21] According to Julius Bab, it was this role that brought out all Pallenberg's qualities: 'you could admire a Pallenberg in the round'. 'Neurotic and amusing, sometimes profoundly indifferent, and often completely passive, he would suddenly leap onto the stage to intervene in a part of the rehearsal.'[22] Max Gülstorff, who played the bewildered and desperate Father, gave to the character the spectral atmosphere that Reinhardt had evoked with the entrance of the Characters. The Mother and Stepdaughter were played more naturalistically by Franziska Kinz and Lucie Höflich. The Son (Matthias Wieman) was particularly noticed by the critics for his melancholy intensity, and photographic evidence reveals an impressive performance from Naftali Lehrmann as the Young Boy – thin pale face, adolescent haircut, and his hand thrust into his jacket pocket as he stares intensely towards the ground (see fig. 4).

Pirandello's play was quickly assimilated into German theatre and thought. As in France, where Copeau passed over the text, there was a certain amount of nationalism in the German approach to the text and its author. The German premiere, in the Raimund Theater in Vienna in the month of 1924, had been directed in Expressionist style by Rudolf Beer, who also took the part of the Director. He substituted a German play, Georg Kaiser's *Kolportage*, for Pirandello's *The Rules of the Game*. Reinhardt, though he directed some Expressionist drama, was on the whole not at ease with it, and used only some of its techniques in his productions. The language, the short sharp phrase, of the reworked introduction shows some similarities with the minimalist writing of the Expressionists, and the use of a

4. The production by Max Reinhardt, Die Komödie, Berlin, 1924. (Photo: Museo dell'Attore, Genoa.)

variety of means to produce meaning in the theatre also owes something to their innovations. Reviewers, whether in Berlin, Frankfurt or Munich, recalled Johann Ludwig Tieck (in particular *Puss in Boots*), Arthur Schnitzler and Frank Wedekind. Pirandello's thought evoked Kant for some reviewers but on the whole his philosophical competence was compared negatively with that of German thinkers.

CHAPTER 6

PIRANDELLO'S PRODUCTION OF THE 1925 TEXT (1925)

TEATRO ODESCALCHI, ROME, 18 MAY 1925, DIRECTED BY LUIGI PIRANDELLO

By the time Pirandello presented his own production of *Six Characters in Search of an Author*, he had had eighteen months' experience in practical theatre. Previously, as an author of new plays, he had read his scripts to theatre companies and attended rehearsals in an advisory capacity. From early in 1924 his interest in theatre had taken a different direction. A group of people (known initially as 'The Twelve', subsequently as 'The Eleven'), who wanted to establish an art theatre in Rome, invited him to join them as its figurehead and to direct the theatre company. The group included the journalist and dramatist Orio Vergani and Pirandello's eldest son, Stefano, himself a poet and dramatist. Lamberto Picasso, who was to become the leading actor of the Teatro d'Arte, the dramatist Massimo Bontempelli, and the publisher Claudio Argentieri, joined the initial group later. Pirandello threw himself into this new venture and became daily involved in the renovations to the little Teatro Odescalchi, where Podrecca had shown his famous puppet company until he began his worldwide tour in 1924. This theatre was to be the home of the Teatro d'Arte, part of a multiple venture, which would nowadays be called an arts centre. Plays, dance, concerts and exhibitions were to be accommodated there. The theatrical company was to be financed separately from the theatre itself and would be expected to tour in Italy and overseas, as well as provide a season of plays in Rome.[1]

The repertoire of the Teatro d'Arte was to consist of plays of quality and to include new plays from a wide range of countries. But when Charles Cochran invited the newly fledged company to England, he stipulated that it should perform Pirandello's plays, and from June 1925 the company was associated with the presentation of Pirandello's own work. With Pirandello's plays as the predominant part of the company's repertoire, it was *Six Characters in Search of an Author* that was the most-performed play in the three years of the company's life: a total of 148 performances in 63 cities (106 in 39 Italian cities, 27 in 18 European cities, and 15 in 6 South American cities).[2] In preparation for the visit to London in the middle of June, the play was presented in Rome. The text was radically different from the one presented four years earlier; indeed in a flyer Pirandello announced it as 'the first complete version, enriched with new details, and different from the famous versions presented in Berlin, Paris and New York'.[3] As Alessandro d'Amico has indicated, 'new details' is rather a low-key phrase for the major changes effected in the text. These include a rewrite of the introductory scene; a new entrance for the Characters who in 1925 appeared from the auditorium; a different presentation of the Characters evidenced from their heavy make-up and stylised clothes; the use of steps that linked the stage with the auditorium, allowing the Director to view the stage from the spectators' viewpoint; a reworking of the 'garden scene'; and a different end to the play to include the reappearance of the Characters minus the children, their projection as shadows, and the laughter of the Stepdaughter as she escapes through the auditorium. Other changes include an increase in the number of characters in the play – the 1925 version divides the Props Man into two parts, introducing a Stage Manager; and enhancements to some of the actors (e.g., the Leading Lady now arrives late carrying a little dog) and to Mme Pace (the wig is introduced in this version, as is her capacity to terrify the actors).[4]

Pirandello also made several structural alterations to the text, as well as amending some of the speeches, which all in all amounts to a substantial revision. These alterations probably began with Luigi Almirante's cuts to the Father's speeches in Niccodemi's version. The Father's part is considerably reduced in the 1925 version. The speech in which he describes the situation at the end of the story ('We three remain, I, the Mother and that son') is removed – this situation is now communicated visually by the new end given to the play. The discussion between the Father and the Director in part 3 is much reduced in length. The Son no longer has a speech complaining that he has been forced to confront what no son should be forced to see – his parents as full human beings with emotional and sexual problems. The attempt at a scene between Mother and Son is removed from the beginning of part 2. The Stepdaughter's speech to her little sister about the make-believe of the stage is now in the third part rather than at the beginning of the second.

Key factors influencing the changes to the playing text were, as already indicated, the productions by Pemberton, Pitoëff and Reinhardt, and Pirandello's involvement with the refurbishment of the Teatro Odescalchi. Pirandello saw the Paris production of *Six Characters in Search of an Author* at its general dress rehearsal with Dario Niccodemi, who disliked the performance. Niccodemi thought the show 'horrible' and the actors 'amateur', but he had the grace to report in a letter to Vera Vergani that Pirandello 'approved, was very pleased and enthusiastic'.[5] Pirandello also saw Pemberton's 1922 production in February 1924, when a special revival was mounted to coincide with his New York visit. However, he did not see Reinhardt's production until October 1925, though, as a dramatist able to read German and anxious to keep up with the fortune of his plays, he would probably have read the scripts and the reviews.

A major area of discussion for anyone directing *Six Characters in Search of an Author* is the presentation of the Characters. Pirandello made it clear in his revised stage directions that the Characters are to be differentiated as fully as possible from the Actors and suggested how this might be done: by costume, the positioning of both groups, especially when the Characters first come on to the stage, and lighting.

He privileged, however, the use of masks as the 'most effective and apposite means'.

> This device will elucidate the play's central message The CHARAC-
> TERS must not, in fact, seem to be phantasms; they must appear as
> figures of created reality, immutable constructs of the imagination: more
> real and more consistent, because of this, than the natural and volatile
> ACTORS. The masks will help to convey that these figures are the
> products of art, their faces immutably fixed so that each one expresses
> its basic motivation: the FATHER's face registering Remorse; the STEP-
> DAUGHTER's, Revenge; the SON's, Contempt and the MOTHER's,
> Sorrow. The MOTHER will have fixed wax tears in the dark hollows of
> her eyes and down her cheeks, like those seen on ecclesiastical images
> of the Mater Dolorosa.[6]

In his description of the Characters' costumes, it also becomes clear that Pirandello wished to distinguish through costume the situation of the two families that make up the group of the six Characters. In both 1921 and 1925, the Mother, Stepdaughter, Boy and Little Girl are in mourning, while the Father and Son are not. To the 1925 directions is added that the Son will be wearing a purple overcoat and a long green scarf. But only in 1925 does Pirandello stipulate that the material from which the costumes are made should be special. Of the Mother, the directions read: 'Her dress, too, while simple, should be some special material and of an unusual design, with stiff folds falling like those of a statue; it must not look like a shop-dress or be of a familiar pattern.'[7]

The key phrase in the new stage directions is 'created reality'. In reviews of both the Pitoëff and Reinhardt productions, the words 'phantasms' and 'phantoms' occur often to describe the effect the apparition of the Characters had on the audience. Pirandello is clear that these are what his Characters are not. With the phrase 'created reality' Pirandello wanted to emphasise the reality, the superior reality of the Characters, rather than a spooky presence. And this reality is to be experienced in contrast to the ordinary, everyday reality of the Actors. As Alessandro d'Amico has pointed out, the changes to the

1925 text resulted in the Characters and Actors always being on stage together, whereas in 1921 the Stepdaughter and the Little Girl, the Mother and the Son, have scenes at the beginning of part 2 without the presence of the Director and any of the Actors.[8] In 1925 Pirandello conveys the difference between the two groups, which he had in mind in 1921, through new stage directions. The audience's reactions are largely controlled by the reactions of the Director and Actors, which are much enhanced in this later version. In 1921 Mme Pace causes 'momentary astonishment'; in 1925 her appearance causes the Director and Actors 'to dash down the steps leading to the auditorium and make for the central aisle and exit screaming with fright'. In 1925 Pirandello adds a substantial stage direction after the Stepdaughter's dance to describe the 'strange fascination' she exerts on the Actors. When she calls the Mother in 1921, she merely beckons her; in 1925 'she draws her to her with almost magic power'. Her laughter increases from four to ten occasions, culminating in the final sound of the play, her laughter as she leaves the auditorium. And Pirandello adds further stage directions to suggest the other time dimension the Characters live in: the Stepdaughter, in addition to the Son, is shown separated from the Mother and two children sometimes and is described as 'abstracted and distant' twice.

The entrance of the Characters also changed. From appearing from the back of the stage in 1921, their entrance is divided into two phases in 1925. They follow the theatre usher through the auditorium and remain at the bottom of the flight of steps that lead up to the stage. The Stepdaughter is the first to rush on to the stage in dialogue with the Director, followed by the Father, with the Mother and two children on the first steps and the Son below, sulky and detached. Two pages of dialogue later, the Father invites the Mother on to the stage and leads her 'with a certain tragic solemnity to the other side of the stage, which lights up immediately with a fantastic light'. The children, Son and Stepdaughter follow – the former to the back of the stage, while the latter leans up against the proscenium arch. This impressive piece of theatrical direction on the part of the Father impresses the Actors who, momentarily silenced, then burst into applause in admiration for the show they have just been shown. And with this new entrance the audience has longer in which to appreciate the Characters' presence.

Another aspect of the play that underwent major changes was the deployment of the theatre itself. The 1925 text was closely connected with the refurbishment of the Teatro Odescalchi, where it was first presented. In fact, in the words of Alessandro Tinterri, the 1925 text, published later in the year, could be seen as 'the transcription into the text of the play of what was staged by the author at the Odescalchi theatre'.[9] The young architect, Virgilio Marchi, who had already attracted attention as the designer of Anton Giulio Bragaglia's Teatro degli Indipendenti, was invited to design the refurbishment, which began on 6 October 1924. His brief was to provide a welcoming space for theatre lovers and a technically advanced space for performers and backstage staff. Pirandello was acutely aware, as were other Italian theatre practitioners of his time, that Italian theatre was hampered by its lack of facilities. In particular, it had not kept abreast with advances in staging and lighting and had in the early 1920s little concept of scenic design and direction. There was, for instance, no word for 'director' in the Italian language until the 1930s because in Italian the leading actor of the company, the *capocomico*, was frequently also both its 'director' and 'manager'. When the function was recognised as separate, the French word '*régisseur*' was used.

Marchi had little space to work with but he used what he had to maximum advantage. He widened the narrow entrance of the old theatre into an elegant space with three arches leading to an impressive staircase to the six-row circle (including two boxes), which he had to construct from scratch to meet the brief of accommodating at least 350 spectators – the final figure he achieved was 348. He designed a spacious-looking bar and buffet in the basement. He provided ample room for wardrobe and properties and nineteen dressing rooms for the actors. He raised the level of the auditorium and provided a rake, and then lowered the stage to avoid the old problem of many an Italian theatre where spectators in the front row of the auditorium could not see the stage. He took especial care with the sight lines. The stage, stalls and circle were designed to allow every spectator to see without the least movement of the head. Spatial limitations (the usable stage area was no more than 53 square metres) did not permit a revolving stage but this was compensated for by an elaborate lighting grid, designed by Albertini of La Scala in Milan. The introduction of a cyclorama, the removal of footlights and the inclusion of front-of-house spots put this theatre in line with other European developments and in the vanguard of Italian theatres. In comparison with other Italian theatres designed for drama, this was a modern, technologically advanced 'jewel of a theatre'.[10] Part of a review of the opening night by Corrado Alvaro provides a contemporary impression of the theatre, revealing both its innovatory aspects in relation to Italian theatres and its comparison with European ones.

> Footlights have been abolished. Lighting is effected by a series of spots placed both front of house and on stage. These spots plunge the stage into pools of colour. With careful control amazing effects of proximity and distance can be obtained. The actor is not highlighted by a shadowless light, like little figures under a stereoscope, but immersed in a warm and general light that can change tone by minute and imperceptible degrees. Provided that is not abused, this method of lighting could be used to compensate for shallow but wide stages like the one at the Teatro Valle. The setting is created emblematically. A large piece of cloth, called a cyclorama, covers the three walls of the stage. Against this, lit by spots of different tonal colours, are placed a few pieces of scenery so as to create the character of the setting. This is a method widely adopted by art theatre abroad. Purple and grey are the informing colours of the whole auditorium, which is raked towards the stage and accommodates three blocks of grey seats on grey carpet; above, a dress circle, six rows deep in silver. A grey curtain with silver edges opens on to the purple carpet of the stage. The walls covered in grey material are lit by baroque lamps, and indeed the whole design of the theatre by Virgilio Marchi could be called baroque. The silver of the decorations, the mother-of-pearl and dove-coloured grey of the wall hangings and velvets, give a

soft tone to the whole theatre. The golden heads of the ladies in the stalls seemed balanced on an antique jewel case.

The lamps cast a prism of light on the grey wall hangings. In the auditorium there is a lyrical quality that is even better discovered on going into the foyer. There, windows, lamps, gratings, blinds form an orchestra of silver, emphasised by the brick yellow of the plaster and by the gleaming muted red of the curtains. The design of the whole theatre, with its system of levels, loggias, balconies, has a musical movement.[11]

Pirandello took a keen interest in the refurbishment, especially the design of the stage. He and Marchi between them hit on the idea of a double flight of steps on to the stage that could assume three different conformations according to the nature of the play being presented: placed together in front of the stage to make a central stairway, or separately to make a double access to the stage; or converging upwards on either side of the stage from the orchestra pit. This was also a feature characteristic of other theatres in Europe. The Champs-Elysées Theatre in Paris, where Pitoëff had presented his production of *Six Characters in Search of an Author*, had steps in front of the stage, which were used by some of the Actors and the Director; so did the Frankfurt Playhouse where Richard Weichert presented the play in October 1924. Reinhardt's Kammerspiele at the Deutsches Theater, opened in 1906, had also dispensed with footlights and had steps from the auditorium on to the stage, though its stage was considerably larger than that of the Teatro d'Arte. The Teatro d'Arte steps were first used for the theatre's opening production, Pirandello's *Festival of the Lord of the Ship*, and subsequently for his production of *Six Characters in Search of an Author*.

Additionally to the elimination of the 'fourth wall', Pirandello made a number of other alterations to the 1921 text. The introductory part was much expanded to include awareness of backstage staff as well as actors: the play now begins with a man hammering on stage, and more of the trappings of theatre are visible to the audience. The Director enters through the auditorium; the Leading Lady's part is expanded to include a late entrance also through the auditorium. In the improvised scene before the entrance of the Director, one of the Actors sits at the piano and begins playing a dance tune while some of the younger Actors dance to it.

Another point where it is possible to see the influence of the new theatre on the 1925 production is in the garden scene. In 1921 the setting for the garden is largely in place before the curtain rises on part 3; now, apart from the garden pond, the Director creates the scene on the spot with the lighting technician. The cutout trees and cyclorama (instead of 'the sky') are lowered, and the Director gives directions to the electricians, which will turn the cyclorama into the sky he wants. The new lighting system is also used to contribute to the revised end of the play. In 1921 the play finishes with the Director sending the Actors home after the agonised cries of the Mother and the Father after the Boy has killed himself:

> THE DIRECTOR: Fiction! Reality! Go to the devil the lot of you. Never has anything like this happened to me before! They've made me lose a whole day![12]

In 1925, after the Director has sent his Actors home, he calls out to the electrician to kill all the lights, which he does, plunging the stage into complete darkness to the annoyance of the Director who asks for a small light, at least, to see by. Immediately, behind the cyclorama, a green light comes on as if by mistake, projecting huge shadows of the Characters, minus the two Children. The Director dashes off the stage in fright (the verb in Italian, *schizzare*, is the same word as was used for the reaction of the Actors to the appearance of Mme Pace) while at the same time the green light and the shadows disappear and the lunar atmosphere returns. Slowly the Characters emerge from behind the cyclorama. The Son and Mother enter first from the back right and then the Father from the left. They come forward to centre stage and remain there as 'figures in a trance'. The Stepdaughter emerges from the left and, pausing on one of the steps, turns round, looks at the three Characters, laughs and runs through the auditorium. At the back of the auditorium, she turns again, laughs, and runs out into the foyer. Her laughter grows fainter and then, after a short pause, the curtain falls.[13]

Some changes are easy to document. For instance, not until 1925 is it made clear that the flats that are brought on stage to provide an outline of Mme Pace's shop are to have pink and gold stripes, in striking contrast with the Stepdaughter's description of the room covered in a floral wallpaper on a white background. In a photograph of Pitoëff's production the flats are clearly striped.[14] Pitoëff's insistence on the separation between Characters and Actors looks to have influenced Pirandello's production as well. Further similarities are also likely to be influences from the three productions mentioned in the flyer. Virgilio Marchi recorded that the merits of all the variations in other productions were weighed up, as the 1925 production was planned.[15] The piano, for instance, in the opening scene, appeared in both Pitoëff's and Reinhardt's productions and both these directors made much more of the introductory part than had the 1921 text. The garden scene has definite similarities with Pitoëff's rewriting of it. The gradients up to the Champs-Elysées stage may also have been influential. Pemberton's production probably suggested the auditorium entrance for the Director and Leading Lady. Some changes in Pirandello's production, however, can be seen as resistance to aspects in other productions. Though the advice to use masks for the Characters may have been influenced in part by Pitoëff's use of heavy, stylised make-up, Pirandello did not accept other details regarding the presentation of the Characters, notably their presentation as phantoms, as in both Pitoëff's and Reinhardt's productions.

The staging of Pirandello's own production of *Six Characters in Search of an Author* in London, Paris and Berlin provided an opportunity to compare the Italian, 'southern' version of the play with 'northern' renderings. In London the comparisons were with the Stage Society's 1922 greenroom production and comments were restricted to the different styles used for the Actors and Characters. The *Times* critic recognised that *Six Characters* was 'another, a different play done in Italian by Italians' and summed up the difference as: 'Everything is a little "more so."'[16]

In France the total dependence in the Italian production on the acting to convey the Characters evinced surprise. In the Italian production the Characters conveyed their mysterious difference by remaining abstracted and immobile when not engaged in their drama, and acting with febrile intensity when they were. The French production conveyed difference by atmospheric lighting and stylised acting. French critics were also impressed by the sheer carnality and sensuality of the Italian acting, in particular that of Marta Abba. Gabriel Boissy described Marta Abba.

> Tall, slim and excitable, dressed in a knee-length short skirt, which revealed two slender legs in black stockings . . . She flashes into laughter and weeps in a way rarely seen on the stage. She succeeds in being both strange and true and presents a figure in the imagination of a life of extremes.[17]

It is only necessary to glance at illustrations of Ludmilla Pitoëff and Marta Abba in the same role to see the wide divergence in interpretation and style of presentation (see figs. 3 and 5).

It was German critics, however, who dared to criticise Pirandello's presentation rather than merely noting differences. By the autumn of 1925, when the Teatro d'Arte reached Germany, Pirandello's theatre had been well explored both on the stage and in the press. German critics could claim an acquaintance with the play unrivalled by any other European country. In Berlin, in particular, the Teatro d'Arte visit was awaited with great anticipation and Pirandello himself was treated as a major celebrity. The sumptuous Hotel Adlon in the Unter den Linden offered free accommodation to the whole company and decked out the hotel in flags for Pirandello's arrival, arranging a phalanx of staff in front of the building to await the distinguished guest. Pirandello, never imagining that such display was for him, used the service entrance, and then had to exit the hotel and reenter by the

5. The first production of the 1925 text, directed by Luigi Pirandello, Teatro Odescalchi, Rome, 1925. (Photo: Museo dell'Attore, Genoa.)

main entrance.[18] In Berlin and other major German cities, the Teatro d'Arte was invited to play in the state theatres – in Berlin this was the first time the Staatstheater was offered to a foreign company. Reinhardt was in the audience and Pirandello, in his speech at the end of the performance, made a point of praising Reinhardt's production and commenting on their differences of approach to the text and, indeed, the differences between the German and Italian texts.[19]

Pirandello thus himself set the scene for the comparisons that were to come from the German critics. Some expressed surprise that the philosophy of the play seemed undercut by its style of presentation. The Italian production appeared to concentrate on presenting the play as theatre rather than as a revelation of the tragedy of the human condition. The acting and movements seemed too light for the psychological depths of the text, the lighting and scenic effects too elementary. Critics were also surprised that Pirandello did not use the black backdrop for the entrance of the Characters, as Reinhardt had done, that there seemed little attempt to present the Characters as creatures from another world, as phantasms, as in Reinhardt's production. On the contrary, they were flesh-and-blood human beings.[20] There was even some suggestion that Pirandello, or at least his actors, had misunderstood his own play.[21] The critics noted the great differences in the presentation of the Director. There was no doubt that the Father was the central male character in Pirandello's version. Egisto Olivieri's frenetic and energetic performance as Director, darting on and off the stage, had none of the tragi-grotesque stature of Pallenberg's interpretation and even appeared 'colourless' (Paul Goldman) and 'mediocre' (Felix Hollaender) to some. The ensemble work of Pirandello's production, however, was appreciated and, for one critic (Franz Köppen), the company was an example in this respect that German theatre would do well to follow.[22] And individual acting was much praised, especially that of Lamberto Picasso (the Father) and Marta Abba (the Stepdaughter), who particularly impressed Reinhardt.

It was in France that the notion of 'southern' and 'northern' interpretations was first mooted – and, it needs to be remembered, the northern was Russian, not French, and did not therefore involve French nationalistic pride.[23] In Germany differences of approach were more personally felt. A number of Germans felt a loyalty to Reinhardt (even if by 1925 Reinhardt's theatre was beginning to appear outmoded to some), and a loyalty to a theatre that had come to depend on new machinery for its amazing effects. In Berlin, where citizens took pride in their theatrical innovations, this kind of theatre was particularly 'German'. Even differences in acting styles were seen, by Alfred Kerr, for instance, as differences in race or stock ('Here two peoples meet, two stocks') rather than as the result of different theatrical traditions.[24] Marta Abba combined the two views, difference in theatrical tradition and different spirit, when recalling how in Dresden the play was performed in both German and Italian:

And if the Germans were better than us for the extraordinary prestige of their staging, with all the machinery of one of the best-endowed state theatres, we excelled for our interpretative ability, for the clarity of our scenic design and for the sharpness of our perception. In fact, because of our acting and not because of our stage machinery. The impetus of our temperament, the harmony of our Latin spirit carried us all.[25]

Despite Pirandello's technological innovations at the Teatro Odescalchi, and his increased use of theatrical devices such as the cyclorama, the Teatro d'Arte's *Six Characters in Search of an Author* exemplified for other Europeans the Italian tradition of the actors' theatre, the commedia dell'arte, at its best.

CHAPTER 7

SIX CHARACTERS ON THE ITALIAN
STAGE (1936–1993)

Productions of Pirandello's plays in Italy can provide a rough guide to the development of stage direction in twentieth-century Italy.[1] An analysis of productions of *Six Characters in Search of an Author* offers a mini history within the larger context. As we have seen, the director was a latecomer to the Italian theatre. Pirandello had written his plays for star performers: for *Six Characters in Search of an Author* he had hoped that Ruggero Ruggeri would take on the Father, and felt that the play was fully realised only when Marta Abba took the role of the Stepdaughter.[2] From 1946, however, productions began to be known for their directors.

From the mid-1940s to the 1960s, the purist trend dominated, involving an adherence to the text. Pirandello himself can be seen as a precursor of this tradition. His careful elucidation of the speeches, his stress on accuracy and authenticity, his insistence that actors 'became' the character they represent constituted a radical, if conservative, approach to theatre-making in a period when speeches or whole sections were often cut from a play to enhance a star's performance.[3] Orazio Costa continued in this approach, bringing to it his own distinctive inventiveness. Both Giorgio Strehler's (1953) and Giorgio de Lullo's productions (1963/64) were also based on an exploration of the meaning of the text. These three productions, quite different from each other, original and arresting, were based on what they perceived to be the author's intentions. The freeing of the text from its author, a dominant trend from the 1970s, led to some exciting and fantastic explorations of Pirandello's plays, highlighted in Giancarlo Cobelli's version of *Six Characters in Search of an Author* (1980) and Mario Missiroli's in 1993.

Before turning to Costa's productions, something needs to be said about the twenty-year period from 1925 to after the Second World War. From 'the dullness of the productions' mounted in this period,[4] two productions stand out: those by Ruggero Ruggeri and Guido Salvini. Ruggeri finally included *Six Characters in Search of an Author* in his repertoire in 1936 and sought Pirandello's advice. In a letter Pirandello reiterated the 1925 stage direction describing the entrance of the Characters, insisting that they were not 'shadows or phantasms but on the contrary superior and more powerful beings'. Rather than masks, Pirandello advocated make-up that would fix certain characteristics to the faces of the Characters. *Six Characters in Search of an Author*, he insisted, was 'a truly classical tragedy renewed in all its elements'.[5] A striking feature of this production was the presence at the back of the stage of a huge enlarged photograph of the head of Pirandello, which acted as a kind of screen through which the Characters entered.[6] Salvini's production of 1941 distinguished itself through its ambitious lighting. Salvini, who had been both a stage designer and director in Pirandello's company, opted to reveal the Characters, 'motionless and spectral',[7] by opening a black curtain at the back of the stage, presenting them against a backcloth of a clear sky. The Characters disappeared at the end of the play 'as if sucked in by the chill, starlit sky against which they stood', leaving the Stepdaughter, alone and isolated, 'who seemed to rip the curtain with her final laugh'.[8] Both the Stepdaughter (Andreina Pagnani) and the Father (Renzo Ricci) gave memorable performances. Pagnani was particularly congratulated for 'her lacerating laugh which grew and grew until it seemed to burst into the suffering of her tormented flesh',[9] a performance that was seen in the Marta Abba tradition ('a force unleashed from nature');[10] Ricci for the intelligence of his performance, and in particular for the way he conveyed his sincere and lonely desperation to be understood.

TEATRO QUIRINO, ROME, 29 NOVEMBER 1946, AND FESTIVAL TEATRALE DI PROSA, VENICE, 18 SEPTEMBER 1948, DIRECTED BY ORAZIO COSTA

Costa's two productions were the first of any distinction of the post-war, post-Fascist period. They were the first Italian productions of the play since Pirandello's own in 1925 to highlight the work of a director in the theatre. Costa was one of a new breed. He was not a member of an actor's family but had the 'normal' education of grammar school and university, graduating from the University of Rome with a thesis on the theatricality of the dialogue in Manzoni's *The Betrothed*. He was one of the first students of the Accademia d'Arte Drammatica in Rome, which Silvio d'Amico had done so much to found. D'Amico was of the view that until a drama school was established, Italy's theatre would lag behind that of other European countries. Costa was influenced by his Russian teacher at the Accademia, Tatiana Pavlova, who taught Stanislavsky's method, and particularly by Jacques Copeau with whom he spent a crucial six months in France. By 1944 Costa was himself a teacher at the Accademia, and it was in this capacity that he directed his second production of *Six Characters in Search of an Author*.[11]

Costa firmly believed that the theatre belonged to the actor. 'The actor is everything . . . The actor represents the author inasmuch as the actor is the text made flesh . . . The actor is the material by which the author's spirit is revealed.'[12] For Costa the actor is a being in whom there exists a very rich potential of multiple life that wants to manifest itself. The actor has two essential attributes – voice and movement, which are supported by two theatrical means – costume and make-up. What the actor says is all-important: the words the actor speaks are not preexisting concepts to be explained to the public, but ideas in the process of being formed, becoming the actor's very thought, the reality of which has to be imposed on interlocutors and hence the audience.[13]

There are echoes of Pirandello's ideas here and elsewhere in Costa's views on acting and the relationship between authors and actors. Niccodemi, the first director of *Six Characters*, recorded how Pirandello insisted that the actors knew their lines so well that the characters' thoughts became theirs.[14] The concept of 'text made flesh' was a frequently recurring one in Pirandello's theoretical writings on theatre and, indeed, is an important motif of the play. Pirandello, however, at least until the mid-1920s, saw this as impossible, owing to the intrusive nature of the actor who, in his view, came between the author and the character.

Some twenty years after Pirandello's own production, Costa chose to present *Six Characters in Search of an Author* as a classic, rather than as an avant-garde or iconoclastic text. And he decided to use the 1921 text, which he considered 'much more spontaneous'.[15] Other reasons could also have persuaded him as they did later Italian directors. The date of the revised text, 1925, was also the date of Mussolini's assumption of power in Italy, while 1921 predated by one year the Fascist March on Rome. During his lifetime and after, Pirandello had been associated with the Fascist party and the regime. As a man of the theatre seeking financial support, he could not afford, and indeed did not want, to stand apart from what he referred to as 'national life'. Hence the ostentation of his affiliation to the Fascist party in 1924, when Fascism was at a low ebb after the murder of the socialist deputy Matteotti, in which the party was implicated. A fortnight after his very public application for membership, Pirandello was in successful negotiations with Mussolini for support for his Teatro d'Arte. In return for the regime's support of the Teatro d'Arte, it was expected that Pirandello would act as 'ambassador' to the regime when touring abroad, and his post-performance speeches, involving both theatrical and political issues, became a well-known feature of the company's presentation.[16]

Pirandello's relationship with the regime was subsequently not so rosy; there is evidence that he found it difficult to barter his prestige for funds and the government's financial support for the Teatro d'Arte ceased in 1928. Pirandello's opinion of Mussolini deteriorated over the years. In a letter to Marta Abba (14 February 1932), for instance, he advised her against any positive expectation of her forthcoming encounter with Mussolini, describing him as 'rough and crude human material, made to command ordinary and mediocre people whom he despises, capable of anything and totally without scruples'.[17]

Though it would be difficult to describe any of Pirandello's literary or dramatic works as apologias for the regime, there is evidence from newspaper articles and interviews that Pirandello liked to be known for his undemocratic views. After his return from the United States in early 1924, he said, in a much-quoted interview with Giuseppe Villaroel for *Il giornale d'Italia* (8 May 1924), that he considered the American way of life too democratic, that the masses needed someone to guide them, and that he himself was anti-democratic *par excellence*, views he repeated more than once during his lifetime. By the time of his death in December 1936, his modest wishes (written in 1911) that there be no funeral, that his body be cremated and his ashes scattered, combined with his views that art belonged to a different realm from politics, were not enough to eradicate the impression that Pirandello belonged to the Fascist period.

It was Costa's task to present a major Pirandello play as fit for the new era. As a classic the play would lose its political implications. In line with the 1921 version, he presented the play behind the proscenium arch. In order to retain its innovatory features, Costa constructed a theatre on stage, thus presenting a theatre within a theatre. At the beginning of the play, two curtains were raised: the normal curtain, the dark red curtain of the Teatro Quirino in Rome, followed by a blue curtain, revealing an empty auditorium and a stage, on which the action took place.[18] With this device Costa intended also to provide echoes of the baroque theatre designer Gian Lorenzo Bernini, and contemporaneously to provide a constant illustration of one of the motifs of Pirandellian theatre, the mirror image.[19] The implication of the design was that the Actors played to the false auditorium and therefore largely with their backs to the audience while the Characters, addressing the Director and the Actors, would play to the real audience. As the drama intensified in parts 2 and 3, Costa dropped the theatre-within-a-theatre motif, demonstrating thereby the greater reality of the Characters.

As we have seen, right until the year of his death, Pirandello retained the same views concerning the presentation of the Characters as 'created reality' rather than as 'phantasms'. It was Costa's intention, however, to emphasise the humanity of the Characters ('authentic human realities') rather than the difference between Actors and Characters.

In 1948, with a company of mainly young actors either at, or just graduated from, the Accademia dell'Arte Drammatica, Costa took his intention of rendering *Six Characters* a classic one stage further: he made it into a costume drama, the first time this had been done. He directed the play, supported by his brother who designed the set, and his sister who designed the costumes.[20] Costa chose costume because he had come to realise that '*Six Characters* had to find its place in history'; for the first time the play 'was seen historically'.[21] The Characters were presented in 1920s dress while the Actors were dressed as pre-First World War old stagers. The production was first presented at the Venice Festival teatrale di prosa.

In 1946 Costa was directing actors of standing, including Camillo Pilotto, Sarah Ferrati and Sergio Tofano. Pilotto had played the Father under Pirandello's direction, though not in the 1925 production, and it is likely that he came to the part with preconceived ideas. In 1948 Costa had a different cast, young people, in the main, whom he knew and had taught – a more malleable cast, as one reviewer put it.[22] Rossella Falk, just graduated from the Accademia, was acclaimed as a revelation in the role of the Stepdaughter. Tino Buazzelli as the Father also received good reviews. In 1948 Costa maintained the notion of a theatre-within-a-theatre but only as an image, partially presented beyond the hooked-up curtain. The maturity and liveliness of this production is evident in the illustrations. In both productions Costa set the Stepdaughter's dance in part 1 ('Prends garde à Tchou-Tchin-Tchou') on a table, thereby increasing the attention given to the scene through the upward gaze and gestures of the surrounding actors. Sarah Ferrati in 1946 was in full mourning. Her full-length dress with long sleeves and high neckline, combined with graceful movements, make her closer to Ludmilla Pitoëff than to Marta Abba. Rossella Falk, in a 1920s cabaret dress in shiny black material, above the knee and décolleté, with long gloves that leave part of the arms naked, a necklace against her white skin, comes across with much greater vitality.

Costa's productions of *Six Characters* are the first to offer an interpretation that took account of both the theatrical and political situation of his times. As Roberto Alonge has observed, Costa was fascinated by 'this revolutionary arrival of a "group of characters" who came to bring a new message to a company that was acting in the traditional style'.[23] In both productions the Actors represented 'text-bound' people of the past, while the Characters were claiming for themselves an existence in the new era that history and society could not yet grant them. The Father's statement, 'We want to live', gains a new poignancy in the different political climate of post-Fascist Italy. Costa's productions deliberately stress the humanity of the Characters, and lessen their otherness. To emphasise this the Characters mingled with the company of Actors, an approach adopted by Giorgio de Lullo in his production of the play in 1963/4.

Costa's productions were influential beyond their time: he set a trend in Italy by opting for the 1921 version of the text; and in his movement from a rhetorical, demonstrative acting style to a more dynamic naturalism in the 1948 production for the Accademia d'Arte Drammatica, it is possible to perceive the beginnings of a fresh acting style in tune with the new political climate.

THÉÂTRE MARIGNY, PARIS, 12 MARCH 1953, DIRECTED BY GIORGIO STREHLER

Giorgio Strehler's great encounter with Pirandello did not occur until 1966. The production was not of *Six Characters in Search of an Author* but of Pirandello's last unfinished piece, *The Mountain Giants*, and 'ranks among the finest of all his stagings'.[24] Its final image of the heavy metallic safety-curtain crashing down and smashing the travelling players' cart signalled for Strehler not the end of theatre (as it did for the players) but 'the death of a dream, one I had pursued and defended for twenty years in the face of increasing opposition'.[25] His encounter with *Six Characters in Search of an Author* was both less original and less foreboding. Giorgio Guazzotti went so far as to characterise Strehler's pre-1966 productions of Pirandello as 'anomalies', insignificant in comparison with his productions of Shakespeare and Goldoni.[26] In addition to his 1953 *Six Characters*, these include a programme of three one-act plays, *The Man with the Flower in His Mouth*, *At the Exit* and *A Dream (But Perhaps It Isn't)* for the Group 'Posizione' at the Guf Theatre of Novara (24 January 1943); *The Man with the Flower in His Mouth*, *The Imbecile* and *The Licence* in the refugee camp at Mürren in Switzerland (1944); an early version of *The Mountain Giants* for the Piccolo Teatro (1947); and *Tonight We Improvise* for the Piccolo Teatro, in 1949–50.[27]

The production of *Six Characters in Search of an Author* was the result of a longstanding invitation from the Théâtre Marigny in Paris. This was to be Strehler's fourth visit and this time he 'felt it necessary to take a Pirandello, moreover, the most famous Pirandello',[28] as well as his production of Goldoni's *Arlecchino, Servant of Two Masters*. Strehler was much influenced by Costa's production, which he described as 'a convincing example' of what he saw as 'the most modern, advanced and correct interpretation of the text'. This interpretation presented the Characters as real, as opposed to the superficiality and convention of the Actors. But for Strehler reality was a social rather than a philosophic or aesthetic reality. He saw the Characters as 'living and real human beings – well defined socially as petit bourgeois – who in the Pirandellian drama come to ask for an explanation for their truly terrible tragedy from society itself, here represented by the inauthentic actors'.[29] In stipulating that the Characters walk on stage 'off the street, from the house next door, from real life', Strehler knew full well that he was challenging Pitoëff's production of some thirty years before, in which the Characters were, in his view, 'a kind of evanescent ectoplasm'.[30] Strehler gave the Characters costumes that placed them in history, just after the First World War, the period in which it was written.

Strehler saw Pirandello's play as 'betrayed by performance', and by implication, Pirandello seduced by this betrayal. By this he meant that Pirandello had submitted to the fascination of the productions by Pitoëff and Reinhardt, the 'European' productions, with their 'shadows' and 'magical superstructures'. The 1925 text had moved away from the essential feature of the earlier version – the Sicilian Pirandello in revolt against the fictions of morality – to provide a play that fitted into European theatre. Strehler opted for the 1921 version because he saw it as the authentic text, the product of the 'great Pirandello', the Pirandello of the Sicilian plays *Liolà* and *The Jar*; Pirandello the Sicilian short-story writer in the Verga line of *verismo*, as recognised by the thinker Antonio Gramsci.[31] In linking the first version of the play with Pirandello the Sicilian, Strehler echoes the comments of the first Father, Luigi Almirante, who, in an interview, claimed that he had no difficulty with Pirandello's language because it was Sicilian translated into Italian. And the link of Sicilian with social reality was also to be echoed later in Zeffirelli's decision to make the family of Characters Sicilian. The choice of text was also influenced by the ending of the two versions. Strehler, in fact, honed the ending of the first version so that the last words came not from the Director, shouting 'Fiction! Reality! Go to the devil the lot of you!', but from the Father (Tino Buazzelli), who, holding the Boy in his arms, cries 'Reality! Ladies and Gentlemen, Reality!' Illustrations of Costa's production suggest an influence here on Strehler's rendering.[32] The French critics, familiar with the play, were well aware of the change Strehler had made.

Strehler's production had a modest life during 1953, at the Théâtre Marigny and subsequently as one-night appearances in Trieste and Parma and for short runs at the Piccolo Teatro in Milan and the Teatro Mediterraneo della Mostra d'Oltremare in Naples. It was influential, however. Giancarlo Cobelli, who was to direct the play in 1980, was a student at the Piccolo Teatro's School of Dramatic Art, and played one of the actors. Romolo Valli, who was to take the role of the Father in Giorgio de Lullo's production, was the Leading Actor in Strehler's.

MALY THEATRE, MOSCOW, MARCH 1963, AND
TEATRO QUIRINO, ROME, 17 JANUARY 1964,
DIRECTED BY GIORGIO DE LULLO

In contrast to Strehler's production, de Lullo's was an international success, beginning life as part of his company's Eastern European tour and figuring also as a much-acclaimed visitor to the London World Theatre Season in April 1965, in addition to substantial runs in Italy. It was also a revelation: Moscow audiences had never seen the play before, and though there had been several productions of it in London and elsewhere in England, none had touched English audiences as this one did. De Lullo's company, the Compagnia dei Giovani (Young People's Company) was invited back the following year to the World Theatre Season, in which it presented *The Rules of the Game*.

A number of factors contributed to the company's success in this play: the particular combination of actors who formed the company, their previous training and working practices, and the moment in the life of the company in which it was presented. The company was formed in the summer of 1954 and comprised Giorgio de Lullo (33) and Romolo Valli (29), both members of Strehler's Piccolo Teatro di Milano, Rossella Falk (28), Tino Buazzelli (32) and Anna Maria Guarnieri (20). None of them came from acting families; de Lullo, Buazzelli and Falk had trained at the Accademia d'Arte Drammatica in Rome, where Orazio Costa was a teacher. Buazzelli and Falk, in fact, had taken the leading roles in Costa's production of *Six Characters in Search of an Author* in 1948. Valli, de Lullo, Buazzelli and Falk had all been or were members of the Piccolo Teatro di Milano: Valli had taken the part of the Leading Actor in Strehler's production of *Six Characters in Search of an Author* while Buazzelli had played the Father. Guarnieri, at twenty the youngest of the group, had just graduated from the Piccolo Teatro school, and was fresh from an outstanding success in Herbert's *The Moon is Blue*. With very different talents – de Lullo was often characterised as the dreamy romantic, while Valli took over much of the managerial role in the company – there was a considerable homogeneity in their backgrounds and training. As they wrote in their first presentation of themselves, they had all been directed by the new directors of their time: Costa, Visconti, Strehler and Squarzina. As a number of observers pointed out, they combined in their work the attention to aesthetics characteristic of Visconti and the strict discipline of Strehler's Piccolo Teatro.[33]

The working method of the group, as explained by Romolo Valli, was highly suited to the mounting of a Pirandello play. The actors did much of their work round the table, rather than in rehearsal with movement. It was Valli's view that actors need a full grip of the words, and how they are spoken, before rehearsing in full. 'To translate into sounds a line that isn't yours, that you have not said, but which 'an other' has said and which you have to make credible, is for our company a work of radical deepening.'[34]

With an approach that recalls Pirandello and Costa, Valli stressed the role of the director in eliciting the meaning from the words on the page. When it comes to interpretation, he explained in an interview in *Il Dramma*, the actor is a co-author: 'someone who has so enriched the existing material as to make it personal'.[35]

Valli spoke in some detail about the creation of the role of the Father, the first Pirandellian role he played for the Compagnia dei Giovani and one that began a series of encounters with Pirandello that can be described as one of the few persistent threads in their work as a company.[36] The creation of a role, which he described as the 'work of possession', began with a notion of the character combined with a synthesis of private emotion and personal rational thought. Through the deconstruction and plumbing of the depths of the text, the actor, according to Valli, reached a kind of everyday familiarity with the themes and characters.[37]

After this detailed, almost grammatical analysis of the text, Valli would then pass to the 'mimetic stage': finding the face and body of the character. The physical aspect of the character came from an image from Valli's own memories and experiences. As he explained, 'I could unveil the secret key which led me through a complex game of mirrors to the physical identity of each character: and here I was much helped by my passion for Proust.'[38] It was after he was confident of 'the physiological and gestural truth' of his character that the most fascinating part of the 'work of possession' began. The unconscious fusion of the different aspects of the character came together, through unconscious forms of sublimation, to a point that was complete only when the curtain rose. This process continued into, and even after, the run of the play.[39]

As Valli pointed out, this method of working, inspired by de Lullo's approach to the text, was particularly fruitful when mounting a play by Pirandello. Working with a Pirandello text was also for Valli 'a continuous learning process'. By the time he was preparing for *Henry IV*, Valli expressed the relationship as a '*terzetto*' or trio: Pirandello, de Lullo, Valli. It was Pirandello who made of him 'an aware actor'[40] and enabled him to realise that acting was a widening of his own human experience. 'If I succeed in giving life to a character invented by a poet, it is clear that I extend my own existence, and I put my existence, my story as a man, at the service of the existence of that character.'[41] But Pirandello was also central to the group as a whole. 'Pirandello became our working method, our structure.' The group learnt that 'behind the appearance of the words that an actor speaks, there are hidden realities which habit has worn away, in some way misted over'.[42]

The year 1963 proved a turning point in the history of the company. They had been working together for nine years and had presented a number of acclaimed productions. Outstanding among these were *The Diary of Anna Frank* (with Valli in the role of Anna's father) and

Brendan Behan's *The Hostage*. In 1962 they received an invitation to go to Moscow, after an official from the USSR's Ministry of Culture had attended a performance of Goldoni's *The Women of Good Humour* in Milan. Towards the end of the summer of 1962, after all the actors had disbanded for several months to do different things, they planned their Eastern European tour. They chose to take the Goldoni play that had so attracted the Soviet official and a restaged version of *The Diary of Anna Frank*. It was at this point that they also decided to tackle *Six Characters in Search of an Author*, as the most important play of the most important twentieth-century Italian dramatist, to which the Soviet people had been denied access because of Stalin's policy of cultural isolation.[43] The three plays enabled the company to reveal a range of abilities: strong characters and realism in *The Diary of Anna Frank*, a delightful entertainment emphasising elegance and visual pleasures in the Goldoni play, and in the Pirandello an intellectual commitment and a search for a new style. The success of the tour, relayed excitedly to the Italian public by journalists, was deemed to have performed an important task in establishing 'new and decisive relationships of cultural diplomacy'.[44]

When presenting *Six Characters in Search of an Author* to Eastern European audiences, de Lullo and his company decided to make of it a costume drama, and to place the drama clearly within a historical context: the play was presented as a classic of the 1920s. The fact that the company was presenting the play to a foreign audience also influenced their decision to make the play as visual as possible. Different considerations prevailed when they decided to present the play in Italy. By the 1960s Pirandello was, in a sense, an embarrassment: a respected writer but not a well-loved one, so different from the reception given to the popular eighteenth-century classic, Carlo Goldoni.[45] From early days Pirandello had been accused of cerebralism, of being overintellectual. The uneasiness concerning his politics made him a difficult choice for some directors. Many people felt that his plays were understandable only within the context of the social and political tensions of his time; others that a proper understanding of his regional roots was a prerequisite to appreciating his themes. Others, again, saw it as important to present Pirandello the iconoclast, the playwright who had proved that theatre was 'impossible'. The company decided to address none of these issues. In line with their developing methodology outlined above, they centred their attention on Pirandello's words, ignoring previous interpretations and paying no attention to historical and political considerations. The actors strove to bring out the naked meaning of the text.[46]

During one of the rehearsals, the designer, Pier Luigi Pizzi, noted that the rehearsals were more effective than the performances: the set and costumes of the 1920s served not to enhance their method of presenting the play but, on the contrary, worked against it. It was this insight that caused a major change in the presentation of the play to Italian audiences. The company would present a *rehearsal* of *Six Characters in Search of an Author*. The stage was totally exposed (in Rome at the Quirino the audience could even see the theatre heaters along the back wall of the stage) and left bare. The back walls were painted white, the 'Emergency Exit' and the 'Do Not Smoke' signs left as they were; the batten of spots was clearly visible. Just a few chairs were added to the bare stage. The costumes were ordinary everyday clothes of the 1960s, with little differentiation for the main Actors, a scarf for the Leading Man, a fur for the Leading Lady. Among the Characters, only Mme Pace appeared different from normal with some element of the grotesque in her costume. The Father wore a raincoat, the Stepdaughter a black skirt, a black-and-white blouse and a black cardigan.

In *Six Characters in Search of an Author*, Pirandello exposed the tricks of theatre and revealed naturalism as 'impossible'; but he also availed himself of theatrical means (in particular, lighting) to convey his points. In its production the Compagnia dei Giovani did not expose theatre so much as intentionally ignore many of its possibilities. No suspension of disbelief was required of the audience in relation to the Characters: no theatrical devices were used to make the audience believe that the Characters were created realities. As the audience began to take their seats, the members of the company walked on to the stage, the minor actors and actresses first. They appeared engrossed in their own thoughts and waiting for someone or something: then Romolo Valli and Rossella Falk came on and at that point the members of the company began chatting with one another. Even de Lullo, the play's actual director, appeared unobtrusively on stage to set the rehearsal going and to signal the breaks. The actors who played the Characters mingled and chatted with the other actors during this opening part of the play.

Some disliked this Chinese-box structure and felt it an unnecessary intrusion, one that attenuated the dramatic effect of the Characters' entrance. Others were impressed that the entrance, interrupting the rehearsal of *The Rules of the Game*, was a surprise, achieved through thoughtful direction of the acting and of the reaction of the company rather than through any special effects focused on the Characters. The Characters entered from back stage left and back stage right in two groups and came together in a pathetic bunch in front of the Director and Actors. The words from *The Rules of the Game* faded from the Prompter's lips, and the comic actor playing Leone Gala stopped beating eggs. The Characters then converged in a semi-circle around the Prompter's box.[47] As Maurizio del Ministro acutely observed, the Prompter's box, emblem of the fiction of theatre, revealed the illusion of their aspiration.[48]

De Lullo's text was a combination of features from the 1921 and 1925 versions. Ferruccio de Ceresa, who played the Director, used the front row of the auditorium to view the rehearsal, as written into the 1925 text, and some of the details of the linguistic revision of the play were kept. But the 1921 version was used at the beginning of part 2, where the Stepdaughter introduces the Little Girl to the stage and where the Mother tries to make contact with her eldest son. De Lullo also expanded parts of the script, most ostensibly in the scene in which the Actors attempt to rehearse the scene in Mme Pace's shop. This allowed for some detailed and, in some people's estimation, exaggerated acting on the part of the Leading Actor (Carlo Giuffrè)

6. The production by Giorgio de Lullo, Teatro Quirino, Rome, 1964.
(Photo: Museo dell'Attore, Genoa.)

and the Leading Lady (Nora Ricci). An important section of this part was the altercation between the Father, the Leading Actor and the Prompter (played by Pirandello's own prompter in the Teatro d'Arte, Luigi Battaglia), over whether the Father said 'È vero?' or 'Spero' ('Is it?' or 'I hope'). These rhyming words (in Italian) clarify what for the Father is a vital point in determining his character. 'È vero?' shows him concerned that this may be the first time the Stepdaughter has prostituted herself and could be interpreted as concern for her, while the statement 'I hope' ('This won't be the first time, I hope') is more obviously concerned with his own pleasure. De Lullo played up this section, adding some phrases to the Prompter's part and having the Actors and Characters involved converging on the Prompter's box, where the Prompter communicated his insistence by the upward thrust of his chin.[49]

De Lullo also expanded the section of the play in the second part when the Stepdaughter is not allowed to undress on stage. It seemed that it was only at this point that she fully realised the fiction of the stage. The expression on her face, both shattered and rebellious, was emphasised by the repetition of the phrase 'I'm not staying here'. De Lullo had her attempt to escape from the fictitious reality of the stage by rushing impetuously to the back of the auditorium, where she is compelled by unseen forces to turn back towards the stage. Like some vengeful Fury, she bangs her fists on the stage. The Director responds in anger by flinging his impossible script into the air, the flutter of the falling pages suggesting the impossibility of his task, and by implication of all theatrical production. The Stepdaughter stands centre stage at this point, preparing for the embrace between the Father and herself. She is visibly moved and the Director responds in sympathy to her emotion (here De Lullo transferred the Director's involvement with the Stepdaughter's emotions from the garden scene to the end of part 2). The Stepdaughter covers her ears with her hands in an attempt to cut out the anticipated cry of the Mother, moves ineluctably towards the Father and, with sudden resolve, bares her arm and buries her head in his chest while the Father, as if in an attempt to refrain from reciprocating, claws at his raincoat as he submits to the embrace. The embrace is caught in the mirrors of Mme Pace's shop. The Mother's savage cry as she rushes to separate the couple is contrasted cruelly by the satisfied and delighted cry of the Director as the brisk fall of the curtain reveals the artificiality of the stage.[50]

This motif of the fiction of theatre is maintained in the final presence of the Characters. They are not presented in shadow play as written into the revised 1925 text but walk slowly from the back of the stage to the front, bewildered and crushed, to reassume their identity as actors, as members of the Compagnia dei Giovani. The production became at that moment not only an image of the impossibility of theatre but also an image of its triumph.

TEATRO ELISEO, ROME, 29 OCTOBER 1980, DIRECTED BY GIAN CARLO COBELLI

In interviews Valli had spoken of the role of Compagnia dei Giovani in reaffirming the primacy of the actor after a period of directorial supremacy and excesses;[51] but, as far as productions of Pirandello's plays were concerned, the period of directorial inventiveness and ideological readings came into its own after the period of the Compagnia dei Giovani.[52] *To Clothe The Naked*, written in 1922 immediately after the two great plays *Six Characters in Search of an Author* and *Henry IV*, lent itself particularly well to alternative readings. In the 1970s and 1980s, there were four major productions of this play.[53] The first, by Massimo Castri (1976) explored a subtext of the play with the help of Maurizio Balò's striking set. Castri's interpretation of the 'cultural revolution, the "third revolution" of Mayakovskian memory' in terms of theatre, favoured the psychoanalytic: it was important to liberate human beings, to make people conscious of the image of society interjected within them as individuals in order to achieve a social revolution.[54] Castri defined his technique as 'perspective realism'. By this he meant that by exploring and revealing the subtext he was able to offer an interpretation of the reality of the play from a different perspective. For Castri, Pirandello's text was 'a web of words which cover an attempt to cover naked bodies, and the presence of one naked body which is prevented from covering itself with words'.[55] Borrowing from Thomas Carlyle, Pirandello had coined the phrase many years earlier of the 'wardrobe of rhetoric'. As Felicity Firth has put it, 'Pirandello gives us words, words which he always recognised and referred to as a kind of fancy dress, while Castri in this production gave us the bodies.'[56]

Many of Pirandello's plays follow the pattern of the well-made play and are set in rooms. *To Clothe the Naked* was no exception. In the text Pirandello provided quite a detailed description of a writer's study in rented accommodation. The room designed by Maurizio Balò was more of 'a nightmare box, a kind of out-of-time prison' of a room. Roberto de Monticelli, who recognised the innovatory quality of Castri's production ('for the first time we are seeing parodistic violence in the Meyerhold tradition, applied to the texts of this dramatist with singularly efficacious results'), interpreted the setting as a 'kind of bunker of the bad conscience of the bourgeoisie'.[57]

The reverberations of Castri's approach were felt in other productions. *Six Characters in Search of an Author*, of course, is not set in a room (though a room is constructed on stage when it is required), but the notion of 'bunker' figured prominently in the reviews of Cobelli's version of the play. The title of Renzo Tian's review was in fact 'Nel bunker del teatro i fantasmi' ('Ghosts in theatre's bunker').[58] Cobelli followed the 1921 version of the play in the main, largely for the political significance of its date. Cobelli and his designer, Paolo Tommasi, with whom he had worked on a number of previous productions, seemed also to have transferred to *Six Characters in Search of an Author* a dominating motif of *To Clothe the Naked*. In the initial stage directions to that play, Pirandello stresses the importance of the window of the writer's study. At crucial moments of the play, notably at the end of the first and second acts, the window is opened and the street sounds – on one occasion an accident involving an elderly man – pervade the stage. The street in this play is the image of the ineluctable rush of life against which we humans have no defence. In the set for *Six Characters in Search of an Author*, Cobelli and Tommasi politicised this idea. Pirandello's play is set in the enclosed world of theatre. Apart from an occasional reference to contemporary theatre, all mention of the world outside is contained within the story the Characters bring with them: Mme Pace's shop, a room in the Father's house and the garden. In Cobelli's production the Characters enter from the outside, bursting through an upper window, which suddenly splits open at the back of the starkly white stage. In addition to seeking a theatrical company, the Characters appeared also to be escaping from the world outside. The Characters come from a place of horror, but that horror is not only a personal one of split families, near-incest and the pain of lack of understanding. As the Characters descended the oblique stairway into the actors' 'bunker', that 'world' beyond was revealed, through a high gate with spiked railings and a city nightscape in the distance beyond. And the sounds of the suffering city came with them: the noise of crowds, the roar of traffic, police whistles and the eerie howl of sirens. These sounds changed their nature in the last act: strains of a Requiem Mass and an explosion: a lament for a world that is disappearing. With this image Cobelli portrayed symbolically his view of Italy in 1921.[59]

The nightscape image also offered other perspectives on the play. Rather than the clarity of daylight, as in Pirandello's text, Cobelli opted for the associations with nighttime: a funereal atmosphere, the dark night of the soul, the plunge into the abyss, the haunting presence of dreams and ghosts.[60] In Pirandello's oeuvre there is a leaning towards the dark and the macabre: descriptions of corpses, suicide and a strong link, from an early childhood memory, between love and death. This, however, is not foregrounded in the text of *Six Characters in Search of an Author*, where the pessimism of the play is expressed in words and the theatrical moments carry echoes of the melodramatic, well-made play. Cobelli, on the other hand, clothed the dark pessimism of the play in the macabre and the baroque. He gave expression to the themes of the play less through Pirandello's words than with his own visual images. References to death abounded; one that struck a number of reviewers was the similarity of the garden fountain to a tomb.[61] And the final image was the advance of the back wall of the theatre to crush the three remaining Characters – Father, Mother and Son – driving them forward, off the stage into the audience.

Some of these images carry echoes of Giorgio Strehler's and Mario Missiroli's productions of *The Mountain Giants*. The use of the back wall, just mentioned, is reminiscent of the iron curtain that crushed Ilse in Strehler's production. The Actors of the company, who are usually portrayed as superficial, out of touch with their emotional selves, became in Cobelli's production of *Six Characters in Search of an Author* strange, phantom-like creatures, closer to the Scalognati of Pirandello's last unfinished play, as directed by both Strehler and Missiroli (1979), or with characters in a Fellini film, than with conventional actors. Pirandello had advised masks for the Characters, but here it was the Actors whose faces were waxen-white or covered with rice flour. Pirandello had advised special costumes made of special material for the Characters; again it was the Actors who sported a wonderful array of carefully designed light-coloured costumes that were both visually pleasing and intriguing. This produced a different take on the contrast between the two sets of characters. After their eruption the Characters, dressed in dark ordinary clothes, seemed drab in comparison, 'small-minded, petit-bourgeois provincials, far more interested in their family squabbles than in their search for realisation'.[62] Their almost offensive ordinariness was again conveyed in images of Cobelli's devising: the Mother takes out some sewing from her shopping bag, the Son behaves like a lout and the Stepdaughter puts on a pair of black stockings. And their unchanging quality, so valued by Pirandello, is accorded less respect than the Actors' yearning to grow. In the early part of the play, the Actors were shown as 'a bunch of perplexed and amazed phantoms' in precious and stylish costumes, wandering about the stage like zombies.[63] They are attracted to the Characters, who seem to them real flesh and blood, and there was a certain appealing pathos in their attempts to mimic the Characters, particularly in the second part of the play when they attempt to rehearse the Characters' 'scene'. This pathos develops into dignity: at the end of the play it is the Leading Man and the Leading Lady who gather up the dead bodies of the two children and carry them slowly and painfully off stage, another echo from Strehler's *The Mountain Giants*, where the dead body of Ilse is borne away by the actors. As the critic Odoardo Bertani put it, with this ritual the Actors achieved something of their own, the enactment of a real event.[64]

A play that was written in part to demonstrate the shallowness of the contemporary actor becomes in this production one that revealed the actor's humanity. It drew attention to 'the fragility of the actor, his need to be consistent, his precariousness and dependence, his compliance and his readiness to submit'.[65] The irony in this is that this view of the actor was not offered by the self-effacing de Lullo but by the much more flamboyant and iconoclastic Cobelli.

Rather than listen to the text, Cobelli had set out to do something new. His was a self-consciously audacious interpretation. In an interview he told Nino Garrone of *La Repubblica* that he was fed up with the hoary old Pirandellian problems of mask and face, illusion and reality; and that the six Characters were in danger of mummifying through too much reverence. He was tired of the conventional following of the text, which produced a Stepdaughter with a slit skirt, a Father whingeing with his hat in his hand and a Director there for comic relief. He had wanted to get behind the text to the reality of Pirandello's situation when he was struggling to write the play: his wife was going mad, his son was a prisoner of war, his daughter had attempted suicide. Thinking in this way, Cobelli found that the stereotypes began to disintegrate and he began to perceive the possibility of what he called 'realistic' theatre or, in Polish director and stage designer Tadeusz Kantor's terminology, a 'theatre of war', something both 'very metaphysical and very concrete'. Cobelli saw the play as a 'struggle for recognition: the Characters don't recognise themselves in the Actors and vice versa'. Cobelli also had a different view of the Director. In this production he was not satirised nor made into a source of laughter. He was portrayed as a troubled, lonely and anxious young man, dedicated to trying to understand a text that remains for him a source of continuous bafflement.[66]

Cobelli's production had a mixed reception. Its importance lay in remaking the text for the Italian 1980s. With a nod to Expressionism, it made use of the multimedia the theatre can offer: Mme Pace was presented through film as a spirit manifestation complete with divan, screen and drapery. With Missiroli's production of *The Mountain Giants*, with which it shared a number of characteristics (a taste for the sepulchral, a similar setting, a final image of catastrophe), it severed links with the past and showed Italian theatre invigorated by the inventive imaginations of its directors. Cobelli had made of the 1921 text not only a commentary on its own period, but also a play relevant to the director's.

TEATRO GRECO DI TAORMINA, 10 AUGUST 1991, DIRECTED BY FRANCO ZEFFIRELLI

Zeffirelli had not directed a stage play since Pirandello's *Right You Are! (If You Think So)* in 1984 and came to *Six Characters in Search of an Author* fresh from his production of the film *Hamlet*. Since introducing Eduardo de Filippo to London audiences in 1973 and 1978, he had felt that his next theatrical production would be a Pirandello, but he was inhibited from presenting *Six Characters* because he could see no way through the 'impasse which blocks us off from Pirandello's original conception'.[67] Since the 1930s the play had, in his view, 'atrophied, buried by directors trying desperately to recreate the *frisson* of the original by making it a study in the absurd, rather than a searing analysis of dramatic truth'.[68]

Zeffirelli sought and found justification for his approach to the text in Pirandello's writings. As frontispiece to the programme,

Zeffirelli printed a quotation from one of Pirandello's last works, his introduction to Silvio d'Amico's theatre history. It reads:

> Theatre is not archaeology. The refusal to tamper with ancient works in order to update and adapt them for a modern audience is negligence rather than respectful scruple. Theatre needs adaptations, and has always benefited from reworkings in all periods in which it has been most alive. The text remains intact for those who wish to read it again at home, for their own edification. Those who want to enjoy the play will go to see it in the theatre, where they will find it cleansed of its withered parts and of its outdated expressions and reworked for contemporary tastes. And why is this legitimate? Because the work of art, in the theatre, is no longer the work of the writer (which can in any case be preserved in another form) but a living thing to be created and enjoyed, moment by moment on the stage, with the participation of the audience.[69]

Zeffirelli's solution was to substitute *The Mountain Giants* for *The Rules of the Game* as the play in rehearsal before the entry of the Characters. *The Mountain Giants*, Pirandello's last, unfinished play, begun in 1928, was in part inspired by an incident experienced by Pirandello and his company when presenting *Six Characters in Search of an Author* while on tour in Sicily in the autumn and winter of 1927. The company had reached Agrigento, the nearest town to Pirandello's birthplace. Dignitaries from a nearby town, Canicattì, invited the company to present a play in their theatre and in order to provide a sizable audience arranged for the local peasant farmers and labourers to attend the performance. The evening made a lasting impression on the company and was recorded by one of its members.

> The public was made up of peasants who came from round about wearing knitted caps, clogs and shawls. The theatre was jam packed, with poor people, of course. The bigwigs were in the boxes. When the curtain came down – or rather didn't – because in *Six Characters* there isn't a curtain – those poor people stayed glued to their seats. We had to go out front and say: 'Look it's finished, it's over.' But still they didn't move, because they thought that phrase was part of the show too. Then, very

slowly, when they saw that nothing else was happening, they shuffled out of the theatre. I remember that we left the next morning at dawn with the curtains of our coach drawn. And when the peasants gathered in the square, Picasso [Lamberto Picasso, the company's leading male actor] had a moment of panic, and said: 'Look, they're getting together, because they think we have played a joke on them.' Because to stage a play of that sort for those kinds of people – a play that did not have scenes, a curtain or even costumes, well . . . And we all drew a sigh of relief once we got onto the train.[70]

This memory of a dire encounter between two groups of people, the players and the peasant audience, is the catalyst for Pirandello's last play. *The Mountain Giants* introduces the remnants of a 'fringe' travelling theatrical company led by Ilse, married to the Count, who are fanatically dedicated to staging a play called *The Fable of the Changeling*. They turn up at the decaying villa belonging to Cotrone, known in the area as a magician, and stay overnight in his zany household. Cotrone invites Ilse and her company to stay on at his villa, La Scalogna, but Ilse and her company are out of sympathy with Cotrone and his household: Cotrone and his companions create magic whereas Ilse and her company interpret a written play. Ilse wants to make art, not magic. The second encounter, and the one that recalls the Teatro d'Arte's Sicilian experience, occurs in the last unwritten act when the company attempts to present its play to the inhabitants of the nearby town. When the company offers the poet's play to the 'giants', that is, the bigwigs of the town, they are too busy to attend and the play is presented to the workforce instead. The workers have no understanding of *The Fable of the Changeling* and destroy the actors' attempt to present it, killing Ilse in the process. Both encounters, of Cotrone and his magic with Ilse and her actors, and of the latter with the local workforce, are clashes of incompatibles. The theatrical company are fanatics of art who have eschewed life while the people to whom they attempt to present the play are fanatics of life who have neither time to spend on art nor understanding of it and thus destroy its practitioners.

The Mountain Giants expressed Pirandello's concerns for the sur-
vival of theatre as an art form in the 1930s. The theatre building in
the town near Cotrone's villa has been left to decay and the people of
the town are thinking of replacing it with a sports stadium or cinema.
Thematically, if it can be assumed that Stefano Pirandello's prose sum-
mary of Act III incorporated his father's ideas, the play repeats in a
different guise, and with a different emphasis, ideas that run through
much of Pirandello's work: the clash between art and life, the spiritual
and the material.

When Pirandello wrote it, *The Mountain Giants* was a pessimistic
statement about the possibility of making art in the 1930s in Italy.
It was also, along with *Six Characters in Search of an Author* and
Tonight We Improvise, a play in praise of theatre and the imagination.
Some sixty years later, however, Zeffirelli saw this last unfinished
play as a work of its author's 'great decline', 'a play that is absolutely
shattered'.[71] As such it had become a prey of the avant-garde (Zeffirelli
presumably had Missiroli's production of 1979 in mind): 'a modernist
piece which prefigures the sort of futurist pieces, loaded down with
avant-garde clichés which are to the theatre of our own day what the
bourgeois comedy was to the Twenties'.[72] In order to preserve *Six
Characters in Search of an Author* as a debate about theatre, and not
to present it as merely a period piece, Zeffirelli cut *The Rules of the
Game*, which made the theatre debate one about bourgeois theatre,
and introduced a different text.

Zeffirelli used *The Mountain Giants* to provide a satirical presentation of contemporary theatre. Knowing that his production was to
have its first night in the open-air Greek theatre in Taormina, which
accommodates about 8,000 spectators, Zeffirelli had a large and popular audience in mind when thinking through his approach. Together
with Luigi Vanzi, he rewrote all of the first part to show preparations
in train for a rehearsal, and part of the rehearsal itself of a vast and
elaborate presentation of Pirandello's last play. The set was a huge
platform framed by metal tubing and lit with hundreds of spots as if
for a rock concert, with cabins for the technicians well in view. The

authors introduced two new characters, given some prominence: an interviewer from the Third Programme of RAI (the Italian equivalent of the BBC) and an *ottimizzatore* (an 'optimiser'). The first was accompanied by a deliberately intrusive cameraman, who helped to establish that the audience were witnessing the preparations in Milan for a dress rehearsal of Pirandello's last play. His presence constructed the polemic against the ubiquitous and all-consuming modern-day television. The second acted as a very visible Assistant Director and provided a bridge between the Director and the Actors and, later, the Director and the Characters.

In performance the stage became a medley of functioning ramps, costume trunks, props and bottles of water. Some actors were seen trying their lines, others their positions, and others again (actors playing the inhabitants of Cotrone's villa) displaying elaborate and colourful costumes. Satire of contemporary theatre – and life – was achieved through the self-important speeches given to the Actors, the pseudo-intellectual utterances of the Director (who expatiated on the subtext), the to-ing and fro-ing of technical staff, the frequent demands for coffee from the bar, and the ever present mobile phone. Visually the whole scene was colourful and frenetic chaos. The opening scene came across as 'an extended improvisation, culminating in a gaudy rehearsal (gold top hats, colourful costumes, rubber breasts, a large throne, psychedelic lighting, weird cries).'[73] The theme of the superficiality of modern theatre, given over to effect and notions of audience consumption, was easily comprehensible.

Into this noisy and colourful rehearsal of a superficially sophisticated Milanese theatre company an unobtrusive family, dressed in black, entered from the back, virtually unnoticed. Soon, however, this unimpressive group of people began to dominate the stage. The superb acting, particularly of Benedetta Buccellato (the Stepdaughter) and Enrico Salerno (the Father) changed the mood of the production from light-hearted satire to intense drama. Buccellato was a particularly powerful presence, with an enormous range, displaying intense sexuality, gentle tenderness and rage. Salerno was also volatile in his mood changes. A nice touch was the way he drank from a small flask kept in his pocket. He brought out excellently the man-to-man complicity between himself and the Director, particularly when he directed his philosophic thoughts not to the audience but to him. Salerno described the Father as 'that sublime Father, impudent persuader and sinner from the provinces'.[74]

As academic as well as theatre critics have pointed out, Pirandello had written *Six Characters in Search of an Author* in two 'languages': the language of the theatre company or the language of comedy, and the language of the Characters or the language of tragedy.[75] Within the latter he had differentiated further: the Father's language of persuasive logic, the Stepdaughter's fragmented passionate speech, and the repetitive and poetic language of the Mother. In Zeffirelli's production the gap between the Actors' and Characters' languages was widened again, because Zeffirelli reverted to Pirandello's script for the Characters, thus creating another dislocation in the script, which strengthened the difference between the two groups. Zeffirelli added a convincing detail: the family that intrudes into the Milanese rehearsal was Sicilian, enhancing the difference between the two groups and stressing the homeliness and basic reality, for the first Sicilian audience, at least, of the Characters.

TEATRO ARGENTINA, ROME, 10 NOVEMBER 1993, DIRECTED BY MARIO MISSIROLI

Missiroli's best-remembered encounter with Pirandello was his production of *The Mountain Giants* in 1979, for which Enrico Job's set of a deeply sloping metal crater, described variously as a chute, a cave of ice under a glacier, a trap and a dustbin, was the most arresting feature.[76] Job was also the designer for Missiroli's production of *Six Characters in Search of an Author*.

As we have seen, a number of directors have felt the imperative to change the first part of the play, either to suit a different culture, or to 'modernise' Pirandello's 1921 play. But no director had taken issue with the text as written by Pirandello, as Missiroli did, declaring that he wanted 'to save the work that came after by cancelling this inert introduction'.[77] The opening, in his view, was 'an excuse, and not the best of excuses', for what followed. A number of people thought Missiroli's choice of *Le avventure della villeggiatura* (*Holiday Adventures*), the second play of a trilogy on holidays in the country by the eighteenth-century dramatist Carlo Goldoni, was chosen in tribute to Goldoni, the second centenary of whose death fell in the year of Missiroli's production. But such considerations were secondary to Missiroli's view of Goldoni as representative of the century of conventionality and rules and therefore an appropriate antithesis to Pirandello's approach to theatre. The choice of this play from among the many that Goldoni wrote was due to three additional factors: it was written in Italian (not Venetian as were many of Goldoni's plays) and therefore accessible, and was set not only '*en plein air*', contrasting nicely with the claustrophobic atmosphere of the Pirandello play, but more specifically in a garden. (Here Missiroli had taken a further licence, for the stage directions of this play make it clear that the opening scenes are set in a ground-floor room with a view of the garden through the open doors at centre back.) But Missiroli took his substitution one stage further than previous directors: Goldoni's play was not presented as a rehearsal but as a performance in order to situate Pirandello's play 'in an environment of a truly authentic fiction'.[78] The elaborate eighteenth-century costume was clearly a major component of this 'authentic fiction' – in an interview Missiroli said that he had 'chosen Goldoni for the costume'.[79]

Missiroli was aware that the text of *Six Characters* presupposes an empty theatre: by choosing performance over rehearsal, he was reinstating the audience. 'Pirandello denied his audience, for me the audience is given as present.'[80] To emphasise this Missiroli had the Director (played by Gianrico Tedeschi) come out in front of the curtain and announce the beginning of the play. The curtain then opened on a lush garden with huge baroque-looking trees – an eighteenth-century

Arcadian wood – and the opening scenes of Goldoni's play in full costume got under way. The Characters, all in black, entered from the
wings in a straggly group, the children appearing first. The Actors,
aware of the intruders, tried to press on with the play until, some
twenty pages later, the Director intervened and the text reverted to
Pirandello's play. Not all critical responses to this were as favourable
as Giovanni Raboni's, who witnessed the contrast between the real
and ordinary people who were the Characters and the fiction of the
eighteenth-century Actors with a *frisson* he had seldom experienced in
productions of the play.[81] Many, in fact, were puzzled as to Missiroli's
intentions, but these became clearer as the play progressed. The trees,
made of cloth, were gradually replaced by a less lush vegetation of
old and scorched trees, which by part 3 had disappeared entirely;
the stage became less and less cluttered as the Characters increasingly
established their reality and dominance. During the course of the
play, the Actors began to shed some of their eighteenth-century costume. For instance, by the time the Leading Man and Leading Lady
played the scene between the Father and the Stepdaughter in part 2,
they were without hats and jackets, and this gradual lessening of for-
mality contributed to the deconstruction of the eighteenth-century
fiction.

The setting for the garden scene was an Enrico Job *tour de force*.
The Goldonian backdrop disappeared; the bare stage with powerful
1920s metallic columns was revealed, and, on a slope between two
funereal cypresses, a plain square fountain appeared under a full moon
supported on a tubular metal support. This stark, rationalist scene
contributed to the sense of the unreality of the eighteenth-century
opening setting. At the end the Actors, still wearing parts of their
eighteenth-century costume, fled down the steps into the auditorium
leaving the Characters 'masters of the space'.[82] The Characters had the
last word, not the Director as in the 1921 script, but Missiroli also cut
the 1925 end. The stark outer reality and inner realism of Pirandello's
twentieth-century theatre had triumphed over the outward show and
rule-bound theatre of the eighteenth-century well-made play.

In addition to his major change to the play, Missiroli's interpretation for a contemporary audience also involved some less radical alterations. The Stepdaughter's dance in part 1 was given elaboration of dance and song to Satie-type music. The Director (Gianrico Tedeschi) was perceptibly Milanese while the Father (Gabriele Lavia) spoke with a light Sicilian accent. In interviews before the first night, Lavia (better known as a director than as an actor) expressed the view that his generation had 'never fully digested the historical and psychological condition of being a parent'. As for himself, he admitted to not having the physique for fatherhood and remembered his own father's authority: 'he only had to raise an eyebrow to ensure silence at the meal table, whereas I, father of two daughters, consume my meals in an atmosphere of utter hubbub'.[83] So Lavia's Father is given a contemporary gloss: rather than expressing his torment through the topos of the '*raisonneur*' as written by Pirandello, Lavia presented a man obsessed by sexual possession.[84] The scene in Mme Pace's shop was one of intertwined bodies, intense caresses and hands fumbling under a skirt. Though Missiroli made no claims for originality for his presentation of Mme Pace, this was arresting: Art Deco screens, Mme Pace as priestess in Liberty yellow and black, which reminded one reviewer of Japanese No theatre, and a leaning towards the fetishistic.[85]

Missiroli's production was variously received. Though visually impressive (and this received some favourable comments), there were a number of people who felt that the text suffered, particularly during the exposition scenes in part 1. For some the theatricality of the acting, in particular during the garden scene, undermined the pathos and exposed what at least one reviewer thought was the laughable outdated quality of the text.[86]

CHAPTER 8

TWO ENGLISH PRODUCTIONS
(1929 AND 1963)

After the Lord Chamberlain's rejection of the text in 1922, a licence for public performance in the UK was slow in coming. Lewis Casson, Nigel Playfair of the Lyric Theatre, Hammersmith, Barry Jackson of the Birmingham Repertory Company, and Philip Ridgeway, with Theodore Komisarjevsky, of the Barnes Theatre all sent in applications and were anxious to accommodate the censors' requests.[1] 'In preparing this new version, we have had in mind the elimination of anything likely to offend', Barry Jackson wrote in July 1925. 'I am particularly anxious to do this play and to alter anything which you have objection to. On these lines it would seem a pity if England is not to have Pirandello's masterpiece,' Philip Ridgeway stressed the following year. Three months later, in 1926, Barry Jackson succeeded in securing an interview with the Lord Chamberlain (quite an unusual event) but not in changing his mind.[2]

The censors, it appears, were divided. G. S. Street had always been in favour of granting a licence but Lord Buckmaster and another reader (whose signature is difficult to determine) were not.[3] By 1924–5 their principal objections hinged on two sections of the play. The unidentifiable reader had been told that the translation is 'very bad' and thought that this was perhaps why he found it difficult to imagine how the play would be realised on the stage. He objected to the brothel scene and revealed his inability to read the play by his statement that the scene is 'aggravated by the extreme youth of the step-daughter, a girl in short petticoats, with her hair in two plaits down her back, when she meets her step-father in the rooms of the procuress'.[4] (The Stepdaughter describes herself in this way when narrating the incident of the Father offering her a hat when she was a schoolgirl.) The second section came at the beginning of the second part and was referred to as 'a somewhat obscure allusion to a very disgusting incident'. This is clarified by Lord Buckmaster, who claimed that he had 'never overlooked the dramatic merits of this play', which he thought 'considerable'; but he felt it necessary to 'repeat that to base a scene upon the horror of a boy seeing his Father and Mother in sexual relationship sickens and disgusts me and I therefore assume it would sicken and disgust a normal audience'.[5] Though it is possible to read the Son's speech in this way (as it has been subsequently, most obviously in Bourseiller's 1978 production at the Comédie française) it is not necessary to do so. The Son's complaint could be understood to imply that he feels he should never have been forced to consider his parents as human beings with sexual and emotional problems. It is ironic that the English public theatre was prevented from staging this play on account of a speech that Pirandello himself excised in his revised 1925 version.[6]

In 1928 Barry Jackson succeeded in his invitation to Lord Cromer to see the play at the Arts Theatre in a 'members only' performance. Lord Cromer still found it 'a most disagreeable play' but felt bound to confess that it was 'quite inoffensively acted' and he therefore issued a licence. As Nicholas de Jongh suggests, 'the lurid fantasising of his mind's eye was soothed by the reticence of the performers'.[7]

FESTIVAL THEATRE, CAMBRIDGE, 10 OCTOBER 1929, DIRECTED BY TYRONE GUTHRIE

In 1925 Alderson Burrell Horne assumed the management of the Cambridge University Amateur Dramatic Club's theatre. Four years later, under the assumed name of Anmer Hall, he took a lease on the little eighteenth-century Festival Theatre with the intention of staging plays during the university's terms. To achieve this he needed a resident director. The person recommended to him was Tony (Tyrone) Guthrie.

Guthrie was twenty-nine, with some varied experience in the theatre. At Oxford he had taken parts in various Oxford University Dramatic Society productions, including Glendower in *Henry IV Part I*, directed by James B. Fagan. His hopes of a career as an actor had seemed on their way to fulfilment when he joined Fagan in his new venture, the Oxford Players, in the new Oxford Playhouse, the old Red Barn on the Woodstock Road. But after six months Fagan had seen fit to dismiss him in October 1924. Guthrie had then been employed by the BBC (he was later to write a number of radio plays); and for two years, 1926–28, he had directed the Scottish National Players in Glasgow. The invitation to direct at the Festival Theatre was timely; Guthrie was depressed and unemployed after the death of his father from cancer in 1928 and the onset of his mother's blindness, and not much enjoying living in London.[8]

Flora Robson had also been a member of the Oxford Players and had been sacked by Fagan at the same time. She had been told that Oxford undergraduates wanted pretty actresses and that her looks did not fit the bill. She returned to her parents' home in Welwyn Garden City and took on a job as welfare officer at the Shredded Wheat factory. In the summer of 1929, before going to Cambridge to take up his new post, Guthrie went to Welwyn Garden City to adjudicate in the amateur dramatic festival. Among the competing groups were the Welwyn Garden City Barnstormers, the dramatic society of the Shredded Wheat factory, directed by Flora Robson. The result of this encounter was her employment by Anmer Hall and the lead role in Guthrie's first production at the Festival Theatre: the Stepdaughter in *Six Characters in Search of an Author*.[9]

The Festival Theatre's eighteenth-century building had been given a modern makeover by its previous manager, Terence Gray: an abstract design of scarlet, black and emerald-green triangles. Accommodating about 500 spectators, it had features that were to become hallmarks of Guthrie's later theatrical practice: no proscenium barrier between stage and audience, no footlights and a modern lighting system. The Festival Theatre, in fact, is remembered for having a lighting system in advance of any in London at that time.[10] In addition, Gray had installed a curved cyclorama, an unusual feature then. The advanced lighting was controlled by a wonderful electrician, Mr Steen, 'who taught Guthrie a great deal about how to light actors and sets without the time-wasting process of trial and error'.[11]

The Festival Theatre was run on a shoestring. Actors took home £3 and 10 shillings a week and were expected to provide their own costumes. An anecdote about Flora Robson illustrates this. She felt that her performance of the Stepdaughter lacked something because she had to wear her 'good' dress for it; the management this time saw her point and provided her with 'a shiny black satin dress, exactly right for the part'.[12] There were few stagehands in addition to Mr Steen and his assistant Mr Smith, so all the actors, including the leading man Robert Donat, were expected to 'muck in'. Flora Robson found a niche for herself as prompter.[13]

Guthrie's opening production of *Six Characters in Search of an Author* was a great success at the time and remembered for years afterwards, in particular for Flora Robson's performance as the Stepdaughter. Raffaello Piccoli, writing in the *Cambridge Review*, comments on a 'magnificent performance, with that character of inevitability which only belongs to a production which has been thought out at once as a harmonious whole and in its minutest detail'. He compliments Frederick Piper on his speedy delivery of the Father's philosophical passages; Leslie Frith, who made you 'feel as if you were actually behind the curtain'; and Flora Robson who was 'very modern, very human, very Italian'.[14] Another reviewer commented that her 'sensitive treatment of the part was the main topic of foyer conversation'.[15] Guthrie recalled going back to Cambridge some thirty years later and reminiscing with a group of Senior Fellows over dinner. 'Unanimously they declared that in thirty years of subsequent playgoing they had never seen a performance to equal its dazzling originality and force.'[16] It was the moment of Robson's comeback after being out in the cold at the Shredded Wheat factory. Her great desire to be an actress and the Stepdaughter's desire for life as a Character came together in her presentation of the role, as she told Nicholas de Jongh in an interview in 1979. 'In the last act I had a speech when the character I played wasn't a real person, just a figment of the playwright's mind, and I had to say, "I sat in the hole of his desk and begged to be born". And that was me in the factory you see – begging and begging to be born, born into acting.'[17]

The play was revived at the Westminster Theatre for a fortnight in 1932 with Robson as Stepdaughter, and it is from photographs of this later performance, in addition to reviews and reminiscences of the actors, that it is possible to see something of Guthrie's approach to the text. The stage was completely exposed: bare brick walls, exit lights, 'Silence' and 'No Smoking' notices clearly visible.[18] Ladders of various shapes and sizes criss-crossed each other in reflected shadows on the curved cyclorama. The Characters were also reflected: one particularly menacing illustration shows the Characters assailing the Director across his table, the shadow of the Father's intense and prehensile hands seeming to claw at the Director's head as he leans forward over the desk in his eagerness to put his point across (fig. 7). Guthrie's feel for the excitement of the play came across in his introduction of the Characters. While the rehearsal of *The Rules of the Game* was in progress, stagehands crossed the stage with parts of the scenery. The Characters came on invisible to the audience behind one of the flats, to be suddenly revealed on stage – a device more usually reserved for the entrance of Mme Pace. 'The stagehands paused centre backstage and – at the appropriate moment when they had moved on – a spotlight came in, and there was this group of mournfully dressed, anxious intruders suddenly and unaccountably slap in the middle of the stage.'[19]

Guthrie kept a balance between the tragic and comic aspects of the play by allowing Leslie Frith to exploit the comic possibilities of his part (the Director) fully. As in Cambridge, the Westminster production was remembered for Flora Robson's performance. She received a standing ovation every night of the fortnight's run: 'the

7. The production by Tyrone Guthrie, Festival Theatre, Cambridge, 1929.
(Photo: Pollard Crowther).

entire audience stood up, cheering and waving programmes, a sight I never saw again during my thirty years in the theatre', Alan Rolfe, a member of the company at the time, recalled.[20] The theatricality of the production also made a lasting impression, as it had in 1929. Then one reviewer had commented that it was 'difficult to believe that we were watching Pirandello's play and not the Festival Theatre people getting ready for it in reality'.[21] In 1929 one of the actresses remained on stage during the interval eating from her lunch box and throwing her banana skins into the auditorium. Alan Rolfe also recalled that he and his partner in the company made their entrances by the pit door; on several occasions they nearly came to blows with angry would-be spectators refused entry because the house was full, who thought that the actors were spectators trying to push past them to the front of the queue.[22]

A moment that was caught particularly well in the 1929 production was the acting out of the 'scene' in Mme Pace's shop. This scene when repeated by the Actors usually ends up as comic and a satire of contemporary acting techniques, despite Pirandello's stage directions that it should not have the least appearance of parody, but be, rather, 'more highly polished'. A critic from Welwyn Garden City with the initials F. J. O commented: 'It is the highest praise to say that Miss Robson made the part live to such an extent that the leading lady's copy of it, quite a pretty piece of work, seemed, as it was intended to seem, good acting contrasted with reality. This, the most interesting and most difficult effect in the play, came off with triumphant success.'[23] And Robert Donat, who played the Leading Man, described by D. T. in *The Gownsman* as 'delicious', was praised for not overacting (a considerable temptation in this part).[24]

Two aspects of Guthrie's production rather tantalisingly suggest that he had some knowledge of the 1925 version of the text, not translated into English until 1954 by Frederick May. Guthrie used the auditorium for some of the actors' entrances and, in the Westminster revival, at least, 'at the very end of the play . . . Flora would leap wildly from the stage into the auditorium to make her exit'.[25]

MAYFAIR THEATRE, LONDON, 17 JUNE 1963, TRANSLATED BY PAUL AVILA MAYER, DIRECTED BY WILLIAM BALL

In 1963 Harry Lee Danziger, a New Yorker who had made his home in London, began adapting the Candlelight Room in his hotel, the Mayfair, into a small theatre, which would hold about 300 people, all accommodated in stall seats in a single tiered and sharply raked auditorium. His brother Eddie saw William Ball's production of *Six Characters in Search of an Author* in an off-Broadway production and Harry decided to make Ball's English production of the play his opening presentation. The text, a new adaptation by Paul Avila Mayer,[26] which took account of the recently constructed theatre, was partly rewritten in rehearsal by Ralph Richardson, who played the Father.[27]

Mayer's version begins with the electrician setting up the lights, in a manner somewhat reminiscent of Reinhardt's 1924 production. As the audience begins to come in, the Director says: 'It's a little early in the game to have visitors, but I've never called a closed rehearsal so you're welcome to watch us at work. At this stage anything can happen but we shall proceed here just as if you weren't there.' The actors start rehearsing a scene called 'The Challenge' containing a character called Mrs Gala. This scene is composed mainly of one-liners delivered very fast, during which the electrician, who has continued with his work during the rehearsal, says, 'Plug it in to 23': the lights suddenly go out and six people 'are seen entering in the dark'. These, the six Characters, are asked to sit in the auditorium with the other 'visitors'. After an interchange between Director and Technician, the play resumes the rehearsal.

Other changes to the text bring the 'Pirandello in his study' section into the first act, in an evocation created by the Stepdaughter, just before her first long fragmented speech, 'Let's put this play on, then you'll see that . . .' At the beginning of part 2, the Son is seen fingering a gun, studied by the Juvenile Lead. The other actors try to persuade him to put it away. The scene between the Stepdaughter and the Little Girl is placed in part 3, as it is in the 1925 version. At the end of the play, the Characters appear together and leave the theatre and, having dismissed his company, the Director puts on his hat and coat and leaves too.

Ball incorporated the newness of the theatre and the unique situation of the theatre being part of a hotel into his production. Indeed, his appreciation of the unfinished state of the theatre ('great for Pirandello')[28] ran counter to the efforts of Danziger's team, who were anxious to get everything ready for the opening. When the stage-hands begin to mock up Mme Pace's shop, the Director advises them to borrow 'a few things from the hotel lobby'. Ball used the resources of both stage and auditorium. He framed the people onstage with groups of half or wholly offstage actors, props men and stage managers. In particular, he made full use of banks of lights, swinging them up, down and sideways, sometimes bringing them down within a few inches of the stage. As the action begins:

> we see a company of actors in the throes of a rehearsal for some unidentified play. The lanky, red-haired director is planning stage movements and coursing, rather distractedly, up and down among groups of his cast and the essential workmen of the theatre, who, as eagerly as he, surge in from the wings, squat by the footlights with scripts or, in the space between stalls and stage, confer in clumps or rest their elbows on the casing of the footlights.[29]

The entrance of the Characters was most effective: they appeared 'as if really refracted from some other dimension'.[30]

Ralph Richardson played the Father. The first time he had come across the play was in 1944 when he, Laurence Olivier and John Burrell were running the Old Vic. They needed a leading lady and they turned for advice to Barry Jackson, who was still directing the Birmingham Repertory Company and in whose company both had worked in the mid-1920s. He suggested they came to see the seventeen-year-old Margaret Leighton as the Stepdaughter in *Six*

Characters in Search of an Author. The result of this trip to Birmingham was her employment in the Young Vic company on what to her was an impressive £17 a week.[31] Ralph Richardson had also seen Ball's off-Broadway production of the play and he, too, was instrumental in getting Ball to come to London to direct an English version of it. Kenneth Tynan noted his performance in this play as one of his outstanding ones; Gary O'Connor mentions it as important in his career for being the first 'poetic' character he had acted for some years; and W. J. Lambert of *The Sunday Times* observed a major development in Richardson's acting:

> Above all, Sir Ralph Richardson lends the Father an agonising self-convicted depth of shame. He has discovered a legato line long missing from his speech. Gone are the outrageous caesuras, the mysterious sforzandi which have for long lent a grotesque and often irrelevant extra dimension to his roles. Out flow the long lines phrased and shaped with a musician's art: and from them echo the regrets, the helpless rages, the incurable dismay of all human weakness.[32]

Richardson was appreciated for his capacity to present the unearthly quality of the part and for his special ability to present sexuality through 'delicate suggestiveness'. Barbara Jefford, who played the Stepdaughter, spoke of how Richardson was able to convey the essence of sexual attraction and remorse in the scene in Mme Pace's shop without touching her. His seduction of her was 'so unpredictable . . . so unpredictable, so naughty; this is the mystery – what is so entertaining about him is that you never know. But he is meticulous, every syllable in the text is rehearsed – he underlines different words in different colours – it's planned down to the millicord.'[33]

Jefford herself presented the Stepdaughter as 'big, black-and-white and beautiful as a Greek fury', bringing 'all her vitality to a part in which she was successively narrator, victim, heroine and actress'.[34]

If a fault was perceived in this production, it was in a lack of balance between the fine acting of the Characters, presented in period costume, and the presentation of the theatrical company and its director. There were several comments on this lack of balance but the critic from *The Times* was the most forthright:

> The purpose of the play is to present a debate between illusion and reality, and therefore the actors . . . should present an equivalent counter-weight to the Six Characters. On this occasion they appeared to be a group of bouncy juveniles led by a director who – in Michael O'Sullivan's gobblingly hysterical performance – seemed to belong to the lunatic fringe of the Actors' Studio.[35]

This presentation in fact runs counter to Paul Avila Mayer's version of the play. In part 2 he had inserted a stage direction, not included by Pirandello, about the Leading Lady when she rehearses the 'scene' suggesting that she is a serious actor. When the Stepdaughter bursts into spontaneous laughter at the Leading Lady's presentation of her, the Leading Lady is 'genuinely hurt and angry; for despite the somewhat flamboyant characteristics of her profession, the Leading Lady is a very real person'.

CHAPTER 9

BECOMING PART OF NATIONAL THEATRE IN FRANCE AND ENGLAND

Pirandello's theatre was much more easily assimilated into the national culture in France than it was in England. As we have seen, *Six Characters in Search of an Author* was not only appreciated in Paris as an innovative play: its production by Pitoëff was also regarded as a catalyst for change in French theatre. Symbolic of the difference in reception was its presentation at the Comédie française some twenty-five years before Michael Rudman's production at the National Theatre in London.

COMÉDIE FRANÇAISE, PARIS, 5 MARCH 1952, DIRECTED BY JULIEN BERTHEAU

Six Characters in Search of an Author was not the first play by Pirandello to enter the repertoire of the Comédie française. *Right You Are! (If You Think So)*, with the title *Chacun sa vérité*, was presented in March 1937, three months after Pirandello's death. It remained in the repertoire (directed by Charles Dullin, designed by Suzanne Lalique, with Berthe Bovy as Signora Frola) from 1937 to 1940, and was revived in 1951 and 1956. The translator, Benjamin Crémieux, declared that no production of a Pirandello play had come as close to Pirandello's dreams as had this one at the 'house of Molière'.[1]

Six Characters in Search of an Author, the second Pirandello play to be presented, formed part of the postwar revival of the Comédie française. The reform in 1946 of the statutes of this national state-funded institution had created considerable unease and unrest; a number of key actors left and André Obey, the first postwar general administrator (a government-appointed post) resigned after only six months in office. He was succeeded by Pierre Aimé Touchard, an academic turned journalist, whose interest in theatre had hitherto concentrated on amateur theatre. He took over a theatre with two separate playing places, the Richelieu and the Odéon, but deprived of a number of its finest actors and deserted by its authors. 'Pat', as he became known, began by wooing back a number of the actors, including Renée Faure; and Fernand Ledoux, who had created the role of Signor Ponza, returned as guest artist. Touchard also engaged a number of new actors: among them Jean-Paul Roussillon, Roland Alexandre, Bernard Dhéan, Jacques Eyser and Jean Piat; and in a move that looked to the future, he employed nearly twenty probationers.[2]

One of the most difficult problems of Touchard's tenure was to find an acceptable use for the second theatre, the Odéon. The revised statutes had stipulated that the Richelieu was to stage French works at least ten years old and foreign works of deceased authors; while the second theatre was to stage works by French and foreign contemporary authors. This had created problems: contemporary authors were not eager to offer their works to the Comédie française and members of the company were not enthusiastic about acting in a second theatre that at the time meant the Odéon on the other side of the Seine. The problem was finally overcome by concentrating on classics in the Richelieu and a selection of plays, some of which were modern rather than contemporary, in the renamed theatre, the Salle Luxembourg. It was here that *Six Characters in Search of an Author* was staged in March 1952. It was deemed a great success and was kept in the repertoire for three consecutive years (109 performances), then revived in 1959.

The director, Julien Bertheau, was a longstanding member of the Comédie française, having joined the company in 1936 at the age of twenty-six. He worked first as an actor then subsequently as a director, and had directed both classical and modern plays, his most recent being Shakespeare's *The Winter's Tale* and Obey's *L'homme des cendres* (*Man of Ashes*). The memory of Pitoëff's 1923 production, which

Pitoëff had revived in 1937, hovered over his approach to the text. Pitoëff's signature, the use of the stage lift to bring on the Characters, had become a mythical moment of Parisian theatre. Bertheau, too, used the lift, yet his production was nevertheless very much his own. Rather than bring the Characters down on to the stage, he brought them up from underground, making associations with the dark of night and the belly of the theatre.[3] The extant script shows the care with which Bertheau planned the Characters' entrance. He placed the Characters in a straight horizontal line in the lift, from audience left: Boy, Stepdaughter, Little Girl, Father, Mother and Son. On the lift's arrival at stage level, all the Characters stepped three paces of differing lengths on to the stage, with the Father (Fernand Ledoux) taking the lead so that the formation became a V-shape with the Father at the apex and the Boy and Son at each end. The Father's eyes were directed first to stage level, then upwards towards the dress circle and then towards the Prompter's box and the Director.[4] It was clearly a moment that he held well and it impressed the audience. Here is one reviewer's appreciation of it: 'I like the way they come out from the earth in the green light reverently kept by Bertheau. They rise up from some mysterious shadowy country, from some hell or some limbo of dramatic creation. And Fernand Ledoux steps forward'.[5]

In part 2 Bertheau brought Mme Pace's little room down from the flies, rather than in from the wings as the script stipulates. The costume for both Characters and Actors was contemporary, but Mme Pace's room was a period piece, with a floral wallcovering of rich material and little table, divan and mirror in keeping with the set. In part 3 the garden was already in place as the curtain rose: five dark and pollarded trees casting shadows against the curved cyclorama. Like Pitoëff, Bertheau used Crémieux's translation of the 1921 text, complete with its errors and, more interestingly, making the Son rather than the Father cry out at the end of part 3: 'Fiction!!! Reality, sir!' Marie-Anne Commène, Crémieux's widow, sat in on all the rehearsals. But the evocative setting for the part 3 garden, designed by Suzanne

Lalique, went beyond Pirandello's 1921 script; the still and lonely garden with its mysterious trees was intended to evoke infinity, as Bertheau explained. 'We take nothing as our starting point to reach out towards infinity, we follow a constant rise to finish with this vertical of Pirandellian thought.'[6]

Bertheau paid detailed attention to the lighting. One of the finest effects would have been at the beginning of part 2. At this point an oval pool of light was thrown centre front of stage for the scene between the Stepdaughter and the Little Girl. The Boy follows his two sisters from back stage left but stands outside the pool of light. When the Stepdaughter forces the Boy's right hand from his pocket to reveal that he is hiding a revolver, the production notes explain that only the revolver is to appear in the ray of light, while he, the Boy, must remain in the darkness.[7] Mme Pace's entrance was also managed in the main by a simple lighting effect. The Father, acting as magician, takes centre stage in a sweeping movement from down stage left, gathers and hangs up the Actors' hats and coats, then moves upstage to draw back the black curtain that acts as doorway to Mme Pace's shop at centre back. He then turns down to front stage left approaching the Director. All the lighting is much reduced, casting most of the stage in shadow, except for three spots, which light the entrance, and the centre of the stage. Mme Pace appears and the Actors press forward.[8]

Georges Neveux, who had seen Pitoëff's production, was able to make comparisons between the 1923 and 1952 stagings. He was particularly struck by the different presentation of the Father by Fernand Ledoux.

> In 1923, Pitoëff had played the Father. His sad gentleness, his subdued vehemence gave us the impression that his true being floated elsewhere and that only his appearance had come down amongst us.
>
> Ledoux has resolutely adopted a different interpretation, that of extreme presence. With his rapid and dental articulation, his brief derisive laugh and those icy blue hypnotising eyes, he has created a character

of excessive logic, one who, nevertheless, quickly becomes as unreal as the ghostly presence of that other interpretation. It is pleasing to be able to praise Ledoux without taking anything away from Pitoëff: if he equals him, it is by quite other means.[9]

None of the reviewers compares the 1952 Stepdaughter with Ludmilla Pitoëff's. However, there were two interpretations of the Stepdaughter in Bertheau's production. The part was initially taken by Renée Faure, but by April Touchard had had to replace her. Maria Casarès was one of Touchard's 'discoveries'.[10] Renée Faure had stressed the provocative and vulgar side to the Stepdaughter's character, while Maria Casarès emphasised the victim, the wounded creature. Less insolent and sensual than Renée Faure, and more contorted, giving the impression of being just this side of a breakdown, she conveyed more mystery and less revenge. The reviewer who made the comparison tended to prefer Renée Faure but conceded that Maria Casarès was probably closer to Pirandello's conception.[11]

In the following year Parisians were able to compare French productions of *Six Characters in Search of an Author* with the Piccolo Teatro's, a situation similar to the one in 1925 when Pirandello brought the Teatro d'Arte company to Paris. Jean Jacques Gautier commented that Bertheau's production presented an appropriate balance between the company of Actors and the Characters while the Italian production did not, putting too great an emphasis on the Characters. He was also unimpressed by the Stepdaughter (Lilla Brignone) whom he accused of out-dated techniques, turning her face too much towards the audience, assuming poses 'presenting her profile and features to such an extent that she appeared more theatrical than the Leading Lady or the Young Juvenile Lead'.[12] Robert Kemp also noted that the Actors were subdued, 'hardened in their affected practices, real soulless mannequins'. But he was full of praise for Tino Buazzelli's interpretation of the Father, particularly in the scene in Mme Pace's shop: 'He has such a troubled air: you feel his age, you sense his fear of the consequences. He is gallant, awkward, embarrassed.' And there is no doubt that in this production it is the Father who has the last anguished cry that affirms the reality of the situation at the end of the play. 'In the tragic final cry, his sincere violence was truly moving.'[13]

COMÉDIE FRANÇAISE, PARIS, 19 OCTOBER 1978, DIRECTED BY ANTOINE BOURSEILLER

The past permeated this production, too. Antoine Bourseiller borrowed Julien Bertheau's script from the Comédie française archives and felt under no compulsion to imagine a different way to bring on the Characters: the stage lift was used again. Two of the actors in Bertheau's production played in this new version: Jean-Paul Roussillon, the Boy in 1952, now took on the Father, and Claude Winter, the Ingénue in 1952, played the Mother. Nevertheless, this was a new production in a number of ways. Claude Winter remembered in particular that the 1952 production concentrated more on the Characters than on the Actors: 'the others [those who were not Characters] were more of a group of onlookers than participants whereas in 1978 each of the players was an individual'.[14] Bourseiller worked with a dramaturge, Dominique Fernandez, known for his psychoanalytic approach to literature,[15] and his production used, for the first time in France, a translation of the 1925 text by Michel Arnaud.

On the whole Fernandez preferred the 1925 text for its greater clarity and theatricality, but there was one cut Pirandello made that, he felt, created an imbalance in the whole play. In the 1921 version the Son and Mother have a discrete scene at the beginning of part 2, during which the great gulf between them is made evident. The Mother expresses both her shame and her reluctance to have her life dramatised and the Son expatiates on his particular predicament. He says, as if to himself, but evidently wanting the Mother to hear (the 'he' in the following quotation refers to the Father):

> And what about me? Hasn't he perhaps acted in such a way that has
> forced me to discover what no son should ever discover? To know that

his mother and father live as man and woman, for themselves, that they have their own life, outside that personality of mother and father which we children attribute to them. Because, as soon as that reality is discovered, our life only remains attached by one sole point to that man and to that woman – a point which can only shame them.[16]

The Son here posits his predicament as comparable in pain and significance to the Father's and the Stepdaughter's. Pirandello cuts this speech entirely in 1925. But for Fernandez this speech provides the Son's character, the motive for his actions: the Son has remained traumatised by what Freud referred to as the 'primitive scene', the Oedipal moment. It is this that constrains him to keep away from his mother. There are, then, in Fernandez's interpretation, two incestuous motifs in the play, between the Father and Stepdaughter and between the Mother and Son.

> The Son can neither distance himself completely from his family nor accept to maintain his role, clouded as he is by a fantasy that he repulses with all his might yet without being able to free himself from it. The two other young illegitimate children repeat, in some way, the figure of the Son. They, completely mute, push the rejection of the Oedipal temptation to the point of suicide. The drowning of the Little Girl and the Boy's revolver shot remain incomprehensible enigmas, if this sense of guilt which bears down on the innocent children is not taken into account.[17]

Pirandello cut this speech because it revealed to him 'the abyss of his own unconscious'. Fernandez went on to suggest that it might even reveal the 'centre of the whole drama', which, rather than the 'scandal of the almost realised incest between the Father and the Stepdaughter' might be the 'dread of the incest between the Mother and the Son' and 'the fascination and horror which every son has experienced for the taboo act'.[18] According to this interpretation, Pirandello was performing for himself his own psychodrama, and faced with the horror of what he had unearthed, sent back to the darkness what he did not want to admit. Fernandez even sees the critique of theatre as some of kind of protection from self-revelation. 'The theme of the theatre on trial hides the anguish of revealing to the public, of revealing to himself, a desire, a conflict, a crime which have to remain hidden. The denouement is rapid, brutal, unexpected: everything returns as quickly as possible to the silence of the censure, to the peace of the unspoken.'[19]

For Fernandez the removal of the Son's speech at the beginning of part 2 has taken from the Son's character everything that makes him interesting. Without it he is nothing more than 'a young male grumbler, rhetorically draped in the proclamation of his "legitimacy"'.[20] So at the Comédie française in 1978, they decided not only to reinsert the speech (in some copies it is written in by hand, in others it is typed), but also to place it at the end of part 1 where it would have even greater impact. It has a special slot – and a special lighting effect – after the Director goes off with the Characters and before the Actors talk among themselves as they, too, leave the stage.

The psychoanalytic and sexual interpretation of the play was also emphasised in the setting for Mme Pace's shop. The bed was no small divan but a large double bed with a headboard and bed end of wrought metal, which were used as images of imprisonment of the Stepdaughter. At the end of the production, which did not follow Pirandello's 1925 stage directions of the shadow play and the Stepdaughter's escape through the theatre, the bed, stashed behind a curtain at the back during the setting for part 3 (a small fountain centre back, two trees and the curved cyclorama of 1952) was momentarily lit as the Characters disappeared.

The Comédie française presented the play as a period piece with Cubist costumes by Sonia Delaunay and, for the Stepdaughter's dance, a foxtrot by Francis Salabert (the music added to the back of the script). This choice was made in order to date the Director's behaviour historically. No contemporary director, Fernandez wrote, would shout 'Silence' to his company, nor would s/he mount a play s/he did not believe in, nor would the actors criticise it as they do in the text.[21] For the Comédie française the Director is largely functional. According to Fernandez, it would be a mistake to make of him a complex person, as he would then compete with the Characters. But he has to be made human. This was achieved by making him responsible for his theatre and sorely troubled that he could find no good plays to stage there. They also added to the role psychological and sociological implications of geography and gender. The Director is portrayed as a chill pragmatic man surprised and fascinated by the arrival of the passionate Sicilian orator. The Director and the Father, coming from very different cultural milieux, find themselves nevertheless drawn together when faced with the devastating frenzy of the Stepdaughter and the Mother's chilling refusal to speak. Fernandez claimed that 'this aspect of the play had never been elucidated before'.[22]

The interpretation of the Stepdaughter (Christine Fersen), the character with the most changes of mood, made her the most perspicacious of all the Characters. 'Clear-sighted, she has all the astuteness the Father lacks. Each time he risks antagonising the Director with his overinsistence, she intervenes to relax the situation, to slip in a note of seduction, of feminine chic.'[23] Fernandez sees in the Stepdaughter's escape from the family a possibility intact within her of ceasing to be the Character imprisoned by her destiny, a possibility of a life as a woman. Christine Fersen emphasised the Stepdaughter's different moods. In part 1 the story about the Father watching her coming out of school and offering her a hat was played with tenderness, without the sarcasm and disgust often highlighted in this episode. The Stepdaughter was revealed wanting to retain a memory of that gift as a touching moment of her childhood, wanting to keep her tiny space of childhood innocence intact. This made the contrast with the Stepdaughter in Mme Pace's shop all the more striking: here she is a vulgar prostitute – there are striking images (in the Comédie française archives) of her and Mme Pace preparing for the entrance of the Father, one with Mme Pace placing a cigar in the Stepdaughter's mouth (see fig. 8). The Father (Jean-Paul Roussillon) was less sympathetically portrayed. In particular, in the speech where he invited sympathy for the sexual predicament of a man in later middle age, too old to be attractive to women, too young to do without them, he was shown as a hypocritical 'dirty old man'.

8. The Comédie française production by Antoine Bourseiller, 1978. (Photo: Claude Angelini, Bibliothèque de la Comédie française.)

The first to use the 1925 script in France, Bourseiller made much of the new opening and added refinements of his own. The evening performances of the play began at 20.23 and the matinées at 14.23 (rather than 20.30 and 14.30), with the consequence that the action began while the audience was still settling. The auditorium was half-lit, the stage fully lit and the curtain up. At 20.22 the stage lift was brought down to below stage level (in preparation for the Characters' later ascent). At 20.23 the Chief Technician (René Arrieu) comes on stage, followed by the Young Leading Man (Philippe Etesse), who approaches the piano back stage right. He begins to play (Julien Risselin's 'Don Luciano' tango), then other actors and actresses gather round. Two actors, Philippe Etesse and Catherine Conti (probably the understudies) rehearse a scene from *The Rules of the Game* (between Guido and Silia) that highlights the image of the mirror. Later in the scene Bourseiller included more of this rehearsal than scheduled by Pirandello – the script has an inserted page 6a with a scene between Leone and Filippo that is repeated after the Prompter has asked permission to put the cover on – in this production – *her* prompt box.[24]

As Pirandello's stage directions stipulate, there are two little flights of steps on either side of the stage leading from the auditorium to the stage, but the auditorium was not used in this production as much as Pirandello suggests. The Leading Lady enters from back stage left rather than through the audience, and the Actors do not rush off stage in fright at the entrance of the Characters. The Director, however, does leave the stage several times, stage right, to watch the rehearsal from front of house.

It is interesting to see Bourseiller's interpretation (aided by his dramaturge) in the light of the central cultural position held in 1960s and 1970s Paris by the psychoanalytic movement. Elisabeth Roudinesco refers to this period as 'Freudian France in Full Array' in her monumental history of psychoanalysis in France.[25] It is perhaps also pertinent to recall the emphasis the British Lord Chamberlain's office put on the Son's speech, making of it a prime reason for refusing the play a licence.[26] In 1920s London the Son's speech, which does not necessarily have to be understood in terms of him seeing his parents making love, was deemed by the authorities to be so shocking as to warrant rejecting the whole play. Perhaps the English censors had more insight than they are usually given credit for in their awareness of the potentially crucial import of this small part of the play.[27]

OLIVIER THEATRE, NATIONAL THEATRE,
LONDON, 18 MARCH 1987, A NEW VERSION BY
NICHOLAS WRIGHT, DIRECTED BY
MICHAEL RUDMAN

As early as 1925 an anonymous critic writing in the *Times Literary Supplement* broached the question of translating Pirandello.

> Beyond a certain point, of course, it is impossible to translate Pirandello. His characters and situations are so invented as to demand Italian pre-conceptions, emotions and gestures. To take a convincing guise in English they really need adaptation . . . Wrong acting could make absolute nonsense of any of these plays, and intelligent acting, con-versely, could lend them a far greater actuality, possibly, than their author ever conceived. Every country, therefore, will need its own particular adaptation.[28]

How to present foreign plays became an increasingly vexed question in the 1960s and 1970s. Between William Ball's 1963 production at the Mayfair Theatre and Michael Rudman's at the National, London theatregoers had had the opportunity to see other Italian plays in English; three de Filippo plays, Franco Zeffirelli's *Saturday Sunday Monday* (1973), *Filumena* (1977) and *Ducking Out* (an adaptation of *Natale in casa Cupiello*, 1982); and Dario Fo's *Accidental Death of an Anarchist* (1979–80).[29] It did not pass unnoticed that comic Italian plays tended to be chosen for the English public and that their comedy was enhanced. Theatre managers and directors are only too aware that theatre has to be marketed, and clearly one of the best ways to ensure a reasonable run is to make people laugh, particularly when something foreign and new is being offered. *Saturday Sunday Monday* was defined as 'the finest and funniest show in London' and 'a warm and lively comedy'.[30] According to Jeremy Kingston and Benedict Nightingale, however, Zeffirelli's production, while conveying well the humour inherent in the play, failed to portray its social tensions and transformed 'a sombre and disturbing comedy into a palatable slice of life'.[31]

The difficulties of presenting de Filippo to the English (Martin Esslin described *Filumena* as 'an exotic plant') had led to different strategies.[32] Sometimes actors were required to speak with artificial Italian accents, as in Zeffirelli's 1973 and 1977 de Filippo productions, to convey 'Italianness' to the audience. Both Dario Fo in Italy and Martin Esslin in the UK have commented unfavourably on the ten-dency to caricature Italians on stage (as a corollary of the way Italians are caricatured off stage).[33] 'Transfer' was the solution Mike Scott adopted for *Ducking Out*, which was transplanted to West Lancashire.

Until recently, notions of loss have dominated much of the critical discussion of translation. These concur in the main with ideas that Pirandello expressed as long ago as 1908 in his essay 'Illustrators, Actors and Translators'. But in the past ten years, different perspectives have emerged that have helped to liberate translation from notions of both failure and inferiority. Aware that no final version of a text is ever possible, because language is in a state of continuous flux, Barbara Godard has articulated the view that holds for many when she affirms that translation is not concerned with 'target languages' and the conditions of 'arrival' but with 'ways of ordering relations between languages and cultures'. 'Translation', she writes, 'is an art of approach.'[34] As Susan Bassnett has put it, 'The task of the translator is to maintain balance, to mediate between cultures and languages, between reader and writer.'[35] Octavio Paz, the Mexican writer and translator, thinks of the translator as a liberator. The original writer chooses words from a range of linguistic possibilities with absolute precision and assembles them into an object that s/he and others consider fixed, the 'work of art'. 'The translator's task is to free up that fixed text, freeing "trapped language" and allowing it to circulate anew in another context.'[36] The translator's task is not to follow old models slavishly or seek to reproduce a faithfulness that is impossible, but rather to liberate the text and give the dead writer a new life in a new language.[37]

These approaches make a useful starting point for an examination of Michael Rudman's production of *Six Characters in Search of an Author*. Nicholas Wright, the National Theatre's dramaturge at the time, adapter of several plays and original playwright, created a new version of the text. To achieve this, since he has no Italian, he worked from a version of the 1925 text made by Gwenda Pandolfi, whose name appeared last in the cast and credit list in the programme for the 'literal translation'. In fact, her version is a lively rendition of the Italian, both readable and 'performable'.[38] But it does not 'liberate' the text, nor does it give it 'new life' for English theatregoers of the late 1980s. Nicholas Wright's adaptation, on the other hand, 'mediates' between the writer and the English theatregoer, negotiating a safe passage for Pirandello's radical text, by addressing those areas that might still vex the West End/South Bank theatregoer. Wright removed *The Rules of the Game* and substituted *Hamlet*, described in the programme as 'a play from the familiar classic repertoire'. He did not see *The Rules of the Game* as 'very relevant to *Six Characters in Search of an Author*'.[39] However, Pirandello's self-reflexive use of one of his own plays introduced, before the entrance of the Characters, concepts concerning acting and role-play. The discussion between the Leading Actor and the Director on the meaning of his speech and how to deliver it (including the advice to 'turn to the audience a bit more – about three quarters profile') already begins to deconstruct conventional theatre practices. The way *Hamlet* is used as the rehearsal play also provided an opportunity for thinking about roles before the entrance of the Characters. The actors in the company are known by the parts they play in *Hamlet* rather than by their personal names, and are so listed in the programme. *Hamlet* created opportunities for other intertextual references as well. The play within the play, and *Hamlet*'s speech about it, has a Pirandellian ring, and the theme of incest chimes neatly. Wright noted that both plays had fathers who have died recently, 'a neurasthenic son, a stepfather, a grieving mother, and a lot of ambiguous guilt'. There are, in addition, what appear to be 'little quotes, whether unconscious or not I don't know. At one point the son says, "Words, words, words". And the final line of the play is "Give me some lights"'.[40]

The last line is a request from the Director for light, because Wright decided to cut the 1925 ending and revert to the 1921 version at this point. He also kept the whole production on stage and did not use the Olivier auditorium. Rather than present the National Theatre Company in the Olivier Theatre in 1987 (one solution for the opening scenes), he and Rudman decided to return to the original production, creating a set on the Olivier stage that would 'recapture the

Roman stage' of the first production in Rome in 1921.[41] The result was a visually impressive setting, designed by Carl Toms. On the deep and wide Oliver stage, an inner stage was erected for the rehearsal of *Hamlet*, and centre back, a rostrum for one of the scenes. Behind the rostrum along the back wall of the theatre were a number of assorted chairs, and two thrones. The lower level of the surround area contained, stage right, a props skip, piano, timpani, the Prompter's chair, the Director's desk and armchair; and stage left, the Stage Manager's trestle table and a cheval mirror. In addition to the scenic material suggested by Pirandello's stage directions, Wright included a further theatre department, that of 'wardrobe' (providing a cameo role for Joyce Grant). So on stage were two wardrobe rails and an umbrella stand back left, and a table and chair for the Wardrobe Mistress, centre left. As well as the stage, raised rehearsal space for *Hamlet* and the rostrum, further areas of the theatre were open to public view. Back stage right was a flight of steps leading to a double door labelled 'USCITA' ('EXIT'); beyond the doors to the right, off stage, a stack of flats; back stage left large double doors, and to the left of them, off stage, a corner with a cluster of furniture and props (a Russian stove, a statue on a plinth, a bird cage, and an old gramophone); and even further over to the right, a number of large house plants. The space under the door marked 'USCITA' was filled with various paint pots, baskets and buckets. These carefully arranged nooks and crannies of the set were works of art in themselves, as the photographs in the theatre's archives demonstrate. The whole stage was fully exposed to the bare walls and plumbing, but the set also included walls with crumbling plaster, revealing the brick beneath and pilasters on either side that gave a slight sense of enclosure (see fig. 9).

Nicholas Wright's 'Italian' setting, complete with its 'USCITA' sign and including details such as letters on the Stage Manager's table addressed to The Director, Teatro d'Arte, Roma, all with Italian stamps, was persuasive. It created a sense of wonder (as a member of the audience, you could discover new details throughout the performance). It was also, however, historically misleading. Pirandello did

9. Production by Michael Rudman, National Theatre, London, 1987. (Photo: Mac Dougall, Group Three Photography.)

not include wardrobe rails and a wardrobe mistress or master in his opening scene for the very good reason that run-of-the-mill Italian theatrical companies of the period did not include such a person. Actors were expected to provide their own costumes. The introduction of scenic and costume design was one of the practices that Pirandello introduced in the mid-1920s while working with his theatrical company, the Teatro d'Arte. When directing Ruggero Ruggeri in the role of Henry IV, Pirandello would in fact have some difficulty in persuading him to wear a different costume from the one he had used in *Hamlet*. If it was good enough for Hamlet, why would it not do for Henry?

Wright's writing for this opening scene, however, provided an animated scene of a theatre at work and much expanded Pirandello's original version. The Wardrobe Mistress, who is the first of the company to be described, hands out practice skirts to the female characters. Throughout the opening scene the Assistant Stage Manager practises a thunder roll on the timpani. The first actor to appear is Polonius, an old character actor who goes over his lines with the Prompter. Ophelia and Hamlet rehearse the nunnery scene. Hamlet and Laertes choose swords. There is a conversation between Laertes and the Lady in Waiting, an earnest young woman much cluttered with bags, about parts in *Mask and Face*. Gertrude arrives late because her train is delayed. When she finally arrives she puts on her practice skirt immediately, pins up her hair, and removes her bracelets and gives them for safe keeping to the Wardrobe Mistress. The Director arrives to a roll of thunder on the timpani (the ASM's second attempt). This prompts the Director to remember that the theatre has an old-fashioned thunder roll produced by rolling cannon balls in a channel that runs around the auditorium, a device that Polonius remembers from his days of playing Mephistopheles in *Faust*. This device is in the process of being resuscitated when the Characters enter. Claudius is rehearsing 'Though yet of Hamlet our dear brother's death/The memory is green' when the menacing rumble becomes a deafening crash from all parts of the auditorium.

As it reaches its climax, the lights black out. The noise decreases, quite slowly,
with many an echo and reverberation. In the blackness we hear
GERTRUDE: It's utterly, utterly real.
HORATIO: It seems to have fused the lights.
POLONIUS: It always did.
We see, picked out in the darkness, six people.[42]

   As can be appreciated from this opening scene, a distinctive feature
of this production is the emphasis it gave, both visually and aurally, to
the theatre. This also extended to acting, its profession and its craft.
The actor playing Polonius refers to theatre as it was in the 'good old
days' when the old commedia dell'arte theatre was in vogue. Wright
built up this part. It is Polonius and the Prompter who get the last lines
of part 1; and it is Polonius who at the end of the play thanks the
Director for an interesting rehearsal. Wright's point, however, goes
beyond the display of theatricality and the presentation of theatre
as an institution with a history; acting itself is seen in process, the
stages of transformation are made visible to the audience. In part 2
the role of the Father is assigned to Claudius. When challenged by the
Father that there is no resemblance between them, Claudius goes to
the Wardrobe Mistress to be kitted out. During the ensuing dialogue
'*the Wardrobe Mistress continues changing his clothes and appearance*
into quite a good approximation of the Father'.[43] The Father expresses
his fears of misrepresentation:

> FATHER: This is what I am most afraid of – that I will be misrepre-
> sented, that it will be a version of me and not me myself which stands
> in the dock when I am judged. (*He and Claudius stare at one another.*
> *They look remarkably alike, with the single difference that Claudius has a*
> *walking stick.*)
> FATHER: I don't know what . . . I can't explain it, but the words I use
> sound false, as though the truth were draining out of them.

At this point he is told by the Director to go and sit down and watch,
which he does, meekly. Later during the 'rehearsal' Claudius indicates
to the Father, as if pointing out a mistake, that he has no stick.

FATHER: No stick.
CLAUDIUS: Do you mind if I try it with?
FATHER: What can I say?
CLAUDIUS: Good fellow.[44]

Throughout the 'rehearsal' the Actors' willingness to try to get it right gives the scene a different tone from the original text. The Lady in Waiting, who plays the Stepdaughter after Gertrude refuses the role, wants to understand the Stepdaughter's motivation (a sly reference to Stanislavsky). The text makes it clear that Claudius is a very able actor.

> It's worth saying at this point, for all the carry-on, Claudius is a very good actor; subtle and probably under-rated. So there's no element of ham or parody in this performance, though it's clearly different from the original. The Lady in Waiting is a promising actress, though inexperienced. However, the Characters are openly appalled, amused or derisive at the acting, whether or not there are lines indicating this.[45]

Wright's version of the play gives sympathetic characterisation to the Actors and Members of the company. This and the fact that National Theatre actors of considerable standing played Actors and Members of the company (for instance, Leslie Sands played Polonius, Joyce Grant the Wardrobe Mistress), makes it unsurprising that it was the Actors rather than the Characters who gained the audience's sympathy. The immediacy of the detailed realism communicated more easily than the intensity of the Characters.

Michael Rudman's production was a London theatre event, if not a consistently appreciated one. Both he and Nicholas Wright were profiled before the performance.[46] The production was reviewed in *The Listener*, the *Times Literary Supplement* and *Plays International*, as well as in the dailies and weekend papers. It figured in the two BBC radio programmes on the arts, *Critics Forum* and *Kaleidoscope*. Reception of the production fell into two fairly distinct categories. Most of those who knew the play well and liked it (including those who knew it in Italian) were firm in their criticism. John Elsom thought

Wright had transformed 'a powerful play into the small change of a British show-biz comedy-drama'.[47] Michael Ratcliffe saw the production as 'a retreat from tragedy and passion'.[48] For John Peter, on the other hand, who had previously thought *Six Characters in Search of an Author* did not 'have the staying power of great art', Rudman's production was a revelation. 'It is flamboyant, tense and tragic, cool, cerebral and melancholy: it bears the stamp of intense authenticity.'[49]

The differences in appreciation were manifest most directly in two reviews in *The Yearbook of the British Pirandello Society*. The first, by Giulia Ajmone Arsan, regretted that 'anglicisation' had 'deprived the play of its depth'.[50] Yet for Katharine Worth the production was 'a triumph of anglicising' that 'opened up Pirandello's play for popular consumption in the English theatre'. She noted, too, that the Characters were 'assimilated to the "natural" mode in which the so-English company excel'. Richard Pasco's impressive performance as the Father did not entirely eliminate a longing for 'a stormier, darker interpretation' such as Romolo Valli could bring to the part. Pasco was a 'quietly reasonable English person, in his middle class and middle aged suit and pullover . . ., deeply ashamed of the near-indecent act he was made to commit but also deeply interested in the idea of being what he is, and conscious of a responsibility to explain it to the bewildered actors'.[51]

In this production English actors concentrated on what they could do well. They brought out the comedy of the play, they made of Pirandello's philosophical debate on reality and illusion a warm, cosy workshop on theatre; in a phrase (Michael Coveney's), they 'tamed the piece'.[52] Put differently, the National Theatre's production might be said to have 'liberated' the text (in Octavio Paz's sense) for an English audience. In mediating between the Italian text of 1921 and English audiences of the 1980s it may even have made it easier for Jonathan Kent to present *The Rules of the Game* and *Naked* at the Almeida Theatre in 1992 and 1998.

CHAPTER 10

MAKING *SIX CHARACTERS*
ACCESSIBLE: ROBERT BRUSTEIN
AND RICHARD JONES

Six Characters in Search of an Author has not escaped the accusation often levelled at Pirandello in English-speaking countries of being too cerebral. In this chapter the focus will be on two productions that, while bringing out the fundamental concepts in the play, have gone out of their way to make the play accessible.

LOEB THEATER, CAMBRIDGE, MASSACHUSETTS, MAY 1984, ADAPTED BY ROBERT BRUSTEIN AND THE AMERICAN REPERTORY THEATRE, DIRECTED BY ROBERT BRUSTEIN

Public experience of Pirandello's plays owes much to scholars with theatrical know-how who have staged his plays. The translations and productions of Frederick May, who as well as being head of the Department of Italian at the University of Leeds during the 1950s and early 1960s was a fine amateur actor and director, did much to put Pirandello on the theatrical map in the UK.[1] In the USA it is Robert Brustein who performed a similar function. He holds a PhD from Columbia University and trained as an actor for the stage. In the 1950s he was his country's leading critical voice in his generation with his trenchant attacks on the philistinism of the American stage.[2] The combination of academic knowledge with theatrical insight has made of Brustein a force to be reckoned with in the theatre. According to the playwright Jules Feiffer, speaking in 1986, 'Bob Brustein

155

is the best artistic director we have in America because he is the best
drama critic we have in America.'[3] In the mid-1960s Brustein came to
the notice of Kingman Brewster, then President of Yale, who invited
him to Yale as Dean of the Yale School of Drama, and since then
he has worked within academic institutions. At Yale he formed an
impressive ensemble group, making of the Yale Rep (later renamed
the American Repertory Theatre) a teaching institution. His aim was
'to wean students away from Broadway and a media culture based on
a perfidious hit/miss mentality', by creating a permanent ensemble
company that would be 'evaluated not in terms of a single production, but in terms of a continuous vision given flesh and blood in
an ongoing dialogue of various productions'. The company fulfilled
its potential with its move to Harvard in 1979 'after one of the most
notorious dustups in the history of American theater'. At Harvard
they had better facilities, the Loeb Theater, 'one of the best-designed
and most technologically sophisticated theaters in America', rather
than the New Haven remodelled church, which had limited the stage
design of the plays presented. Better facilities meant the possibility of
more opulent productions. These included adaptations of Molière's
Sganarelle and Gozzi's *The King Stag*.[4]

Soon after moving to Harvard, Brustein mounted *Six Characters in
Search of an Author*, which remained in repertoire for some years. He
has a longstanding interest in Pirandello. Years before this production,
he had included a chapter on Pirandello in his book *The Theatre of
Revolt* (1965). If somewhat sceptical of Pirandello's plot structure and
use of dramatic materials, which he described then as 'conventional'
(Pirandello 'keeps us confined amidst the ugly paraphernalia of the
cluttered drawing room'), Brustein concluded that Pirandello was 'the
most seminal dramatist of our time' whose influence on twentieth-
century drama was 'immeasurable'.[5] In 1986 he told William Harris
of the *New York Times* that 'Pirandello is perennially relevant, perennially significant'.[6]

Brustein is considered to be a text-based director, but this does not
mean that he takes the text as he finds it. He is also a pragmatist.

He once said that it is necessary to violate the writing of Pirandello's dramas in order better to keep their intent, and his treatment of *Six Characters in Search of an Author* is a good example of his approach. Without a female character actress to play the part of Mme Pace, he changed the Spanish seamstress and brothelkeeper of Pirandello's text into a Latino pimp initially named Emiliano Pace, subsequently Paz, defending himself by a reference to Shakespeare's practices.[7] To heighten the tension the play was presented without intermission and the text was reduced (though not as much as some reviewers would have had their readers believe). Cuts were made to some of the interchanges between the Father and the Director (in this case, the Senior Actor of ART, Jeremy Geidt). One key speech by the Father concerning the efficacy of words was dropped. The language of the translation was contemporary American. Brustein's text, which in 1996 he described as 'liquid, spontaneous, improvisatory', adapts to different circumstances, both topographical and temporal: in Boston there was a reference to the Freedom trail and the department store Filene's Basement, a quip about a rival university theatre (the Huntingdon), and a useful explanation for the absence of explicit sex on the stage – unsuitable for the Boston matinée audiences.[8] In 1984 Emiliano Pace was '[a] lithe man with rouge on his cheeks and spangles on his eyelids, heavily jewelled, dressed in a vulgar but stylish suit, wearing a curled blond wig, and holding a long cigarette holder in his hand'. By 1996 he is '[a] lithe, well-built man, with long black hair, wearing vulgar clothes without a shirt, pendants hanging from his neck. When discovered, he is taking a sniff of cocaine through a tube.' In 1996, as he had no wig, the Mother hurls her handbag at him, rather than ripping his wig from his head.[9]

In early productions of *Six Characters in Search of an Author*, directors had cast the companies' stage staff as the stage staff of the play.[10] Brustein went further and had the actors of the ART play themselves. The play the company is rehearsing is not *The Rules of the Game* but one currently in repertoire, *Sganarelle* in 1984, *The King Stag* in 1996, both directed by Andrei Serban. This led to some good-natured grousing on the part of members of the *Six Characters'* company about Serban's tendency to abandon a production once it is mounted, leaving the Senior Actor Jeremy Geidt with the job of keeping it up to scratch. In contrast with the immediate reality of the company, Brustein cast the Characters as Italian, products of Pirandello's imagination and 'with Italian concepts of honor and moral codes'.[11]

In 1996 Brustein wrote that a production of *Six Characters in Search of an Author* 'should make the audience's flesh creep', since Pirandello's play 'is a metaphysical ghost story about the transparent nature of reality'.[12] The opening was low-key: a Technician, Anthony, was seen by the audience several minutes before the play began, sweeping the stage. Careful attention was given to magic or stage tricks. Brustein introduced a loading door at the back of the open stage to facilitate the Characters' entrance. Before the entrance of the Characters, the scrim over the door would begin to tremble (through the use of a wind machine) then turn transparent. The loading door lifted slowly, revealing the six Characters brilliantly lit from the back. The Characters swayed eerily from side to side. In the introduction to his printed version, Brustein suggests following the six, but especially the Father, 'with a special light different in quality, intensity and color from the lighting on the rest of the stage'.[13]

'The scene' between the Father and Stepdaughter was greatly enhanced by the use of a huge mirror, a dance mirror brought down from the flies. Lighting from behind rendered the mirror's material (mylar) transparent, with the result that when Paz appeared, evoked by the Father, the furniture, assembled by the stage crew on the Father's and Stepdaughter's instructions, was exactly parallel to the crude props placed in front of the mirror. Additionally, the mirror was able to project back into the room the image of an actor standing in front of the mirror. Thus scenes were played in front of the mirror and behind the mirror at one and the same time. When the Father and Stepdaughter sat on the couch in front of the mirror, they appeared to the audiences (both on stage and off) to be facing them; and when the Mother hurled her handbag at Paz behind the mirror, it seemed in front that she had hit him in the face. As Brustein explains, 'scenes were played in front of and behind the mirror at once'.[14] Reviewers were quick to notice that the 'dance mirror shows the audience looking at itself looking at the theatrical illusion'.[15]

Brustein multiplied the time levels in the play by bringing some of the memory scenes directly into the present. In the first part of the play, the Stepdaughter taunts the Father by remembering how he would watch her come out of school, and, on one occasion, offered her a brown-paper parcel containing a straw hat. In Brustein's version, the actors played rather than remembered the scene, the Father caressing the Stepdaughter's cheek, the Stepdaughter replying in a little girl's voice. Later, the Father and Son recall how the Stepdaughter, the Mother and her two other children came to the Father's house. Again, this scene was played in the present with the Stepdaughter demanding money and pleading to be taken home to the Father's house.

Brustein saw the garden scene as the most difficult and potentially most effective one of the play. Anthony, the Stagehand, takes out the mirror and lowers a white drop and a cardboard wafer moon, and provides a mysterious blue light. The cast hit on the idea of light booms ('in the wings') for the trees, blue plastic ('in one of the roadboxes') to stand in for the pond. When the Son is finally forced to speak, he tells the story of how he saw the Little Girl approach the pond. At the same time the Mother crosses the stage to get closer to the Son, thus focusing attention on the Little Girl with the Stepdaughter standing helplessly behind her. The blue plastic on which the Little Girl was lying began to descend very slowly – Brustein used a lift for this – while the plastic filled with water and the child's clothes were drenched. The Stepdaughter, sobbing gently, reached down and carried the dripping body off stage.

In the next section of the end of the play, Brustein also used mirror effects to convey the confusion of realities. The scrim again turned transparent to reveal a parallel reality behind. The Boy appeared to be standing 'by a real tree as a real moon casts its image on the pond at which he's looking'.[16] The action of the Son, pointing his finger at his head, was seen to parallel that of the Boy pointing a revolver at his head. When the Boy fell the lights went out and the Actors rushed in pandemonium behind the scrim while the other Characters disappeared off stage. As electric power was restored, the cast gathered together again, lingering, upset by the day. The Senior Actor, Jeremy, confirmed that they would meet the next day to rehearse *The King Stag*. Scott, the Stage Manager, helped to clear the stage and expressed a concern for Jeremy, the last to leave. Jeremy called up to Anthony to kill the lights and was then plunged into darkness. Suddenly, from behind the white drop, the loading doors began to rise again. The six Characters were there, as at their entrance, eerily swaying as before. Snatches of earlier dialogue sound out into the theatre: 'We're looking for an Author'; 'Leave me out of it'; 'It's happening now. It's happening all the time'; 'You could be our play'; 'My suffering is alive for ever'; 'Take me home with you'. Then suddenly the six Characters fell forward with a loud crash on to the floor; and the audience realised that they were life-size colour photographs.

Part of the effect of this ending, which takes its cue from Pirandello's 1925 text, is realised through the reactions of the Actors to the experience. The spookiness of the day's experience was particularly well caught by the Actors in the last moments of the play. The Characters could not have left the theatre in any ordinary sense, they conclude, because the doors were locked. Members of the cast go to check. Tommy, one of the Actors, claims that the Boy's death was no trick – he has blood on his hands – but Jeremy contradicts him: 'There's no blood, Tommy.' In the last moments the tension mounts, as members of the company try to dispel their disquiet by arranging evening activities with each other. After the fall of the dummy Characters, Anthony returns to sweep the stage, as he had at the beginning of the performance.

ART keeps excellent records of its work and among the archives in the Harvard Theater Collection are details of the tour performance of Brustein's *Six Characters in Search of an Author* in 1984. The stage manager's notes, brief though they are, offer a reminder of the ephemeral nature of theatre, and the very real problems of touring. Kansas City's theatre had a large auditorium, accommodating 2,200 people, but a small stage, which meant that 'the table and all chairs were on the rake'. In Madison there was 'a new light board and an incompetent and hostile light board operator. The show was about staying in control of both.' In Lincoln the performance began late because the cross-fader on the board broke down half an hour before the start; there was no moon and 'the mirror moved slowly and noisily'; there was no blackout when the Boy killed himself. Occasionally there were problems with the actors, too. One actor turned up just ten minutes before the start because he was listening to a play-off game and could not get radio reception backstage. Another, playing the Son, 'did three very peculiar walks for his three crosses to try to escape' without warning his colleagues. 'He was very lucky the whole company didn't burst into laughter.'[17]

YOUNG VIC THEATRE, 9 FEBRUARY 2001, A NEW VERSION BY DAVID HARROWER, DIRECTED BY RICHARD JONES

The Young Vic has a special place among London theatres. It opened in 1970 as part of the National Theatre's programme for young people while the Old Vic was the first home of the National Theatre.[18] Its building of breezeblock and steel, meant to last about five years, provided a venue for classics old and new until 2004 when reconstruction and refurbishment began. As the programme notes say, 'it's small enough to house a whole society and just big enough to be filled by a single gesture'. The auditorium holds about 500 people who sit in unnumbered seats usually around a thrust stage. The theatre caters for young people. A teaching programme aimed at local schools and colleges accompanies each main house production. There are also opportunities for young people to be involved in theatre production through workshops, work experience and apprenticeship programmes. Audiences are wonderfully varied: black, Asian and white, young people in woolly hats, the elderly, tourists, middle-aged bourgeois couples and singles, the trendy and not so trendy, people of the theatre, businessmen and women all gather together in a democratic community to participate in the Young Vic presentations.

Six Characters in Search of an Author might be considered a brave choice for this heterogeneous clientele. Richard Jones, perhaps better known as an innovative director of opera than of plays was, however, able to present the play in ways that made it both challenging and immediate to a wide range of people. He worked from a new version of the play by David Harrower; a direct, contemporary version of the 1925 text that presents Pirandello's thought in crisp accessible language.[19] As with the versions of *The Rules of the Game* and *Naked* by David Hare and Nicholas Wright, this version of *Six Characters* was produced by a dramatist in his own right. All these versions deploy a dramatic style of late twentieth-century English drama – the punchy phrase, the paratactic sentence – and transform, without loss of meaning, Pirandello's early twentieth-century Italian into contemporary English stage prose.

Jones enhanced the accessibility of the play with his own directorial innovations. The first of these concerned the space. Productions are usually presented in the Young Vic on a thrust stage with the audience on three sides. For his *Six Characters Looking for an Author*, Jones transformed the space into a proscenium-arch stage with the audience sitting on period chairs set in tiers in an auditorium bedecked with chandeliers. The immediate impression was of a period piece, in keeping with the spirit of the play. To an *habitué* of the Young Vic, used to actors appearing on the open thrust stage at the beginning of a play, the change of space might be seen as an inverse analogy of the way Pirandello confounded his audience in 1921 with his open curtain and unprepared stage. The first part of Jones's production was set in a rehearsal space; in the second part a whole theatre was presented on the small stage, complete with boxes and footlights; in the third part, this theatre was reduced to the stage only. Only in this last part was the auditorium also used as theatre space. The changes, which extend Pirandello's notions, are theatrical signs to indicate that 'there is no such thing as stable space'.[20]

Jones also made changes to Pirandello's and David Harrower's text. One concerned the entry of the Characters; another the placing of the scene between the Stepdaughter and Little Girl at the beginning of part 2 (where it had been in Pirandello's 1921 text); and a third concerned the end of the play, which did not follow the stage directions concerning the projected figures of the Characters against the backdrop.

The performance was framed by the aria 'Vesti la giubbia', from Leoncavallo's opera *I pagliacci* (first performed in 1892). While *Six Characters* is about a company failing to mount a play because the life of the Characters takes over, in *I pagliacci* the real life of the actors overwhelms the comic plot, with terrible consequences. In both, comedy becomes tragedy at the moment when acting crosses the boundary into life. The aria 'Vesti la giubbia' comes at the end of the first act of this two-act opera. It expresses the anguish of the actor Canio, a member of the company of travelling players who are to stage a comic opera for a small village community in southern Italy. He must prepare for the comic part of the cuckolded clown (*Il pagliaccio*) rather than attend to the real drama of his wife's betrayal of him. 'You must put on your costume, paint your face . . . you must transform your despair into laughter; and make a jest of your sobbing, of your pain.'[21]

While hearing Gigli's tenor in the 1934 recording, the audience is also seeing on the white paperlike curtain before them a 1920s typewriter with hands over the keys, a cigarette smouldering in the ashtray to the right, sheets of paper torn up: the author in the throes of composition. As the curtain opens, the image fades and a Stagehand is seen sawing wood while the aria continues and then fades and a fussy Director's Assistant, in a 1950s coat and skirt, flurries to and fro. This mix of genres and moods, combined with temporal crossings (a 1920s play presented in 1950s dress to a 2001 audience in a simulated 1920s theatre), set the tenor of the performance: tragic, comic, ironic or just '*umoristico*' to use Pirandello's word, with a fine intellectual edge, using fully the means of theatre, with all its tricks of the trade, to question the basis of theatre.[22]

Jones considered it impossible to do the play in contemporary dress because of the value systems inherent in it: the play is about a society with definite values and was written nearly half a century before the sexual revolution. The production needed to signal that it was aware that the play was written in a particular period, but that it was still able to communicate directly with a contemporary audience. The place of its composition was also effectively conveyed: in the first part there was a sign reading 'TEATRO' indicating the way to the theatre; in the second part, when the stage was the theatre, the sign 'USCITA' pointed to the exit, an actress read an Italian magazine, *Grazia*, and the sounds that came through the window when the shutters were opened had an Italian feel to them. The audience is asked to accept that this is an Italian play without having to endure the gimmick of Italo-English that has dogged too many productions of Italian plays in this country.[23]

Economies prevented the Young Vic from employing a large cast of actors. The company, in fact, consists of the Director's Assistant, an anxious maid-of-all-work who combines the roles of Secretary, Stage Manager and Prompter and who looked as if she would have been more comfortable in an office than a theatre, Leading Actress (who does not enter through the auditorium), Older Actress, Young Actress, Leading Actor, Young Actor, Young Actress, and Stagehand. This put restrictions on the opening improvised scene when the company assembled for the rehearsal of *The Rules of the Game* (which both Harrower and Jones kept). The Director's Assistant put out several chairs for the company, tripping in and out with tiny mincing steps. The Actors came on individually and sat on the chairs, separately. Their laconic movements and speech contrasted nicely with the Assistant's neat fussiness and provided a clearly delineated opening. The small company also influenced the characterisation of the Director. A director with a larger theatrical company would have had opportunities for greater narcissism.[24] Darrel d'Silva, quite a large man, dressed in a light suit, the jacket stretched over his stomach and fastened by just one button, played the part as a competent, emphatic director, clearly under strain (he pops pills on entering and again at the end of the play, and smokes on the job), who is given more space than in Pirandello's 1925 text. In some ways the play becomes his attempt to assert himself, his failure to do so and his intellectual and psychological collapse at the end of the play.

Changes to the text were accompanied by directorial inventiveness, as seen in the Characters' entrance. During the rehearsal of *The Rules of the Game*, just after the explanation of the significance of the egg and shell (where one of the actresses came to the Director's aid), the Director gives the cast a talk on Pirandello. The basics of Pirandello's life and art (taken from Eric Bentley's *The Making of Modern Theatre*), is accompanied by slides, shown on a white paper screen. At a certain point in the lecture, the Characters tear their way through the screen and emerge on to the stage. In keeping with the rest of the production, the Characters' entrance had nothing of the mystery and otherworldliness required in the stage directions. This was a simple but effective theatrical trick, carrying with it associations of birth and that moment of transition from narrative to theatre that Pirandello explored so movingly in *Tonight We Improvise*.[25]

For Mme Pace's entrance, a simple well-tried theatre trick was extremely effective. The Father sets the hats and coats and begins to conjure her up, lights flash and flicker, and a strong beam focuses on the exit down stage audience left; the door opens and the audience gaze left with expectation at the open, brightly lit entrance. No one comes. . . and then there she is, 'Mme Pace in person' among the Actors on the other side of the stage.

The end of the play was a further innovation by Richard Jones. Part 3 began without a fountain. When the need arose, a trapdoor was opened and a stage ladder lowered for a tree. The Boy hid in the tree, up the ladder, rather than behind it. There were no cut-out trees, as Jones eschews romanticism.[26] We see the Technician change the gels on the footlights and the fussy Director's Assistant trips round with a mist machine. When the Boy kills himself, a dummy of him falls from the ladder. Pirandello's end to the play was deliberately drained of any possibility of sentimentalism. There was no shadow play of the Characters, nor did the Stepdaughter run laughing through the auditorium. Rather than concentrating on the family, the end makes the Director the focus of attention. In his frustration at his wasted day and his growing uncertainty about his state of mind, he hurls the dummy to the back of the stage. The lights go out, including the working light, and then a light appears. When the Director touches the trapdoor/fountain, it spurts water at him and he discovers there is blood on the dummy Boy. The three members of the original family – Father, Son and Mother – go out through the auditorium. The white curtain of the beginning of the play drops, creating a gauze effect. Behind the curtain the Characters assemble, including the Stepdaughter. The Director slits open the curtain and begins to emerge through it (echo of the Characters' entrance in part 1), appearing in the middle of the Characters, as if he had become one himself, a large flesh-and-blood man in existential agony between hazy figures. The company of Actors then assembles behind the curtain. The curtain is raised and we see the Actors dressed in ordinary clothes to take their bow, while music from *I pagliacci* reminds the audience of the theme of the production: this was a production less about reality and illusion than about 'acting reality'.

No production of this play can convince unless the acting is of a very high quality. Richard Jones was well served by a team of excellent performers. Dressed in a pinstripe black suit and carrying a hat, Stephen Boxer as the Father made the argument in the text convincing, and his lean, lined face enhanced the pain and passion of his delivery. Leah Muller's Stepdaughter put paid to the oft-repeated assertion that only an actress of some years' experience can bring out the complexity of this part. By February 2001 she had only two stage productions to her name, having graduated from the Guildhall School of Music and Drama in the summer of 2000. She was dressed as both 'woman' and 'child': above-the-knee pleated black dress with some white edging on the bodice, black jacket, black round hat and small black handbag; stockings, white socks and high-heeled shoes. It was the combination of stockings, socks and high heels that gave her that adolescent look. Her eyes were heavily made up in green. Her movements were energetic, febrile, yet she had a certain fragility. The intensity of her expression and gaze, her vulnerability, the inwardness of her reaction after the song and dance in part 1 ('Besame mucho'), her obliviousness to her surroundings in her sexual expression made it possible to see in her the sexually abused teenager so often missed by performances from older actresses.[27] The scenes with the Little Girl, with her Mother and with the Father as client in Mme Pace's shop evinced a vitality and vulnerability seldom seen in the portrayal of this character. Within the framework of an accessible English production, the sexuality of the play was better expressed than in most productions. The scene with the Father in Mme Pace's shop was impressive. Both Characters remove some clothes – the Stepdaughter was sitting demurely in her jacket and hat – and lie on the sofa in a passionate embrace, making it easier to catch the 'only just in time' quality of the Mother's entrance usually not achieved with standing embraces.

Unlike some directors who have a long period of acquaintance with Pirandello's work and a desire to direct it, Jones took on *Six Characters in Search of an Author* because he was asked to by David Lan, artistic director of the Young Vic, who also put him in touch with David Harrower. He read up on Pirandello, then threw away his notes and directed the play. His production was an excellent example

10. Production by Richard Jones, Young Vic Theatre, 2001. (Photo: Keith Patterson, Young Vic Theatre.)

of what can be done by commercial theatre – the Young Vic generates 63 per cent of its income – with able and dedicated professionals. It made those who knew the text look at it anew; it introduced a classic to a number of people never confronted with it before; and it provided a thoughtful, exciting and moving experience for many audiences.

CHAPTER II

PUSHING AT THE FRONTIERS OF THEATRE: KLAUS MICHAEL GRÜBER AND ANATOLI VASILIEV

Two late twentieth-century productions approach *Six Characters in Search of an Author* as an opportunity to explore theatre rather than to introduce a foreign classic to its audiences. In different circumstances – Grüber presented his production in a mainstream theatre in a country with a history of Pirandello productions while Vasiliev first presented his as a diploma exercise for theatre arts students in a country with limited knowledge of Pirandello – both productions looked beneath the surface of the text and presented arresting versions of the play.

At the beginning of his international career, Pirandello's plays were much talked about in Germany and productions were plentiful. One of his last plays, *Tonight We Improvise*, was so related to the German theatrical scene that its first two productions took place in Germany and a year later it failed to resonate within an Italian context when it received its Italian premiere in Turin.[1] From the mid-1930s to the mid-1940s, however, there was a decline in interest in Pirandello's plays. Whereas the two plays jointly written by Giovacchino Forzano and Benito Mussolini were performed twenty-six times between 1933 and 1944, productions of Pirandello's plays amounted to six.[2] Pirandello's translator, Hans Feist, was Jewish and this may well account for the decrease in interest. Another translator, H. F. Redlich, was also Jewish, which could explain the decline in popularity of the libretto for Malipiero's opera *The Changeling*. This was initially well received in 1934 at the Landtheater in Braunschweig, where it was premiered, but it was then banned because it was found to be 'subversive and contrary to the policy of the German State'.[3] Max Reinhardt was likewise a Jew and this may have some bearing on the lack of 'Aryan' productions of *Six Characters in Search of an Author*. In the 1942–3 season there were productions of *Henry IV* in three German cities but none of *Six Characters*. There was one performance in Berlin, however, in 1935: for Jewish audiences, presented by Berlin's Jüdischer Kulturbund.[4]

FREIE VOLKSBÜHNE, BERLIN, 21 MARCH 1981, DIRECTED BY KLAUS MICHAEL GRÜBER

Since the early 1950s there have been more than fifty productions of *Six Characters in Search of an Author* in Germany, spread over a number of cities.[5] Of the more recent ones, the most interesting was by Klaus Michael Grüber at the Freie Volksbühne, West Berlin, in 1981.

By the time he came to direct *Six Characters*, Grüber was a director of some twelve years' experience and was known throughout Europe for his original and challenging approaches to theatre. Expelled from the Piccolo Teatro in Milan, where he had trained with Strehler, for his explicitly political and anti-American production of Adamov's *Off Limits* in 1969, Grüber returned to his native Germany. Since then he has directed in Germany, France and Italy (in 1988 he was invited back to the Piccolo Teatro, where he directed *La Medesima Strada* [*The Same Road*]). In 1973 Peter Stein asked him to join him in the Antiquity Project at the Schaubühne in Berlin. Grüber was to direct Euripides' *Bacchae*.

Grüber, with other directors in the 1970s, for instance Peter Zadek, had felt constrained by German theatres as playing places. Despite a vast programme of theatre building after the Second World War, most theatre architecture was disappointingly conventional. So the performance of *Bacchae* took place in an exhibition hall, the first of a series of productions that Grüber was to mount outside a theatre. Already in this production, some of the characteristics of Grüber's theatre-making were apparent: strong visual images, a deliberate dislocation between image and the actors' delivery of the text, and an uncompromising relationship with the audience. Horses and meat-devouring dogs were brought on stage. Agave dripped with heavy clots of blood after murdering her son. Dionysus was wheeled on to a dazzlingly white stage on an operating trolley. Much of the text was chanted in Ancient Greek.[6] In some productions Grüber abandoned play texts altogether. *Winterreise* (*Winter Journey*), presented in 1977 in the Olympic Stadium in Berlin, was based on Hölderlin's novel *Hyperion*. *Rudi* (1979) was based loosely on a novella by Bernard von Brentano and staged in the deserted rooms of a much-loved Berlin hotel, the Esplanade. The choice of playing places was not only a rejection of institutionalised theatre. In *Winterreise* Grüber was able to integrate the historical resonance of the Olympic stadium, which had staged the Olympics in 1936, with the historical significance of Hölderlin's winter journey.[7]

Those who have worked with Grüber stress his capacity to listen. He commands great loyalty from his actors because he does not prescribe. Rehearsals are a journey of discovery: 'theatre as journey is at the heart of Grüber's practice'.[8] But he also asks actors to listen to themselves and each other. As Angela Winkler, who played the Stepdaughter in 1981, remembered, Grüber would insist on the necessity of listening and the benefits this would bring: 'Listen to yourselves. If you do that, nothing can become rigid, fixed. Your ears and eyes must be everywhere. In this way, you will grasp everything and you will be able to react in a flash if necessary. You can even come out of your role, you can just listen and look.'[9] Grüber's emphasis on listening and watching is a step towards the state of complete awareness. In this state actors will be able 'to be' on stage rather than 'to act'. As Angela Winkler again explained, 'It is enough for one actor not to be in a state of awareness for everything to wobble.'[10] To help actors to understand the difference between 'acting' and 'being', Grüber will introduce a child or an animal into a production. To bring actors to this state of awareness, to render them as children again, requires a long and steady process of stripping away old techniques and psychological resistance. As Angela Winkler described it with a telling image, Grüber works to make actors sensitive to themselves again, 'he discreetly removes their breastplates, which they wear so as not to be wounded'.[11]

Though he works in a number of languages and considers the text just one element among many, the delivery of the play's words is a matter that demands much of Grüber's attention.[12] Antirhetorical in his approach, he is known for his use of the whisper; words seem at times hardly to detach themselves from silence, as if silence were part of the text. He also stresses clarity of enunciation. When directing Racine's *Bérénice* for the Comédie française (1984), concern for Racine's words was uppermost: he said he wanted to be able to hear Racine's pen on the paper. Actors should feel a complete harmony between their breathing and their speech and be in total control of the emission of their words. He wanted the exclamation 'Hélas!' to be 'a warm breath on the hand'; and that breath to spread through the Comédie française.[13] Reflecting after the production, he said that he had learnt that 'one can weep in alexandrines'.[14]

Lighting is a hallmark of Grüber's theatre. He has been helped in his exploration of light by the choice of his stage designers, most of whom are artists (Gilles Aillaud, Eduardo Arroyo, Lucio Fanti and Antonio Recalcati). Sometimes this is particularly dramatic, as in *Hamlet* (1982), when a laser beam, projected from the sky down to the room like a stroke of lightning, caught the sword of Hamlet (played by Bruno Ganz) and the reflections of the ghost's breastplate.[15] Grüber seldom uses light to bathe the stage in full light in the manner of Peter Brook.[16] Characters are often placed in semi-darkness, isolated and individual. Angela Winkler recalled that in *La Medesima Strada*, Gilles Aillaud had projected a shadow on the wall and that as Antigone she was encouraged to take refuge in that shadow. She remembered her difficulty in doing this, as she always gravitated naturally towards the light when she was explaining her position to Creon. But she gradually realised that Antigone had no need to convince anyone of anything. 'She simply is, she simply states her position, that is her greatness', so it was right for her to remain in the darkness, 'it gave me repose, helped me not to be distracted by trivia'.[17]

There is considerable affinity between Pirandello's ideas concerning acting and the stage and Grüber's approach to acting. In their search for true theatre, both strive to point out the falseness of imitation and to expose actors' wiles. Grüber, however, also exposed Pirandello's text. At the beginning of *Six Characters in Search of an Author*, Pirandello presented the introduction of the theatrical company as matter to be both seen and heard by the audience. There is no doubt that the Actors' and Director's entrances, and the mounting of the rehearsal of *The Rules of the Game,* are written in for the audience's entertainment. It is Pirandello's method of setting up his thesis. Only in part 2, when the Stepdaughter and Mme Pace speak in hushed tones, is the audience brought face to face with the obvious truth about presenting plays in a theatre: if actors speak as they would normally in such a situation, then most of the audience cannot hear. Making the play accessible makes it untrue. In Grüber's production Pirandello's dialogue, written with an audience in mind, is transformed into theatre chat among the company, inaudible to much of the audience (which remonstrated in force, as reviewers were eager to point out).[18] Grüber's stage, like Pirandello's, presented a sense of unreadiness for performance, but Grüber extended the notion of the unreadiness of one particular theatre stage into an image of failed hopes for theatre in general. Rubble and junk appear to have fallen down from the flies and jut out over the forestage; lighting installations, boards and metal beams lie scattered on top of each other. To the right of this image of chaotic decline and decay, Grüber placed the well-dressed Artistic Director of the Freie Volksbühne, Kurt Hübner (a notable German director in his own right), who played the Director in the play, sitting in a large black leather armchair, in front of his directorial desk complete with typewriter, smoking a cigar.[19]

Grüber's handling of the Characters' entrance was equally arresting. While the audience were still laughing at a joke from Kurt Hübner (interpolated by Grüber), the Stage Manager appeared at the back of the stage announcing that 'there are some people here'. Thunder rumbled, the theatre was plunged momentarily into darkness, and in the gloom, from among the mysterious junk, six dark figures in wet raincoats appeared, leaning on metal poles that hung on long ropes from the flies (and are usually used to lift pieces of scenery). A dim light emanated from the fallen lighting installations. In the light of these lamps, the illuminated junk appeared to be the remains of a sacred space. Titina Maselli, the stage designer, had suggested to Grüber that he could distinguish the Characters by presenting them as photographic negatives, that is, by inverting black and white. Her suggestion, which Grüber did not take up (he told her that he had no desire to paint his actors' teeth black), prompted another solution: he dressed the Characters in dripping raincoats of dark, reflecting material that gave the impression that they were made of celluloid.[20] For Helmut Schödel of *Die Zeit*, the line of Characters recalled Richard Oelzes's painting *Expectation*, in which 'men like the Father look up to the sky where clouds are brewing menacingly'.[21] Irene Böhme of the *Süddeutsche Zeitung* saw the Characters as refugees from Turkey, or 'poor travelling people having a rest at the roadside – associations of forlornness in the twilight'.[22] Luc Bondy commented that Grüber did not present Pirandello's 'irruption of strange elements into a theatrical rehearsal, a rupture at least as grave as incest, as a *coup de théâtre*, put on stage for voyeurs; on the contrary these strangers seem more surprised and humiliated than the theatre people present'.[23]

Pirandello's Father is articulate, a man with definite ideas; he knows what he wants. A character abandoned by his creator, he wants to live. He is looking for an author, but is, in a sense, his own author: he knows his own story and insists that it is played as it happened. 'His tragedy is not a question of form but of life.'[24] Grüber's Father (Peter Roggisch), with his long hair, untrimmed beard and old tie, was a mysterious, ramshackle figure, closer to a homeless person, with his restless eyes and little schnapps flask, who stared at the audience in bewilderment and always doffed his hat to the Director. He was 'either pushing and insistent'[25] or stammered out his sentences hesitantly, almost syllabically, as if they were dreadful discoveries he could not face.[26]

Peter Szondi has described the Stepdaughter as a Strindbergian character, insistent on her point of view and claiming the stage for herself.[27] There was something of this Strindbergian egocentricity in Angela Winkler's Stepdaughter. Described by Helmut Schödel as 'one possessed, like a witch', she was desperately aggressive: she raged, screamed and sang, totally self-absorbed.[28] The Mother (Barbara Morowiecz) conveyed a secret pain: the image that impressed reviewers was of her sitting on the stage in a state of despair, her two children leaning up against her, peeling an orange.[29]

Theatre in Germany was, and still is, heavily subsidised, by both state and local government: just before unification, for instance, only about 15 per cent of the total costs were covered by box-office income. Theatre buildings, often criticised for their conservative structure, are exceptionally well equipped. These facts help to explain the anger of some reviewers and audiences when confronted with Grüber's rendering of *Six Characters in Search of an Author*. Struck by the extraordinarily impressive visual images of some of his earlier productions, they were left irritated by the visually difficult *Six Characters*. Günther Grack spoke for many in his review:

> Nowadays artistic directors appear to have hardly more urgent worries than to ask the State or the lottery for the provision of extra money for the acquisition of further batteries of spotlights but then the directors do not use them. We might get the most wonderful lighting bridges, colour mechanisms and all sorts of electronic sparklers, but it gets darker and darker on stage.[30]

Others, however, saw Grüber's parsimonious use of light and sound as essential elements of his rendering of the play.

Pirandello's play was both a denunciation of the theatre of his time and place and a play in praise of theatre. Theatre as place of magic, a theme that he explored more fully in his last, unfinished play,

The Mountain Giants, was given greater emphasis in the 1925 version of *Six Characters in Search of an Author* than in 1921. In 1925 Mme Pace's entrance, conjured by the Father's words and the props of her trade, is a key moment in the second part of the play; and the garden scene, as we have seen, was much revised, inspired by Pitoëff's production and by the newly installed lighting equipment and cyclorama in the Odescalchi Theatre. Reinhardt, recalled by a number of the reviewers of Grüber's production, explored the theatre's capacity to the full in his rewritten introductory section of the play. In Grüber's production theatre has lost its old magic. This is epitomised by Mme Pace's entrance. As Helmut Schödel described it, her entrance was 'nearly the most inconspicuous of the whole evening. She just comes on. The revolving stage does rotate a little but it seems to be a technical error rather than magic'.[31]

Grüber's return to a conventional theatre building to direct a play that denounces theatre made a provocative statement not missed by the reviewers. The desolate setting and a lighting plot that put the key moments of the play in gloom and minor characters in the spotlight – at one point the Father had to thrust his face under the lamp on the Director's desk in order to be seen – is part of a coherent thesis. The opening up of the workings of the theatre, which had been so fascinating in Reinhardt's version, contributed in 1981 to the impression of gloomy repetitiveness and the banality of stage work. The Actors were reduced to a staring audience, lonely apathetic individuals.[32] High above the stage on the lighting bridge, a technician appeared time and time again; he switched on a light, waited for the lift, descended to stage level and disappeared, only to reappear again.[33] The stage lift and the big iron bars that are used to lower and raise scenery became not fascinating voyeuristic glimpses into the forbidden area behind the scenes but grey images of the boredom and pointlessness of making theatre.

In the 1920s technical innovations were not simply mechanisms with which to create effects or modify the ways a stage could be organised; they were also expressions of theatre's entry into history, of its ability to adapt to new social forces with the integration of new products and technologies.[34] Grüber's rejection (or deliberate 'misuse') of the Freie Volksbühne's technical facilities reflected both industrial and theatrical 'burn-out'. Georges Banu's words concerning 'lassitude' and 'fatigue' as keynotes of Grüber's work seem particularly relevant to this production.[35] It denounced theatre as not so much an 'impossible art' as a part of the 'institutionalised lie'. 'No director has ever turned more severely against the theatre than Grüber has done. Grüber is ironical, if not cynical; he destroys a myth, a piece of the European hypocrisy culture.'[36]

Yet one aspect of theatre prevailed in this production: the expression of feeling. Grüber's assistant, Ellen Hammer, who has worked with him since 1972, claimed that he is not interested in psychology, but in the expression of feelings and emotion, and that this interest is a constant in his work.[37] His work with actors is aimed at facilitating true expression of feeling. Roland Wiegenstein noted that Grüber's approach to *Six Characters in Search of an Author* allowed the real pain and real tragedy to emerge. He drew the truth from the banal story of Pirandello's script. Emotions were presented in such a way that the audience forgot their ephemeral causes and concentrated on the experience of naked feeling. 'Angela Winkler's tirades, acted out without fear of becoming ridiculous, upset us. They constitute again and again a new, tragic play in the old, worn one. Peter Rogisch's excuses, his helplessness and talkative attempts to explain, become relevant, they constitute the Characters the author denied.'[38] And there were other moments in the production when an emotion impressed. The Leading Lady (Libgart Schwarz) knew that she had to wait at the side of the stage for the rehearsal to continue. After some time she expressed her annoyance by strutting round the whole stage to the exit. But then she appeared again – she had forgotten her script – so she walked round again. All her anger was in that walk. Another impressive moment of expressed emotion involved Libgart Schwarz again: she banged the Stepdaughter's head against the door of the recently installed Mme Pace's room in frustrated anger.[39]

A number of people have commented that Grüber's theatre avoids chorality. He works individually with actors and does not concentrate on ensemble work. And his approach to spectators is similar. His theatre tends to address individual spectators rather than the audience. Georges Banu puts it like this: 'Beings, like words, are clearly distinct, and none blends with the other. Each exists on the stage. Each has a dignity because Grüber offers his characters the right to solitude. And the same can be said of his approach to spectators. He addresses each individually.'[40]

This solitude came across to a number of the reviewers of the performance. As one of them put it, the author who is sought is sitting in the auditorium, as Grüber's production allows the play to develop further in each spectator's mind.[41]

Critics were torn between criticising Pirandello's play as outmoded and criticising Grüber's production for not representing Pirandello's text. From the earliest productions Germans have tended to be sceptical about the novelty of Pirandello's thought (largely because they can see their own philosophers in it) and they tended to see his 'thought' as an excuse for theatrical effects. Grüber denied the script many of its theatrical effects, and so misrepresented the German view of the play. It can be argued, however, that Grüber's approach (for cognoscenti at least, as the production could hardly have served as a meaningful introduction to the play) conveyed rather carefully Pirandello's views as they were expressed over the years. Pirandello saw himself as one who enjoyed provoking his audiences, as his correspondence with Virgilio Talli over *Right You Are (If You Think So)* demonstrated.[42] For 1981 German audiences Grüber's provocation with economic use of light and sound might be seen as a fitting analogue for what Italian 1921 audiences saw as lack of structure. In 1921, when theatre was an established part of Italian middle- and upper-class culture, Pirandello took delight in presenting theatre as an 'impossible art'. During the mid- and late 1920s, however, the expression of his attitude to theatre changed. His kind of theatre – text, character and actor based – was under attack, from two fronts: the new art of the talking film

and theatrical technical innovation. *Tonight We Improvise* gleefully
satirises both 'the talkies' and the directorial and mechanistic excesses
of the German theatre, in favour of an actor-based art. Grüber's presentation of the wornout mechanics of theatre and his concentration
on the individual actors' discovery of their feelings can be seen as
a late twentieth-century expression of Pirandello's later ideological
stance.

ANATOLI VASILIEV'S PRODUCTIONS IN MOSCOW, 1986–7

Anatoli Vasiliev first presented *Six Characters in Search of an Author*
at the State Institute of Theatre Art in Moscow (GITIS) in the
autumn of 1986. This presentation then became the production with
which Vasiliev opened his own theatre, the School of Dramatic Art in
Vorovsky Street, Moscow on 24 February 1987. Subsequently Vasiliev
has toured with this production in Western Europe and America:
Vienna, Milan, Frankfurt, Avignon Summer Festival, London
(London International Festival of Theatre), Canada and the USA,
Mexico and in Grotowski's theatre in Wroclaw, Poland. Productions
of plays by Pirandello – Vasiliev has also directed *Tonight We Improvise*
and *Each in His Own Way* – have spanned some ten years of Vasiliev's
working life. For many people in countries outside Russia, the production of *Six Characters in Search of an Author* was their introduction
to Vasiliev's work.

   Before proceeding to an analysis of these productions, it will be
helpful to have some understanding of Vasiliev's ideas and his position in contemporary Russian theatre. Born in 1942, Vasiliev spent
his early childhood under Stalin. Since the death of Stalin in 1953,
Russians have lived through a succession of historical periods: the
post-Stalin 'thaw' (1953–68), the years of the post-Prague invasion
(1968–85, referred to by the theatre critic Anatoly Smeliansky as 'the
frosts'), *perestroika* (1985–90) and the period that some post-Soviet
intellectuals call '*nomenklatura* capitalism' (from 1990). Throughout

the Soviet period theatre had continued to enjoy the high status in Russian society it had held during the nineteenth century and received generous state funding. Stalin embraced Constantin Stanislavsky and his Moscow Art Theatre, founded in 1898; 'socialist realism', developed from Stanislavsky's practice, became the dominant mode of theatre production. The theatre's response to the strict censorship that gradually accompanied official support was to develop a style of acting that went beyond the text to communicate a system of allusions. The 'ability to speak and comprehend a subtext became an integral part of the performance'.[43] Participating in theatre, whether as artist or audience, was therefore a political experience, and rather different from a night out in the West End of London or New York Broadway, as Victor Borovsky explains:

> Together with the troubled audience, [the actor] looked into the hearts of the characters portrayed and easily evaded the barriers of censorship through which a play had to pass before it could reach the stage. In intonation, colouring and timbre of voice, in the rhythm of the acting, in a glance, a turn of the head, in pauses between words and actions, [the actor] expressed what everyone felt but was strictly forbidden to say openly. Innocuous material, approved and published after careful checking, then took on a meaning alarming to the authorities.[44]

For theatre the loosening of the tight discipline of the Soviet regime brought with it not only less stringent censorship but also less welcome consequences: overt ideological differences and financial problems. The division in May 1987 of the Moscow Art Theatre into two, one on each side of Tverskaya Street can be seen as 'the perfect image of a divided country'.[45] Moscow Art Theatre 2 directed by Tatyana Doronina became the symbol of Soviet Russia. Very soon freedom of expression, yearned for under an oppressive regime, ceased to be exceptional. Expenses mounted and subsidies no longer covered half of a theatre's expenses. Some theatres, for instance, opened up casinos and nightclubs to raise funds. In the first flush of 'freedom', the Russian theatre began to lose its special status in society and to become a form of entertainment as in the West.

Vasiliev started his theatrical training at the beginning of the backlash ('the frosts') and did not find it easy to establish himself in the theatre, let alone run his own theatre. After a brief career as a professional chemist (including three years' national service spent with the Russian fleet), at the age of twenty-six, in the autumn of 1968, he joined GITIS, where his main teachers were Andrei Popov and Mariya Knebel, both pupils of Stanislavsky and Michael Chekhov. The training at GITIS was tough and particularly difficult for someone with ideas of his own developed through years of amateur theatre and who did not like to conform. His teachers, in his own words, 'declared war on him'; 'they conscientiously and systematically destroyed his images'.[46] Nearly turned out at the end of his first year, he learnt to submit to the traditional discipline of social and psychological realism and the Stanislavskian method of GITIS. Later, Vasiliev was to speak warmly of the dedication and discipline of his teachers; and, despite major differences in approach to theatre, he still describes himself as revisionist Stanislavskian.

He began work at the Moscow Art Theatre in 1973, where he met Igor Popov, a professional architect. Vasiliev persuaded Popov to work as a designer in the theatre and he has collaborated with him ever since. His first production was with 'the old guard', a group of actors who had worked with Stanislavsky and Nemirovich-Danchenko, the youngest of whom was seventy-one and the oldest eighty-two. After experiencing the dubious distinction of being driven out of the Moscow Art Theatre, this *enfant terrible* with long dark hair and a seaman's hat from Rostov eventually found a temporary theatrical home in the latter part of the 1970s. The Soviet authorities offered his former teacher, Andrei Popov, the Stanislavsky Drama Theatre. Popov took three of his former pupils with him.

It was here that Vasiliev began to make his presence felt in Moscow. With Igor Popov he mounted in 1978 a production of the first pre-revolutionary version of Gorky's *Vassa Zheleznova* and followed this in 1979 with a text by a contemporary author, Viktor Slavkin, *The Grown-up Daughter of a Young Man*. These two productions gave

Moscow theatre audiences hope that a new theatre had been born, a new 'theatrical family', as Russians understood their best companies to be, where experienced actors lived and breathed theatre along with less experienced colleagues. Vasiliev already had a distinctive style: a new approach to psychological realism that, before his major encounter with Pirandello, showed Vasiliev's conception of human beings 'not as a tight unity but as a set of possibilities'; while his work with actors seemed to enable them to present 'their flesh and spirit in a new unity'[47]. His lyrical genius conjured up tension not so much from the words but from the very atmosphere he created on stage. But the productions proved too much for the Soviet authorities. Not only had Vasiliev, who did not consider himself as a politically active dissident, used the first version of Gorky's play, he had also created on stage, in minute evocative detail, the era of 'the thaw'. As Anatoli Smeliansky put it, writing of the production of *The Grown-up Daughter of a Young Man*:

> From the swamp of stagnation, from the disgrace of submission and mental impoverishment, Vasiliev transported us back to the era of the Thaw. By musical and three-dimensional means he recreated the pitiful yet beautiful image of our 'homeland in Time'. Drainpipe trousers, crepe-soled shoes and jackets with massive shoulder pads were rescued from attics, ties were knotted in unbelievable fashions, and records of underground boogie-woogies were played that had been made by our virtuosi using old X-ray plates (this was known as 'jazz on the bones'). Vasiliev was calling the dance of a whole generation – a dance of liberation, of despair, of failed hopes.[48]

The authorities sent Popov back to the Moscow Art Theatre, a new artistic director was appointed to the Stanislavsky Drama Theatre and Vasiliev left. He and his actors were given refuge at the Taganka Theatre by its director, Yuri Lyubimov. Here he revived *Vassa Zheleznova* (1981) and then staged a second play by Viktor Slavkin, *Hoopla* (1984). While Vasiliev was at the Taganka, Lyubimov defected to London (1983), and in the following year Anatoli Efros was appointed as Taganka's director. Vasiliev and his company were allowed to stay at the Taganka until Efros's death in 1987.

Some consider *Hoopla* to be Vasiliev's best production. The plot is very simple. A forty-year-old man invites some friends and neighbours to his country house for a weekend. They go through the processes of setting up the house after its winter hibernation, reminisce together, prompted by letters and dresses and the old game of hoopla found in the attic, and attempt to pick up the threads of their past lives and friendships. But their individual isolation makes this impossible. They pack up the house again and depart.[49] Again it was Vasiliev's ability to create atmosphere that was so impressive. He seated the audience around the house, leaving a little space between the players and audience but with no formal marker such as footlights. As with the previous Slavkin play, he conjured much of his atmosphere by music, producing what Michael Chekhov had called a 'musical score of atmospheres'. (This meant that in the two years of rehearsals his cast learnt to dance and sing; one actor, Albert Filozov, learnt to play the piano.) Through this 'musical score' the audience was invited to glimpse another reality. The characters, presented with great clarity, became a means to 'creating a mystical and lyrical mood'.[50] Vasiliev complemented his 'musical score' with visual effects. The characters sat around a table covered by a starched white cloth, drinking from exquisite glasses holding garnet-coloured wine and with texts from the Russian 'Silver Age' in their hands. The whole scene came across as 'a spellbinding mixture of theatre and spiritualist séance'; the actors 'emptied themselves' and 'let the past "sing *them*"', as Grotowski would put it'.[51]

In addition to working at the Taganka Theatre, Vasiliev was invited in 1981 to GITIS as a teacher. And it was here that he first worked in depth on *Six Characters in Search of an Author*. It was the now elderly Andrei Popov who handed over his class to Vasiliev with instructions to use this play. 'He knew it would work. He knew I would continue his work. He knew how keen I was on Pirandello.'[52]

The GITIS presentation was not Vasiliev's first encounter with Pirandello. In 1967, which he spent in his hometown of Rostov before going to GITIS, Vasiliev was for a short time the artistic director of the student theatre at Rostov University and he mounted a collage with its main theme drawn from *Six Characters in Search of an Author*. He called it *The Bridge has to be Crossed*. The Russian word for bridge was the acronym for the Youth Student Theatre. The title also carried echoes of Arthur Miller's *A View from the Bridge*, a play that was very popular in Russia at the time. But the most important significance for Vasiliev was a symbolic one: he intended it to mean that it was possible and necessary to 'stride through the aesthetics of the young student theatre and leave them behind'.[53] But the production did not please the university management, and it was forced to close after two performances. Later, as a student at GITIS, he had taken part in a short scene from *Six Characters in Search of an Author* with his teacher Andrei Popov.

Vasiliev has said that he does not choose texts to work on: the texts choose him.[54] The plays of Pirandello (with those of Anton Chekhov) have a special place in his conception of theatre for they hold within them the possibility of two approaches to presentation: the psychological and the ludic. According to Vasiliev, *The Seagull* can be played in two ways. 'You can present it as a play about art. You could also stage it as a play about people who make art.' The first produces a play of ideas and the acting will be ludic; the second asks for a psychological approach.[55] As an actor, 'when you use the psychological approach you are inside the character you are playing, when you use the *ludo* approach, then you are outside the character'.[56] Vasiliev has referred (in a lecture given in 1996 translated into French) to the years he spent working on Pirandello as the 'space between';[57] Pirandello's 'intermediate' writing, then, with its mixture of psychology and game, became a springboard for his later launch into fully ludic texts (Pushkin, Gogol and Dostoyevsky). In the case of Dostoyevsky, as he explained in a workshop on *The Meek One*, a psychological approach 'produces something very gloomy, heavy, insane, impossible to watch, incomprehensible. If you use the *ludo* system it comes out funny, light, even if it is something like *The Idiot* or *The Devils*.'[58]

There are many affinities between Pirandello and Vasiliev. On occasion Vasiliev sounds like Pirandello shaken free of his pessimism. But perhaps the greatest link between them is in their theories of art. In his long essay on humour 'L'umorismo', Pirandello stresses the moment of reflection in art. His characters are self-conscious, seeing themselves in what they are doing, their reflections thrown back at them by the mirror. Reflection blurs the boundary between tragedy and comedy. As an exemplification of his theory, Pirandello refers frequently to Dostoyevsky's characters. Pirandello's theory was remarkably close to what Vasiliev refers to as the ludic approach.

The actor is another major concern of both theatre practitioners. Pirandello's early theoretical writing, asserting the notion of acting as an 'impossible art', focused mainly on the predicament of the dramatic writer, forced to see travesties of his conceptions on stage. But some space is allocated to the problems of the actor. The actor may experience 'the author's vision and will as an outrage'. The actor thinks and feels differently from the writer and perceives the character in his own way.

> The image that has already been expressed must be taken back and restructured inside him so that it can become the movement which will carry out and make it real on stage. For the actor too, the process of making has to come out of the process of conception, alive, and only because of that can it have being, through movements suggested by the image itself as it lives and is active not only within him but by becoming one with him, body and soul. Incarnation.[59]

Likewise, Vasiliev is fascinated by the problem of incarnation in the theatre: initially, making actors into psychologically real characters; later, making ideas flesh. *Six Characters in Search of an Author* marks the beginning of his philosophical inquiry into theatre and his movement away from the psychological realism of Stanislavsky. Borrowing terms from Grotowski, he later explained his work as directed towards the 'vertical', the sphere of ideas, rather than the 'horizontal', the level of real, natural life.[60] 'To the style of research of the exploration of material reality, I wish to oppose the style which explores the metaphysics of life.'[61] It is to this end that he later concentrated almost entirely on the spoken word, exploring the nature of dialogue, as in his versions of Plato's dialogues.

Notwithstanding his movement away from psychological realism, Vasiliev approached plays within the framework of Stanislavsky's analysis. Each play had an 'initial' and 'principal event'. In the case of *Six Characters in Search of an Author*, the 'principal event' was the Boy's suicide, as Vasiliev explained in a seminar in Moscow in the spring of 1996. It is the Boy's death that brings together the two planes of the play 'on the level of the relationship between the beings: the Father, the Stepdaughter, the Mother . . . and on the level of the relationship between the ideas: the discussions on theatre, art, the sense of truth and illusion'. For Vasiliev the hidden sense of the meeting between the Father and the Director is the reality of the Boy's suicide. And in that reality the 'hidden ideas of the text are resolved: the death of the Boy erases the frontiers between truth and lie, between theatre and life'.[62]

As it was for Stanislavsky, the actor is central to Vasiliev's concept of theatre. His *Six Characters in Search of an Author* marked the beginning of more intensive work on the training of the actor. Rather than mounting productions for an audience, Vasiliev explores theatre with his actors through working on a text. This has taken him to abandon theatre as performance and to concentrate entirely on theatre as workshop and research. As John Freedman has pointed out, Vasiliev has not mounted a complete production since *Six Characters in Search of an Author*, though sometimes audiences are invited to see what he is doing.[63] Vasiliev, who was always sceptical of commercial theatre, sees theatre as more akin to a religious mission, and his school as a monastery.[64] To work on a play, therefore, is to train actors: 'The actor must be first-rate, free, authentic and life-like. But the actor evolves in an artificial form. And this is the problem: to bring into being a natural and authentic actor in the artificial form of the drama.'[65] For Vasiliev, to bring an actor into being is a kind of self-effacement. The director has to be inside the actor. But here is the paradox. For it is important to find a harmony between two mutually exclusive ideas, otherwise the director risks destroying both the actor and himself.

At first Vasiliev saw working on *Six Characters in Search of an Author* at GITIS as 'just part of the study process'. He tried to involve his students in a new methodology, but they were able at that stage only to respond in the way they had been taught. 'All they were capable of doing was little skits based on the play. Nothing more than comic skits. And this lasted for three hours. And they were all improvisations.'[66] Then, at a certain point in their work, Vasiliev watched four hours' worth of forty improvisations and saw that there was 'a motif, a theatrical motif. A very subtle one; and a very absurd one. I felt as though there were some very high note, a very tender note of absurdity. It was just a second.'[67] He arranged with the students to return to the text the following year.

At GITIS the play was rehearsed and presented in one of the classrooms, an almost square room with two doors on the left leading out to a corridor, and three windows on the right, looking out over a roof. Vasiliev decided to take both doors off their hinges, creating the impression that the room was broader. The scenery consisted of the back wall, painted green at his request ('a sort of very juicy green') and a makeshift curtain set diagonally across the acting space 'so that one end of the curtain went out into the corridor'.[68] The diagonal division of the stage made the stage look 'much bigger than it was' and had already appeared in two earlier productions also designed by Igor Popov, Gorky's *Vassa Zheleznova* and Slavkin's *The Grown-up Daughter of a Young Man*.

Vasiliev's first version of *Six Characters in Search of an Author* was presented as a diploma exercise, and people who came to it did so in the expectation of seeing students show their paces. 'People came because, after all, they just thought they were going to see a run-of-the-mill diploma work. I had to do it; it was part of the requirement.' But as he watched it, 'a miracle happened. It was remarkable, absolutely superb work, I saw that myself. I could not believe how well they acted, a lot of humour and daring.'[69] After the performance people told him that it was a show and should be presented as such.

It was at this juncture that Vasiliev was given his own theatre in Vorovsky Street. That was how *Six Characters in Search of an Author* came to be the opening play at the School of Dramatic Art. As with many first nights, events of the evening become part of the mythology of the production. Vasiliev remembers with affection the problems people had in literally getting into the theatre. It was winter; the weather was 'a disaster' with 'lots of snow'; the entrance to the theatre was steep so 'everyone had to slide down it to get into the theatre'. Icicles hung from the tall building. Despite the weather conditions and lack of advertising, 'lots of people came to see it'.[70]

Very little was changed from Vasiliev's original room plan: just the 'wonderful green wall at GITIS' was replaced by a white wooden arch to create depth.[71] Igor Popov explained the practicalities. It took two days to assemble the walls, floor and ceiling in the new venue. The importance of what he calls the 'room plan', rather than stage design, is to enable the actors to 'exist' on stage. However casual it may look, the room is not just any setting but the milieu for the specific play. The atmosphere is created gradually in the course of rehearsals, depending on their progress and on the choice of acting material.

In 1925 Pirandello unsettled the audience by his self-conscious use of space: Actors and Characters 'invaded' the audience's domain. In Vasiliev's 1987 production confusion is generated by more radical configurations of the audience/stage space. In 1921 the play was presented in a conventional theatre, in 1925 in a newly refurbished art theatre, but both, of course, separated the audience from the stage. The Italian audience was disorientated by the open curtain and unprepared stage. In Vasiliev's production the confusion begins with wondering where to sit. In part 1, though the audience is placed more or less in front of the acting area, it is impossible to tell who is actor and who is spectator. In part 2, set in Mme Pace's shop, audience and actors intermingle in the acting area, and the chairs are set out as for a cabaret. In part 3, in which Pirandello's text is more closely followed, the audience sits formally in front of the acting area. In each of these configurations, Vasiliev experiments with distance: in part 2, for instance, members of the audience become potential clients in Mme Pace's brothel and are chatted up by the Stepdaughter, setting up a variety of experiences among the audience, separating them one from another.

The creation of the room plan continued with touring. In Canada the theatre had an orchestra pit and the company changed the lighting plan. 'We played in a completely different milieu and it became a completely different Pirandello.' In Mexico they built a new stage from materials found in Canada.[72] In England the company used the Brixton Academy in south London, a venue more often associated with rock concerts than classical plays. On entering the vast arena, the spectators found themselves in a reproduction of Venice, with various *calle* (street) signs and a reconstruction of the Rialto Bridge. Vasiliev's production was set in one curtained-off corner of the room. The whole effect was to create a magical atmosphere of wonder, of the unusual and unexpected.

In the presentation of *Six Characters in Search of an Author* at the School of Dramatic Art and elsewhere, the improvised exercises, created and honed at GITIS, remained as part of the performance. The first part of the play becomes a series of developed improvisations (similar to commedia dell'arte performances where improvisation becomes largely 'fixed' for performance), a series of '*intermezzi*'. The play begins with an open stage as in Pirandello's stage directions, but divided diagonally by the simple makeshift curtain on runners. Dividing the stage enabled Vasiliev to create two mirroring worlds. As the German reviewer of the performance in Avignon pointed out, almost every actor in *Six Characters in Search of an Author* comes into contact with the curtain at some time during the performance, either playing with it, or around it as the Boy and Little Girl do in the game at the beginning of part 2, or using it functionally, to close off or to reveal.[73] The theatre curtain, used by Pirandello in his text at the end of part 2 to denote the impossibility of understanding between the two worlds of the Characters and the Actors, becomes in Vasiliev's presentation the fluid, elusive point of contact between reality and illusion, a constant reminder of both life's flux and human creativity.

At the start of the play, a stagehand is revealed, dozing among the folds of the curtain. On waking he begins to play with it, and as he does so the curtain begins to assume shapes through his manipulations: a woman, a body, a dress – and then reveals under its folds a pair of shoes. This initial '*intermezzo*' sets the atmosphere of the production, one of creativity, wonder, irony. The following '*intermezzi*' show the slow process of getting the theatre ready for rehearsal. For instance, two men, a comic duo, attend to the curtain, walk off, remove their hats. A ladder is brought on and two other men practise stage walks. One stagehand seems to be in the wrong place: he is a young Italian inspired by neorealist films and had no place in Pirandello's script. In Vasiliev's he tells his life story, of how his father left the family when he was only seven, of how they met up again later: if the Characters have the right to tell their stories, why not an electrician?

And if life can be seen in so many ways, as Pirandello tells us, why not act a line in many ways? In Pirandello's text, when the Director comes on stage at the beginning of the play, his Secretary hands him a newspaper and a script. He asks if there are any letters, to which the Secretary replies, 'No, this is all there is.'

Vasiliev plays the micro-scene in various ways.

> DIRECTOR: Any letters?
> SECRETARY: No, this is all there is.
> DIRECTOR (with consternation): There aren't any letters?
> SECRETARY (distressed): No, this is all there is.
> DIRECTOR (almost hysterical): There aren't any letters?
> SECRETARY (firmly): No, this is all there is.
> DIRECTOR (first with suspicion, then decisively): There aren't any letters?
> SECRETARY (indignant): No, this is all there is.
> DIRECTOR: No! This then is all there is (*goes out*).[74]

Not only is there a multiple variation of verbal repetition; the lines are delivered from different parts of the acting area. A similar exercise in variation on a line occurs with an elaboration on the Prompter's request to set up his box in another part of the acting area. By the time the production reached London, there was a further variation: some of the interchange was in Russian, some in Italian.[75]

Another example of variation and multiplication to express Pirandello's perspectivism theatrically is evident in the multiplication of characters and exchange of roles. So in this production there is more than one Father, Director and Stepdaughter. Vasiliev's work with these changes and interchanges in *Six Characters in Search of an Author* prefigures his later work. By taking phrases from another part of the play, or giving one Character's words to another, he not only offers radically divergent interpretations of the same text, he also creates a kind of musical score, built on a theme and variation. In subsequent work, for instance in readings from parts of the Bible or from Plato's dialogues, Vasiliev has concentrated on speech, what can be done with words, the relationship of one sound with another. In these performances there is a minimum of 'theatre', both in terms of visual effect and in terms of relationship with the audience; in the earlier *Six Characters in Search of an Author*, on the other hand, both visual effect and audience awareness were paramount.

Apart from those aspects already mentioned, such as the different positioning of the audience for each act, it is in the expression of sexuality that Vasiliev's production was particularly effective. The theatrical expression of the erotic lies at the heart of Pirandello's challenge to theatre in this play. There were two moments in Vasiliev's production when he succeeded perhaps better than in any other production in conveying the anguish of sexuality in a totally convincing manner. One occasion occurs in the first part, where the erotic encounter between the Father and the Stepdaughter is shown as shadow play. The two Characters sit on wooden chairs, the Father behind the Stepdaughter, and their encounter is expressed as a rocking movement, reflected on the screen behind. The second moment occurs in the

11. The production by Anatoli Vasiliev, School of Dramatic Art, Moscow, 1987. (Photo: F. Bezukladnikov, courtesy of Birgit Beumers.)

second part when the Stepdaughter writhes against a pillar in the scene with Mme Pace.

It is the philosophical quality of Pirandello's writing that attracted Vasiliev. Much has been written on the significance of the inner story of the six Characters, but Vasiliev was not interested in it. This was made clear in the programme note to the performances given at the 1989 Pepsico International Performing Arts Festival of the State University of New York at Purchase. The note begins by narrating the Characters' story, then continues:

> We have stressed the intricacy of the plot solely because this did not interest the Dramatist nor the Director. The old variations of the incest theme, in this case the fatal meeting of the Stepdaughter and the Father, have already been exhausted. Therefore in our show the plot only serves as a basis for a series of improvisations and for philosophical discussions of the heroes. For example, the Father and the Director represent two different approaches to reality in all its manifestations: life, theatre, illusion, and the nature of being.[76]

For Vasiliev the hub of the play is the attempt by the Actors to present the Characters. The Director and Actors are not satirised as in Pirandello's text; Vasiliev does not show an out-of-date, lacklustre theatre company confronted by novelty, but his own company, puzzled by the experience of confronting the Characters and their story. In the second part the most moving moment is not the Stepdaughter with her stepfather in Mme Pace's shop, nor the Mother's scream as she rushes to separate them, but the Leading Actress's distress at her inability to render the part of the Stepdaughter.

As Antonio Alessio has put it, Vasiliev's production of this play was not an example of 'cultural vandalism' but rather suggested an organic orchestral unity.[77] The production was in fact suffused by the gentle melody of the Spanish song 'Besame mucho', accompanied on a guitar by one of the Actors, sometimes sitting, sometimes moving among the audience. The production was an excellent example of a theatre that believes passionately that each generation needs to find its own means of expression, its own version of a text, or, as Vasiliev might put it, its own version of itself through giving expression to a text.

CHAPTER 12

A BRIEF LOOK AT *SIX CHARACTERS* IN OTHER MEDIA

Pirandello was interested in a number of art forms during his productive career. He was an amateur artist (a collection of his paintings was reproduced in 1986 by the Centro Nazionale Studi Pirandelliani as part of the celebrations marking the fiftieth anniversary of his death, based on an exhibition in 1984)[1] and he took a lively interest in the adaptation of some of his plays into libretti for operas. But the art medium that figured most prominently in his life, apart from theatre, was film. He is thought to have attended showings in Rome in 1896 of Louis Lumière's early short films. He wrote a novel, *Quaderni di Serafino Gubbio* (*Serafino Gubbio's Notebooks*), which shows him well versed in film techniques;[2] contributed, in times of great financial stress, numerous scenarios to film studios; and adapted several of his own works for the medium.

Film is the form of artistic expression that can 'best give us the vision of thought' Pirandello declared in Paris in 1924, when in discussion about the proposed film by Marcel L'Herbier of his novel *The Late Matthias Pascal*. Inspired by a First World War Russian film, *Otets Sergeij* (*Father Serge*) by Jacob Protazanov, Pirandello concluded that 'this young art' could render dream, hallucination, madness and the doubling of personality better than either theatre or the novel.[3] Little wonder, then, that he set great store by his attempts to create a film of *Six Characters in Search of an Author*. Some of the effects in the play, which, he had earlier discovered, worked better on the stage than in fictional form (and whose presentation he strove to improve in the 1925 text of the play), he subsequently realised would be even better suited to film. At this stage of his thinking on art forms, Pirandello distinguished film from theatre similarly to the way he separated theatre from narrative in earlier theory.[4] These attempts began in 1926 with a Prologue to a screen adaptation. Two years later, Pirandello prepared a scenario for a silent film (written in German with Adolf Lanz), and in 1935 he collaborated with Saul Colin, his English language secretary in the USA, to produce in English *The Treatment for Six Characters*, intended as the basis of a scenario for Max Reinhardt's projected film (Reinhardt had emigrated to the USA in 1933). Detailed discussion of these documents goes beyond the compass of this book, for none resulted in a production. Suffice to say that they reveal a Pirandello well versed in techniques of film-making, conversant with the latest work of contemporary directors, and a wily negotiator with the leading film companies of the day.[5] The scripts also reveal a thinker pushing at the boundaries of his own ideas and familiar with psychoanalytic theory. In particular, the scenario written with Adolf Lanz, which presents, as do the two other documents, the Author as a character, provides a fascinating insight into Pirandello's view of the artistic creator; in the words of Nina Davinci Nichols and Jana O'Keefe Bazzoni, the Author character 'plays outsider *and* insider, a feeling, suffering father-god-artist-creator and destroyer'.[6] As Pirandello himself explained in 1929, he wanted to explore through the visual images of film what he had only touched on in the play: 'how the Six Characters and their destinies were conceived in the author's mind and, imbued with life, made themselves independent of him'.[7]

The indefatigable scholarship of Francesco Càllari has revealed that no less than forty-nine attempts were made to produce a film version of *Six Characters in Search of an Author* between 1926 and 1986. In addition to Reinhardt, would-be directors include Vittorio de Sica, Eduardo de Filippo, Jean-Luc Godard, François Truffaut, Vittorio Gassman, Ingmar Bergman and Ettore Scola.[8] None of the proposals reached production stage. Versions for television, however, have been more successful and provide some indication of how visual effects can communicate thoughts and feelings. Bill Bryden's direction of

Michael Hastings's adaptation of Felicity Firth's text for the BBC in 1992, for instance, devised an impressive entrance for the Characters: a huge warehouse door cranked slowly open to reveal a line of people, who cast increasingly large shadows as they began to approach the group of Actors; the sense of opposing groups had an air of menace as each advanced upon the other. The Characters' exit was equally effective as the huge door slowly and ineluctably closed with a hopeless finality.[9] Other televised versions include Giorgio de Lullo's stage version adapted for Italian television, David Giles's version for the Canadian Broadcasting Company, and Stacy Keach's adaptation for Hollywood Television Theater. This last was set in a television studio and effected the entrance of the Characters by an electrical interference that replaces the images of the scene on the video screens with that of the six Characters. Keach's production also found a new way of differentiating the two families: the first family is white while the stepchildren are black – a felicitous innovation for an updating of the play. All these versions made the play accessible to a larger public than before; none explored fully the visual facilities offered by film or television to convey Pirandello's thought. They are, in the main, televised narratives rather than visual explorations.

Pirandello made no attempt to create an opera of his world famous play, perhaps believing that the medium, suitable though it was for some of his works (for example *La giara* (*The Jar*) and *Il figlio cambiato* (*The Changeling*)) could not successfully convey the meaning of *Six Characters in Search of an Author*. There is, however, one attempt: by the American composer, Hugo Weisgall.[10] Weisgall is known for the intellectual tenor of his work, and in this instance he was well supported by Denis Johnston's libretto. Taking both the 1921 and 1925 texts (that is, keeping the opening to the second part from 1921 and partly keeping the 1925 ending), Johnston created an impressive verse libretto with moments of fine language. The play-within-a-play becomes an opera-within-an-opera (the cast is rehearsing Weisgall's *Temptation of St Anthony*) and includes intentionally banal musical wit and moments of intense drama. The creation theme is more fully developed in the libretto than in the play: the motif of the author's creative powers is carried through in explicit references to God's creation. The Stepdaughter's speech about the temptation of the author in the darkening room is moved from part 3 to part 1 and stresses the author as creator (she sings 'O, my creator,/Picture the scenes that we could play before you') and when the Director defends the operatic profession in part 2, he begins by referring to the divine creation of the singers ('Male and female created He them/With upper and lower registers,/With pitch and tone and volume'). Some of Pirandello's dramatic concerns are altered. For instance, the two children, the Boy in particular, become more autonomous and are not always close to their mother, though they do remain silent; it is therefore less easy to see them as the embodiment of the Mother's guilty thoughts. Psychological motivation gives way to intense operatic moments; why the Boy takes his life is less clear than in the play; and the Oedipal theme is dropped, for the Son, while being forced to play out the last scene, hits his mother rather than overpowering his father.

In the play the difference between Character and Actor is partly effected by language. As Olga Ragusa has pointed out, the language of the Characters 'is again and again the more powerful one and repeatedly engulfs and drowns out the more trivial language of the Actors'.[11] In an opera that differentiation needs to be effected through the music. Weigall achieves this well in the rehearsal scene in which the coloratura (the Leading Lady of the play) is a caricature of opera singers and contrasts well with the Stepdaughter; but in the main, as the *New York Times* critic put it in 1960, Weisgall 'has not found the musical means' to convey the distinction between the two groups 'with consistent force and eloquence'. Musically both groups resemble each other, with the result that 'too often the style oppresses the theme'.[12]

CONCLUSION

Unlike a number of modern seminal plays that began their theatrical life in experimental or avant-garde settings (Oscar Wilde's *Salome*, directed by Aurélien Lugné-Poe, was presented at the Théâtre de l'Oeuvre; Beckett's *Waiting for Godot*, directed by Roger Blin, at the Théâtre de Babylone), *Six Characters in Search of an Author* was first staged at the elegant Teatro Valle, a leading theatre in Rome, dating back to 1726, which had hosted all the major Italian theatrical companies from the mid-nineteenth century. By this choice Pirandello made clear that his challenge was to mainstream theatre, his audience the well-heeled members of the bourgeoisie. Pirandello's productions for the Teatro d'Arte, which included the 1925 *Six Characters*, and his ambition to establish an Italian national theatre, confirm that his aim was to set 'good theatre' at the centre of Italian cultural life. During his period as director, he considerably enlarged the Italian theatre's repertoire: he introduced nine foreign plays to the theatregoing public and staged fifteen world premieres, mainly of contemporary Italian plays. He was excited by innovatory approaches to theatre and introduced some of them, such as scenic design and mood lighting, into his productions. But, unlike Brecht, Pirandello was not interested in finding a new audience; rather, he strove passionately both to improve the fare for existing audiences and to refine their theatrical sensitivities. Subsequently, as we have seen, *Six Characters in Search of an Author* has attracted both established and experimental directors, from Max Reinhardt to the 'bad boy' of Russian theatre, Anatoli Vasiliev, and has been equally successful whether presented in a theatre of high repute or in some small, lesser-known venue, including the Institute of Occupational Therapy at Pomaz near Budapest, as therapy for a group of schizophrenics.[1] (There are, however, limitations. The play's power was dwarfed in the Olivier Theatre of the National Theatre in London, and every French critic had something negative to say about the vast open space of the Théâtre de la Ville in Paris, formerly the Théâtre Sarah-Bernhardt, as a suitable space for *Six Characters* when it was staged there in December 1968 to inaugurate the theatre.)[2]

In 1921 Pirandello's challenge to theatre came as a trenchant indictment of naturalism. With the assimilation of avant-garde theatre into mainstream theatre, particularly after the presentation of *Waiting for Godot* in 1953, the challenge to naturalism no longer disturbs. As the play became a classic, directors were faced with a question: is it more important to preserve the iconoclasm of the play by devising new ways of confounding the audience, or to promote the play by making it accessible to new audiences? Some (for instance, Michael Rudman and Richard Jones) chose to open up the play to contemporary audiences (and audiences of a much greater heterogeneity than those of Pirandello's day), others (such as Klaus Michael Grüber and Anatoli Vasiliev) to stress its iconoclastic quality by finding new means of confusing and startling the audience.

Pirandello was a literary dramatist. When he wrote *Six Characters in Search of an Author*, it was the written text that was for him the dominant feature of that collection of phenomena that go to make a theatrical performance: actors, audience, costume, director, lighting, set and text. In essays he had written of the author's agony as he experiences the travesty that other elements of theatre make of his creation. It would be easy, therefore, to see replicated in the productions of some of the more innovative theatre directors that old tussle between the author's word and the director's vision; to say that those (such as Rudman and Vasiliev) who presented the play with an emphasis on the creative endeavours of the actors got it wrong – it was Pirandello's intention to expose the inadequacy of actors, to present theatre as an 'impossible art' precisely because the actors cannot reproduce the dramatist's creation. Such a conclusion would be misleading, however. Pirandello may have based *Six Characters in*

Search of an Author on the dichotomy between text and performance as expressed in 'Illustrators, Actors and Translators', but during his lifetime his ideas changed, as we have seen. Later, he was to value the work of the actor in a theatre that he was to see as overmechanised, and which had to hold its own against the new art of the film. Productions that valorise the actors' endeavours can be understood to be inflecting their productions with intimations of a later Pirandello, even if this was not their overt intention.

Few directors adhere verbatim to a written text. All directors of productions analysed in this book have exercised their right to see *Six Characters in Search of an Author* within the contexts of their culture, language and historical point in time. Pitoëff introduced his own stage directions (resulting in a lift for the Characters' entrance), differed from Pirandello in his interpretation of the Characters and rewrote the garden scene. Reinhardt, delighting in the recently available new means of theatre-making, emphasised a theatre at work. Italian directors made their choices between the 1921 and 1925 texts, sometimes for political reasons; some made their own amalgam of the two. One even substituted a costume play for the rehearsal of *The Rules of the Game*. The Russian director Vasiliev departed the most radically from the letter of Pirandello's texts.

It is significant that, despite his strictures on the theatre, Pirandello incorporated into his 1925 version many of the alterations made by others to his 1921 script. Furthermore, he continued to work on *Six Characters*, not as a play but as a film. Here, in his three attempts to provide a film script, ideas in, and about, the play concerning phantoms, incest, the father/son relationship, doubling, the woman as victim and seductive Other, the male gaze, the role of the author and images of creation, continue to engage Pirandello's attention. In one version even Reinhardt's entrance for the Characters, rejected in the 1925 stage version, appears validated. The third section of the 'Scenario' mentions 'mist from which vague figures emerge slowly', who 'assail the Author like figures in a nightmare'. The author is 'besieged by these unruly ghosts'.[3] In the three versions city scenes figure strongly. From the perspective of film, these can be seen in conjunction with the German 'city' and 'street' films, such as Karl Grune's *Die Strasse* (*The Street*, 1923), Bruno Rahn's *Dirnen tragödie* (*Streetwalker's Tragedy*, 1927) and G. W. Pabst's *Die Fraudlose Gasse* (*The Joyless Street*, 1925).[4] From the perspective of productions of *Six Characters*, the emphasis on the street and city shares links with Corbelli's nightmare vision of the city skyline in his 1980 production. Innovations made by Vasiliev, in particular the multiplicity of Fathers in his version, appear also to reflect Pirandello's 'Scenario' where, in sections 43 and 44, Pirandello describes two Fathers: one remembered by the Mother and the other imagined by the Author. The first is 'an extremely intellectual type, distinguished and refined, with a tormented expression on his face, rather like a Beethovenesque mask' while the second is 'a professorial type without particular distinction'.[5]

These cases of directors' innovative insights into the play text, which share links with Pirandello's own later work on *Six Characters in Search of an Author*, can be seen in conjunction with other instances of similarities between productions where there appears to be no direct influence. Richard Jones had wanted to have the Characters burst forth from a huge image of Pirandello, an entrance actually used in Ruggero Ruggeri's production in 1936, with Pirandello's approval. And in the film script Pirandello uses the device of superimposing images on the author's face or head as a means of suggesting creation. Vasiliev used the evocative Spanish song 'Besame mucho' in his production, having it accompanied on a guitar and used as a refrain during the performance. This is also the song that Jones chose for his production, without any knowledge of Vasiliev's use of it. In fact, Jones's production is fascinating for the echoes it carries of other productions.[6] The creation of the whole theatre on the stage is close to Orazio Costa's set (1946 and 1948), though Costa's replicated theatre faced the audience while Jones's was presented sideways on. A grouping of the seated family in part 3 during discussions between the Father and the Director recalled a similar grouping in de Lullo's version (1960). Another instance that caught a moment of the past came at the end of part 1 when the Director and Characters go off to consider the ways of staging what is to be the company's new play. The house lights came up while the Actors, still on stage, discussed their reactions. After the Actors had left the stage, the Young Vic audience remained confused: should they clap, was this a break, the interval? Their reaction brought to mind that time when Pirandello's company performed *Six Characters* near Agrigento to country folk who remained utterly bemused at the end of the performance and then quietly shuffled out of the theatre.

These echoes and similarities suggest that *Six Characters in Search of an Author* is indeed a classic, in the best sense of the term. Sufficiently flexible to accommodate widely different approaches, it calls even the most divergent back to itself, its inexhaustible ideas living on inviolate to daunt and to challenge. Latent ideas and images in the play that continued to burgeon in Pirandello's mind call out to future directors. The words, even the sequence of the narrative, may change, but the dark heart of the text continues both to entice and to control those who approach it.

SELECT PRODUCTION CHRONOLOGY

Teatro Valle, Rome, 9 May 1921
Directed by Dario Niccodemi
Father: Giorgio Almirante
Stepdaughter: Vera Vergani
Producer/Director: Alfonso Magheri

Kingsway Theatre, London, 26 February 1922
Translated by Mrs W. A. Greene
Directed by Theodore Komisarjevsky
Father: Franklin Dyall
Stepdaughter: Muriel Pratt
Producer/Director: Alfred Clark

Princess Theater, New York, 30 October 1922
Translated by Edward Storer
Directed by Brock Pemberton
Father: Moffat Johnston
Stepdaughter: Florence Eldridge
Producer/Director: Ernest Cossart

Comédie des Champs-Elysées, Paris, 10 April 1923
Translated by Benjamin Crémieux
Directed by Georges Pitoëff
Father: Georges Pitoëff
Stepdaughter: Ludmilla Pitoëff
Producer/Director: Michel Simon

Die Komödie, Berlin, 30 December 1924
Translated by Hans Feist
Directed by Max Reinhardt
Designed by Hermann Krehan
Father: Max Gülstorff
Stepdaughter: Franziska Kinz
Producer/Director: Max Pallenberg

Teatro Odescalchi, Rome, 18 May 1925
Directed by Luigi Pirandello
Father: Lamberto Picasso
Stepdaughter: Marta Abba
Producer/Director: Egisto Olivieri

Festival Theatre, Cambridge, 10 October 1929
English version by H. K. Ayliff
Directed by Tyrone Guthrie
Father: Frederick Piper
Stepdaughter: Flora Robson
Producer/Director: J. Leslie Frith

Westminster Theatre, London, 18 February 1932
English version by H. K. Ayliff
Directed by Tyrone Guthrie
Designed by Mollie McArthur
Father: Henry Oscar
Stepdaughter: Flora Robson
Producer/Director: Morland Graham

Teatro Quirino, Rome, 29 November 1946
Directed by Orazio Costa
Father: Camillo Pilotto
Stepdaughter: Sarah Ferrati
Producer/Director: Sergio Tofano

Festival teatrale di prosa, Venice, 18 September 1948
Directed by Orazio Costa
Father: Tino Buazzelli
Stepdaughter: Rossella Falk
Producer/Director: Manlio Busoni

Comédie française, Paris, 5 March 1952
Directed by Julien Bertheau
Translated by Benjamin Crémieux
Designed by Suzanne Lalique
Father: Fernand Ledoux
Stepdaughter: Renée Faure/Maria Casarès
Producer/Director: Jean Meyer

Théâtre Marigny, Paris, 12 March 1953
Directed by Giorgio Strehler
Designed by Gianni Ratto and Ebe Colciaghi
Father: Tino Buazzelli
Stepdaughter: Lilla Brignone
Producer/Director: Nico Pepe

Malmö City Theatre, Malmö, 21 November 1953
Directed by Ingmar Bergman
Designed by Per Falk
Father: Åke Fridell
Stepdaughter: Gertrud Fridh
Producer/Director: Benkt Åkerlund

Maly Theatre, Moscow, March 1963, and
Teatro Quirino, Rome, 17 January 1964
Directed by Giorgio de Lullo
Designed by Pier Luigi Pizzi
Father: Romolo Valli
Stepdaughter: Rossella Falk
Producer/Director: Ferruccio de Ceresa

Mayfair Theatre, London, 17 June 1963
Translated by Paul Avila Mayer
Directed by William Ball
Father: Ralph Richardson
Stepdaughter: Barbara Jefford
Producer/Director: Michael O'Sullivan

Comédie française, Paris, 19 October 1978
Translated by Michel Arnaud
Directed by Antoine Bourseiller
Designed by Sonia Delaunay
Father: Jean-Paul Roussillon
Stepdaughter: Christine Fersen
Producer/Director: Philippe Rondest

Teatro Eliseo, Rome, 29 October 1980
Directed by Gian Carlo Cobelli
Designed by Paolo Tommasi
Father: Turi Ferro
Stepdaughter: Carla Gravina
Producer/Director: Warner Bentivegna

Freie Volksbühne, Berlin, 21 March 1981
Directed by Klaus Michael Grüber
Designed by Titina Maselli
Father: Peter Roggisch
Stepdaughter: Angela Winkler
Producer/Director: Kurt Hübner

Compagnia Teatro Mobile, Bergamo, 18 February 1983
Directed by Giuseppe Patroni Griffi
Father: Giulio Bosetti
Stepdaughter: Lina Sastri
Producer/Director: Massimo de Frankovich

Loeb Theater, Cambridge, Massachusetts, May 1984
Adapted by Robert Brustein and the American Repertory Theatre
  Company
Directed by Robert Brustein
Designed by Michael H. Yeargan
Father: Robert Stattel
Stepdaughter: Lisa Hilboldt
Producer/Director: Jeremy Geidt

School of Dramatic Art, Moscow, 24 February 1987
Translated by N. Tomashevsky
Directed by Anatoli Vasiliev
Designed by Igor Popov
Father: Grigori Gladi, Vitautas Dapscis, Nikolai Cindyakin, Yuri
  Ivanov, Valeri Simonenko
Stepdaughter: Ludmila Drebneva, Svetlana Cernova, Irina Tomalina,
  Natalia Kolyakanova
Producer/Director: Vitautas Dapscis, Yuri Alscits, Nikolai Cindyakin,
  Oleg Belkin, Yuri Ivanov, Valeri Simonenko, Roustem Fatykhov

The National Theatre (Olivier Theatre), London, 18 March 1987
A new version by Nicholas Wright
Directed by Michael Rudman
Designed by Carl Toms
Father: Richard Pasco
Stepdaughter: Lesley Sharp
Producer/Director: Robin Bailey

Teatro Greco di Taormina, Taormina, 10 August 1991
A new version by Franco Zeffirelli and Luigi Vanzi
Directed by Franco Zeffirelli
Designed by Franco Zeffirelli and Raimonda Gaetani
Father: Enrico Salerno
Stepdaughter: Benedetta Buccellato
Producer/Director: Sergio Basile

Teatro Argentina, Rome, 10 November 1993
Directed by Mario Missiroli
Designed by Enrico Job
Father: Gabriele Lavia
Stepdaughter: Monica Guerritore
Producer/Director: Gianrico Tedeschi

Shaw Festival, Niagara-on-the-Lake, 19 August 2000
A new translation by Domenico Pietropaolo
Directed by Tadeusz Bradecki
Designed by Peter Hartwell
Father: Norman Browning
Stepdaughter: Kelli Fox
Producer/Director: Barry MacGregor

Young Vic Theatre, London, 9 February 2001
A new version by David Harrower
Directed by Richard Jones
Designed by Giles Cadle and Nicky Gillibrand
Father: Stephen Boxer
Stepdaughter: Leah Muller
Producer/Director: Darrel d'Silva

NOTES

Introduction

1. Felicity Firth, *Pirandello in Performance* (Cambridge and Alexandria, VA: Chadwyck-Healey, 1990), p. 16.

2. See for instance, 'Arte e coscienza d'oggi' ('Art and Consciousness Today'), 1893, and 'Arte e scienza' ('Art and Science') and 'L'umorismo' ('On Humour'), both published in 1908. See Luigi Pirandello, *L'umorismo e altri saggi*, ed. Enrico Ghidenti (Florence: Giunti, 1994).

3. Luigi Pirandello, *Lettere giovanili da Palermo e da Roma*, ed. Elio Providenti (Rome: Bulzoni, 1994), pp. 148–9.

4. Alfredo Barbina (ed.), 'Lettere d'amore da Luigi ad Antonietta', *Ariel 3* (1986), p. 213.

5. Luigi Pirandello, *Epistolario familiare giovanile*, ed. Elio Providenti, (Florence: Le Monnier, 1986), p. 22.

6. See Susan Bassnett and Jennifer Lorch (eds.), *Luigi Pirandello in the Theatre: A Documentary Record* (Chur: Harwood Academic Publishers, 1993), pp. 87–148.

7. An English version of this poem from Heine's volume *Romancero* (1851) is in Hal Draper (transl.), *The Complete Poems of Heinrich Heine* (Boston: Suhrkamp/Insel, 1982), pp. 592–3.

8. Pirandello, 'L'azione parlata' in *L'umorismo e altri saggi*, p. 314. See also Bassnett and Lorch, *Luigi Pirandello in the Theatre*, p. 21.

9. *Ibid.*, p. 314 and p. 21.

10. Pirandello, 'Illustratori, attori e traduttori' in *L'umorismo e altri saggi*, p. 195. See also Bassnett and Lorch, 'Illustrators, Actors and Translators' in *Luigi Pirandello in the Theatre*, p. 27.

11. *Ibid.*, p. 198 and p. 29.

12. See Claudio Vicentini, *Pirandello: Il disagio del teatro* (Venice: Marsilio Editori, 1993), pp. 22–31.

13. The interview 'En confidence' was published in *Le Temps* (20 July 1925).

14. See Vicentini, *Pirandello: Il disagio del teatro*, pp. 173–5.

15. See G. Corsinovi, '*Questa sera si recita a soggetto*: il testo. Tra progettazione vitalistica e partitura musicale' in Enzo Lauretta (ed.), *Testo e messa in scena in Pirandello* (Rome: La Nuova Italia Scientifica, 1986), pp. 105–32, especially pp. 115–21; and G. Corsinovi, '*Questa sera si recita a soggetto*: Dalla "rappresentazione scenica" alla "creazione scenica"' in J. C. Barnes and S. Milioto (eds.), *Le due trilogie pirandelliane* (Palermo: Palumbo, 1992), pp. 63–70.

16. Francesco Càllari, *Pirandello e il cinema* (Venice: Marsilio Editori, 1991), p. 10.

17. Pirandello, 'Se il film parlante abolirà il teatro' in *L'umorismo e altri saggi*, pp. 339–45. See also Bassnett and Lorch, *Pirandello in the Theatre*, pp. 153–7.

18. See in particular Vicentini, *Pirandello: Il disagio del teatro*, chapter 7, 'La fragilità del teatro', pp. 179–204.

19. Luigi Pirandello, 'Discorso al Convegno "Volta" sul teatro drammatico' in *Saggi, Poesie, Scritti varii*, ed. Manlio Lo Vecchio-Musti (Milan: Mondadori, 1973), p. 1037. See also Bassnett and Lorch, *Pirandello in the Theatre*, p. 173.

20. See Victoria de Grazia, *The Culture of Consent: Mass Organization of Leisure in Fascist Italy* (Cambridge University Press, 1981), pp. 162–4.

21. Pirandello, 'En confidence'.

22. See M. L. Aguirre d'Amico, *Vivere con Pirandello* (Milan: Mondadori, 1989), p. 124.

1. *Six Characters in Search of an Author* – the play (1921)

1. This chapter will discuss the 1921 text. Guido Davico Bonino includes this version in Luigi Pirandello, *Sei personaggi in cerca d'autore* (Turin: Einaudi, 1993) and Edward Storer's English version is in Luigi Pirandello, *Three Plays* (London and Toronto: J. M. Dent & Sons Ltd, 1923).

2. 'Pirandello's Introduction to Six Characters in Search of an Author', transl. Felicity Firth, in Luigi Pirandello, *Collected Plays* II (London and New York: John Calder and Riverrun Press, 1988), p. xvi.

3. See Alessandro d'Amico's Introduction to *Sei personaggi in cerca d'autore*
   in Luigi Pirandello, *Maschere nude* II (Milan: Mondadori, 1993),
   p. 622. Other stories carry the same theme: for instance, 'Personaggi'
   ('Characters'), 1906, 'La tragedia di un personaggio' ('The Tragedy
   of a Character'), 1911, and 'Colloqui con personaggi' ('Conversations
   with Characters'), 1915. See also Ann Hallamore Caesar, *Characters and
   Authors in Luigi Pirandello* (Oxford: Clarendon Press, 1998), chapter 2,
   'The Rise of the Character: Six Characters and the Drama of Creativity',
   pp. 35–63.
4. Susan Bassnett and Jennifer Lorch (eds.), *Pirandello in the Theatre:
   A Documentary Record* (Chur: Harwood Academic Publishers, 1993),
   p. 56.
5. *Ibid.*, p. 57.
6. *Ibid.*, p. 58.
7. 'Our identity depends on the novel, what others think of us, what we
   think of ourselves, the way in which our life is imperceptibly moulded
   into a whole. How do others see us if not as a character from a novel?',
   Philippe Sollers in *Logiques*, p. 288, as quoted in Jonathan Culler, *Structuralist Poetics* (London and Henley: Routledge & Kegan Paul, 1975),
   p. 189.
8. See Bassnett and Lorch, *Pirandello in the Theatre*, pp. 20–34.
9. Caesar, *Characters and Authors in Luigi Pirandello*, p. 167. See chapter 6
   of her book for an interesting comparison between Victor Turner's concept of liminality and Pirandello's 'marginal' characters.
10. The second and third texts, printed in 1923 and 1924, are in fact iden-
    tical, the 1924 text being a reprint of the 1923 edition with a different
    title page. It is not clear whether this 1923/4 text was ever presented
    on the stage. It is clear, however, that Pirandello worked sequentially
    on his texts: the 1923/4 is a revision of the 1921, the 1925 a further
    amendment of the 1923/4 text.
11. F. T. Marinetti, *Teatro* II (Rome: Vito Bianco Editore, 1960), pp. 305–
    10.
12. David Bradby, *Beckett: Waiting for Godot* (Cambridge University Press,
    2001), p. 2.
13. The phrase 'temporal perspective' was coined by Nino Pirrotta in Nino
    Pirrotta and Elena Povoledo, *Music and Theatre from Poliziano to Mon-
    teverdi*, transl. Karen Eales (Cambridge University Press, 1982). Nino

Pirrotta uses the phrase to refer to the 'compression of time' in a play based on the unities, which was 'akin to the artificial compression of space by either linear or theatrical perspective' (p. 129).

14. It is difficult to catch the haunting rhythms and evocative repetitions of this speech in English. In the Italian they bring to mind the poetry of the thirteenth-century Franciscan poet Jacopone da Todi.

15. The other two plays are *Ciascuno a suo modo* (*Each in His Own Way*) and *Questa sera si recita a soggetto* (*Tonight We Improvise*).

16. Peter Szondi, *Theory of the Modern Drama*, ed. and transl. Michael Hays (Cambridge: Polity Press, 1987), p. 80.

17. Firth, 'Pirandello's Introduction to Six Characters in Search of an Author', p. xiii.

18. Bassnett and Lorch, *Pirandello in the Theatre*, p. 56.

19. Firth, 'Pirandello's Introduction to Six Characters in Search of an Author', p. xxiv

20. *Ibid.*, p. xv.

2. The first production: Teatro Valle, Rome, 9 May 1921, directed by Dario Niccodemi

1. Arnaldo Frateili, *Idea Nazionale* (11 May 1921) quoted in Alessandro d'Amico's Introduction to *Sei personaggi in cerca d'autore* in Luigi Pirandello, *Maschere nude* II (Milan: Mondadori, 1993), p. 630.

2. Orio Vergani, 'L'ora dei Sei Personaggi', *Corriere della sera* (15 December 1936), quoted in Gaspare Giudice, *Luigi Pirandello* (Turin: Unione Tipografica-Unione Torinese, 1963), pp. 355–6. See Susan Bassnett and Jennifer Lorch (eds.), *Pirandello in the Theatre* (Chur: Harwood Academic Publishers, 1993), pp. 11–12, for English translation.

3. Lucio Ridenti, 'Addio a Orio Vergani', *Il Dramma* 284 (May 1960) quoted in Luigi Pirandello, *Sei personaggi in cerca d'autore*, ed. Guido Davico Bonino (Turin: Einaudi, 1993), pp. 202–4.

4. *Ibid.*, p. 204.

5. Sabatino Lopez, *Dal carteggio di Virgilio Talli* (Milan: Treves, 1931), p. 143. See also Bassnett and Lorch, *Pirandello in the Theatre*, p. 46.

6. D'Amico's Introduction to *Sei personaggi in cerca d'autore* in Pirandello, *Maschere nude* II, p. 639.

7. *Ibid.*, p. 633.

8. Silvio d'Amico, *Cronache del teatro* (Bari: Laterza, 1963), p. 227.

9. *Ibid.*, p. 234.

10. *Ibid.*, p. 233.

11. D'Amico's Introduction to *Sei personaggi in cerca d'autore* in Pirandello, *Maschere nude* II, p. 628.

12. Dario Niccodemi, *Tempo passato* (Milan: Treves, 1929), p. 82. (See Bassnett and Lorch, *Luigi Pirandello in the Theatre*, pp. 59–61 for a translation of this memoir.)

13. Niccodemi, *Tempo passato*, p. 86. (See Bassnett and Lorch, *Luigi Pirandello in the Theatre*, p. 60.)

14. D'Amico's Introduction to *Sei personaggi in cerca d'autore* in Pirandello, *Maschere nude* II, p. 631.

15. Niccodemi, *Tempo passato*, pp. 82–3. (See Bassnett and Lorch, *Luigi Pirandello in the Theatre*, p. 59.)

16. Niccodemi, *Tempo passato*, p. 87. (See Bassnett and Lorch, *Luigi Pirandello in the Theatre*, p. 60.)

17. D'Amico's Introduction to *Sei personaggi in cerca d'autore* in Pirandello, *Maschere nude* II, p. 630.

18. Fausto Maria Martini, *La Tribuna* (11 May 1921); Adriano Tilgher, *Il Tempo* (11 May 1921). These reviews and others are also in the Appendix to Luigi Pirandello, *Sei personaggi in cerca d'autore*, ed. Davico Bonino, pp. 207–71. For Adriano Tilgher's review, see also Bassnett and Lorch, *Luigi Pirandello in the Theatre*, pp. 62–5.

19. D'Amico's Introduction to *Sei personaggi in cerca d'autore* in Pirandello, *Maschere nude* II, p. 632–3.

20. Marco Praga, *Illustrazione Italiana* (4 October 1921). (See also the Appendix to Luigi Pirandello, *Sei personaggi in cerca d'autore*, ed. Davico Bonino, p. 244.)

21. Tilgher, *Il Tempo* (11 May 1921); Fausto Maria Martini, *La Tribuna* (11 May 1921). (See also the Appendix to Pirandello, *Sei personaggi in cerca d'autore*, ed. Davico Bonino, pp. 212 and 225.)

22. D'Amico's Introduction to *Sei personaggi in cerca d'autore* in Pirandello, *Maschere nude* II, p. 632.

23. Praga, *Illustrazione Italiana* (4 October 1921); Massimo Bontempelli, *Industrie Italiane Illustrate* (7 October 1921); Umberto Fracchia, *Comoedia* (October 1921). (See also the Appendix to Pirandello, *Sei personaggi in cerca d'autore*, ed. Davico Bonino, pp. 244, 247 and 254.)

24. See Felicity Firth, *Pirandello in Performance* (Cambridge and Alexandria, VA: Chadwyck-Healey, 1990), pp. 15–16.

25. Carlo Tamberlani, *Pirandello "nel teatro che c'era"*, *Quaderni dell'Istituto di Studi pirandelliani* III (Rome: Bulzoni, 1982), p. 99.

26. D'Amico's Introduction to *Sei personaggi in cerca d'autore* in Pirandello, *Maschere nude* II, p. 636.

27. Ferdinando Taviani, ' "Sei personaggi": due interviste in una al primo padre', *Teatro e Storia* 7, 2 (1992), p. 325.

28. Mario Apollonio, *Prologo ai "Sei personnaggi"*, *Quaderni dell'Istituto di Studi pirandelliani* I (Rome: Bulzoni, 1973), p. 33.

3. Two early productions in London and New York (1922)

1. See letter to the *Observer* (21 June 1925) from W. S. Kennedy, the Stage Society's chairman, at the time of the Teatro d'Arte's visit to London.

2. Norman Marshall, *The Other Theatre* (London: John Lehmann, 1947), pp. 73–6 and 219.

3. Theodore Komisarjevsky, *Myself and the Theatre* (London: William Heinemann Ltd, 1929), p. 163. For further information about Theodore Komisarjevsky, see Marc Slonim, *Russian Theatre: From the Empire to the Soviets* (London: Methuen, 1963), pp. 207–11; Marshall, *The Other Theatre*, pp. 218–20; John Gielgud, *Early Stages* (London: Macmillan & Co. Ltd, 1939), pp. 105–13, 144–6, 202–5, 239–40, 252–3, 292–300; and John Gielgud, *An Actor and his Time* (London: Sidgwick & Jackson, 1979), pp. 97–103.

4. Komisarjevsky, *Myself and the Theatre*, p. 166.

5. Gielgud, *Early Stages*, p. 113.

6. Marshall, *The Other Theatre*, p. 72, and Komisarjevsky, *Myself and the Theatre*, pp. 157–8.

7. Komisarjevsky, *Myself and the Theatre*, p. 157.

8. 'Something New' in Desmond McCarthy, *Drama* (London and New York: Putnam, 1948), pp. 161–5 (see also Bassnett and Lorch, *Pirandello in the Theatre*, pp. 65–6).

9. 'Young Boswell Interviews Brock Pemberton', *New York Tribune* (2 December 1922). This reference, and others from US newspapers in this chapter, are to be found in Brock Pemberton's Scrapbooks in the Billy Rose Collection, New York Library for the Performing Arts,

Lincoln Center. A fuller version of this section on Pemberton's production is in Simon Gilson, Katherine Keen and Brian Richardson, *Theatre, Opera and Performance in Italy from the Fifteenth Century to the Present: Essays in Honour of Richard Andrews* (Leeds: Society for Italian Studies, 2004).

10. Frederick May, 'Alfred Wareing and the Production of Pirandello in the West Riding', *The University of Leeds Review* (June 1966), pp. 1–2. Another possible author of the programme note is Allan Wade, mentioned in W. S. Kennedy's letter to the *Observer* (21 June 1925), as the person who drew the attention of the Stage Society's Committee to *Six Characters in Search of an Author*. A copy of both the Stage Society programme and the Princess Theater programme are in the Billy Rose Collection in the New York Public Library for the Performing Arts, Lincoln Center.

11. Antonio Illiano, 'The New York Premiere of Six Characters: A Note with Excerpts from Reviews', *Romance Notes* 13 (1971), pp. 18–25.

12. *Theatre Magazine* (January 1923), p. 23; *New York Evening World* (31 October 1922).

13. *New York Evening World* (31 October 1922).

14. Stark Young, 'Brains', *New Republic* (22 November 1922).

15. Kenneth Macgowan, 'New Plays', *New York Globe* (31 October 1922); *Theatre Magazine* (January 1923), p. 23.

16. *Theatre Magazine* (February 1923), p. 9.

17. *NEA Service Cleveland* (21 November 1922).

18. *Zit's Weekly* (11 November 1922).

19. Alexander Woolcott, 'Caviar at the Princess', *New World Herald* (31 October 1922).

20. *Story World* (April 1923); *New York Owl* (December 1922).

21. Young, 'Brains'.

22. J.M.B.K., 'As seen from Down Front', *Daily Hotel Reporter* (4 November 1922).

23. Young, 'Brains'.

24. J.M.B.K. 'As Seen from Down Front'; *Theatre Magazine* (January 1923).

25. Young, 'Brains'.

26. *New York Owl* (December 1922).

27. *Daily Hotel Reporter* (4 November 1922).

28. The special revival was staged at the Forty-Fourth Street Theater; see Alessandro d'Amico's Introduction to *Sei personaggi in cerca d' autore* in Luigi Pirandello, *Maschere nude* II (Milan: Mondadori, 1993), p. 641.

29. See Burns Mantle, *The Best Plays of 1922–1923 and the Year Book of the Drama in America* (New York: Dodd, Mead and Company, 1934), and Samuel L. Leiter, *Encyclopedia of the New York Stage 1920–1930* (Westport, CT, and London, England: Greenwood Press, 1985).

30. For instance, at The Playhouse in Cleveland during the 1922–3 season; in New York at the Portal Playhouse under the auspices of the Hospitality League of the First Unitarian Society, 3–6 October 1923, and at the Punch and Judy Theater (1924) in a special matinee by arrangement with the Foreign Press Service under the auspices of the Italy-America Society.

31. *Christian Science Monitor* (25 January 1923); Alice Rohe in the *New York Times Book Review* (10 December 1922).

32. See Helen Augur in the *New York Times* (4 March, 1923) and Alice Rohe, 'The Theatre's Latest Genius', *Theatre Magazine* (January 1923), pp. 23 and 58.

33. John Hutchens, 'Spring Reckoning', *Theatre Arts Monthly* 15, 6 (1931), p. 450.

34. See the record of performances in the New York Library of the Performing Arts, Lincoln Center.

4. Pitoëff's production in Paris (1923)

1. Paul Renucci, in his edition of Luigi Pirandello, *Théâtre complet* (Paris: Gallimard, 1977), pp. 1360–1.

2. Georges Neveux, cited by Renucci in Pirandello, *Théâtre complet*, p. 1357.

3. Paul Brisson, *Annales* (23 April 1923), cited in Anna Frabetti, 'Pirandello a Parigi. L'interpretazione del teatro pirandelliano in Francia nei primi anni venti', *Filologia critica* 24, 3 (September–December 1999), p. 412.

4. Georges Pitoëff, *Notre Théâtre*, textes et documents réunis par J. de Rigault (Paris: Librairie Bonaparte, 1949), p. 8.

5. Pitoëff, *Notre Théâtre*, p. 9.

6. See Luigi Pirandello, 'Introduzione al teatro italiano' in Silvio d'Amico (ed.), *Storia del teatro italiano* (Milan: Bompiani, 1936), pp. 25–6.

7. Renucci in Pirandello, *Théâtre complet*, p. 1356.

8. Jacqueline Jomaron, *Georges Pitoëff, metteur en scène* (Lausanne: l'Age d'Homme, 1979), p. 139.

9. For further details, see Jennifer Lorch, 'The 1925 text of *Sei personaggi in cerca d'autore* and Pitoëff's production of 1923', *The Yearbook of the British Pirandello Society* 2 (1982), pp. 32–47.

10. Luigi Pirandello, *Six personnages en quête d'auteur* (Paris: Gallimard, 1927), pp. 102–3, and Georges Pitoëff's production copy, p. 111. I am grateful to his son, Sacha Pitoëff, for allowing me access to this script.

11. Felicity Firth's translation of *Six Characters in Search of an Author* in Luigi Pirandello, *Collected Plays* 2 (London and New York: John Calder and Riverrun Press, 1988), p. 8.

12. Pitoëff, *Notre Théâtre*, pp. 45–5.

13. Roberto Alonge, 'Le messinscene dei *Sei personaggi in cerca d'autore*' in Enzo Lauretta (ed.), *Testo e messa in scena in Pirandello* (Rome: La Nuova Italia Scientifica, 1986), p. 65.

14. L. Gillet, 'Deux pièces étrangères à Paris' in *Revue des Deux Mondes*, (1 May 1923), p. 226.

15. Antonin Artaud, *Oeuvres complètes* II (Paris: Gallimard, 1961), p. 160. This review was first published in *La Criée* (24 May 1923). *La Criée* was published in Marseilles, where Artaud saw the production.

16. From an anonymous review in *Le Théâtre et Comoedia illustré*, cited in Alonge, 'Le messinscene dei *Sei personaggi in cerca d'autore*', p. 66.

17. *Ibid.*, p. 67.

18. Pitoëff's production copy, p. 19.

19. Jomaron, *Georges Pitoëff*, p. 143.

20. This image, and others, can be seen in *The Yearbook of the British Pirandello Society* 2, 1982, and in Jomaron, *Georges Pitoëff*.

21. Jomaron, *Georges Pitoëff*, p. 143

22. Artaud, *Oeuvres complètes* II, p. 162.

23. See Renée Lelièvre, *Le théâtre dramatique italien en France (1850–1940)* (Paris: Armand Colin, 1959), p. 410.

24. Jean Hort, *La vie héroïque des Pitoëff* (Geneva: Pierre Cailler, 1966), p. 178.

25. See Lelièvre, *Le théâtre dramatique italien en France*, p. 417.
26. L. Gillet, 'Deux pièces étrangères à Paris'; see also Frabetti, 'Pirandello a Parigi. L'interpretazione del teatro pirandelliano in Francia nei primi anni venti', p. 415.
27. See Frabetti, *ibid.*, p. 414.
28. H.-R. Lenormand, *Les Pitoëff, souvenirs* (Paris: Odette Lieutier, 1943), p. 118.
29. *Ibid.* p. 118.

5. Reinhardt's production in Berlin (1924)

1. For Pirandello's reception in Germany, see Oscar Büdel, 'Pirandello sulla scena tedesca' in Sandro d'Amico (ed.), *Pirandello ieri e oggi, Quaderni del Piccolo Teatro* 1 (1961), pp. 99–122, and Michele Cometa, *Il teatro di Pirandello in Germania* (Palermo: Edizioni Novecento, 1986).
2. See Michael Patterson, *The Revolution in German Theatre, 1900–1933* (Boston, London and Henley: Routledge & Kegan Paul, 1981), pp. 23–4.
3. See John Willett, *The Theatre of the Weimar Republic* (New York and London: Holmes & Meier, 1988), p. 24.
4. Claudio Vicentini, *Pirandello: Il disagio del teatro* (Venice: Marsilio, 1993), p. 128.
5. Stephen Lamb, 'Staging Change, Changing the Stage in the Weimar Republic', *Pirandello Studies* 19 (1999), p. 31.
6. *Ibid.*, p. 30.
7. Cometa, *Il teatro di Pirandello in Germania*, p. 14.
8. Rudolf Pechel, *Deutsche Rundschau* (January–March 1925), pp. 239–40; see also Susan Bassnett and Jennifer Lorch (eds.), *Luigi Pirandello in the Theatre: A Documentary Record* (Chur: Harwood Academic Publishers, 1993), p. 71.
9. Patterson, *The Revolution in German Theatre*, p. 35.
10. Edward Braun, *The Director and the Stage* (London: Methuen, 1982), p. 97.
11. *Ibid.*, p. 98.
12. *Ibid.*
13. See Patterson, *The Revolution in German Theatre*, p. 36.

14. Alessandro d'Amico, Introduction to *Sei personaggi in cerca d'autore* in Luigi Pirandello, *Maschere nude* II (Milan: Mondadori, 1993), pp. 640–41.
15. *Ibid.*, p. 641.
16. Cometa, *Il teatro di Pirandello in Germania*, p. 51.
17. See Hermann Krehan's design in Cometa, *Il teatro di Pirandello in Germania*, fig. I. (See also figs. II, III, IV and V for further illustrations of Krehan's designs.)
18. The opening scene is printed in full in *ibid.*, pp. 60–76, from Max Reinhardt, *Ausgewählte Briefe, Reden, Schriften und Szenen aus Regiebüchern* (Vienna: Prochner Verlag, 1963), pp. 185–93.
19. Cometa, *Il teatro di Pirandello in Germania*, p. 69.
20. *Ibid.*, p. 51.
21. *Ibid.*, p. 77.
22. *Ibid.*, p. 79.

6. Pirandello's production of the 1925 text (1925)

1. For a detailed chronology of the Teatro d'Arte years, see Alessandro d'Amico and Alessandro Tinterri, *Pirandello capocomico* (Palermo: Sellerio, 1987); see also Susan Bassnett and Jennifer Lorch, *Luigi Pirandello in the Theatre: A Documentary Record* (Chur: Harwood Academic Publishers, 1993); pp. 87–150.
2. D'Amico and Tinterri, *Pirandello capocomico*, p. 140.
3. *Ibid.*, p. 132.
4. For changes to the text, see d'Amico's Introduction to *Sei personaggi in cerca d'autore* in Luigi Pirandello, *Maschere nude* II (Milan: Mondadori, 1993), pp. 643–5; Jennifer Lorch, 'The 1925 text of *Sei personaggi in cerca d'autore* and Pitoëff's production of 1923', *The Yearbook of the British Pirandello Society* 2 (1982), pp. 32–47; and J. Møestrup, 'Le correzioni ai *Sei personaggi* e il Castelvetro di Pirandello', *Revue Romane* II (1967), pp. 121–35.
5. See d'Amico's Introduction to *Sei personaggi in cerca d'autore* in Pirandello, *Maschere nude* II, p. 641, note 2. Niccodemi's letter to Vera Vergani was published in the newspaper *La repubblica* (13 January 1990).

6. Felicity Firth's translation of *Six Characters in Search of an Author* in Luigi Pirandello, *Collected Plays* II (London and New York: John Calder and Riverrun Press, 1988), p. 8.

7. *Ibid.*, p. 8.

8. See d'Amico's Introduction *to Sei personaggi in cerca d'autore* in Luigi Pirandello, *Maschere nude* II, p. 644.

9. Alessandro Tinterri, 'Two Flights of Steps and a Stage Direction: Pirandello's Staging of *Six Characters in Search of an Author* in 1925', *The Yearbook of the British Pirandello Society* 3 (1983), p. 36.

10. D'Amico and Tinterri, *Pirandello capocomico*, p. 55.

11. Corrado Alvaro, *Cronache e scritti teatrali* (Rome: Abete, 1976), pp. 76–86; for a translation, see Bassnett and Lorch, *Luigi Pirandello in the Theatre*, pp. 104–8.

12. Translated from the 1921 text of the play. See Luigi Pirandello, *Sei personaggi in cerca d'autore*, ed. Guido Davico Bonino (Turin: Einaudi, 1993), p.155.

13. For the stage directions in greater detail, see Pirandello, *Maschere nude* II, p. 758, and Firth's translation in Pirandello, *Collected Plays* II, p. 68.

14. For this photograph, see *The Yearbook of the British Pirandello Society* 2 (1982), photographic insert between pp. 34 and 35.

15. Virgilio Marchi, quoted in d'Amico's Introduction to *Sei personaggi in cerca d'autore* in Pirandello, *Maschere nude* II, pp. 641–2.

16. *The Times* (16 June 1925); see also Bassnett and Lorch, *Luigi Pirandello in the Theatre*, p. 113; and d'Amico's Introduction to *Sei personaggi in cerca d'autore* in Luigi Pirandello, *Maschere nude* II, p. 642.

17. D'Amico and Tinterri, *Pirandello capocomico*, p. 144.

18. Federico Vittore Nardelli, *Vita segreta di Pirandello* (Rome: Vito Bianco Editore, 1962), p. 187.

19. Michele Cometa, *Il teatro di Pirandello in Germania* (Palermo: Edizioni Novecento, 1986), p. 231.

20. Oscar Büdel, 'Pirandello sulla scena tedesca' in Sandro d'Amico (ed.), *Pirandello ieri e oggi*, *Quaderni del Piccolo Teatro* 1 (1961), p. 102.

21. See d'Amico's Introduction to *Sei personaggi in cerca d'autore* in Luigi Pirandello, *Maschere nude* II, p. 643.

22. Cometa, *Il teatro di Pirandello in Germania*, pp. 234–6.

23. Gabriel Boissy, *Comoedia* (13 July 1925), cited in d'Amico and Tinterri, *Pirandello capocomico*, pp. 142–4.
24. Alfred Kerr in d'Amico and Tinterri, *Pirandello capocomico*, pp. 148–50.
25. Marta Abba, 'La mia vita d'attrice', *L'Italia letteraria* (15 March 1936), p. 7, cited in Cometa, *Il teatro di Pirandello in Germania*, p. 238.

7. *Six Characters* on the Italian stage (1936–93)

1. Felicity Firth, *Pirandello in Performance* (Cambridge and Alexandria, VA: Chadwyck-Healey, 1990), p. 13.
2. See Pirandello's letter to Marta Abba of 21 April 1930 in which he relays to her the effusive praise of Dr Lehrmann (who had seen her performance at the Schauspielhaus in Berlin), with which he, Pirandello, fully concurs: Luigi Pirandello, *Lettere a Marta Abba*, ed. Benito Ortolani (Milan: Mondadori, 1995), pp. 404–5.
3. Susan Bassnett and Jennifer Lorch (eds.), *Luigi Pirandello in the Theatre: A Documentary Record* (Chur: Harwood Academic Publishers, 1993), p. 148.
4. Alessandro d'Amico's Introduction to *Sei personaggi in cerca d'autore* in Luigi Pirandello, *Maschere nude* II (Milan: Mondadori, 1993), p. 646.
5. Letter from Pirandello to Ruggeri (21 September 1936), in Guido Lopez (ed.), *La 'cesta' di Ruggero Ruggeri* (Milan: De Carlo Editori, 1980), p. 66.
6. Umberto Onorato, 'Ultimo incontro', *Illustrazione d'Italia* (6 December 1946).
7. Review by Francesco Càllari, *Film* (14 March 1942); cutting held by Civico Museo Biblioteca dell'Attore del Teatro Stabile di Genova.
8. *Ibid.*
9. *Ibid.*
10. Review by Renato Simoni, *Corriere della Sera* (19 November 1941).
11. For a fuller (and illustrated) version of this section on Costa's productions, see Jennifer Lorch, 'Pirandello for the new Italy: Orazio Costa's productions of *Sei personaggi in cerca d'autore*, in George Talbot and Pamela Williams (eds.), *Essays in Italian Literature and History in Honour of Doug Thompson* (Dublin: Four Courts Press Ltd, 2002), pp. 103–16. For details of Costa's early life and career, see Giacomo Colli, 'L'educazione teatrale di Orazio Costa' in Paola Quarenghi and

Aida de Lellis (eds.), *Orazio Costa, pedagogia e didattica del teatro* (Rome: Università di Roma, 'La Sapienza', 1987–8), pp. 1–30. See also Franco Perrelli, 'Colloqui con Orazio Costa', *Il castello di Elsinore* 38 (2000), pp. 127–34.

12. Orazio Costa, 'La regia teatrale', *Rivista italiana del dramma* 3, 2 (1939), pp. 196–7.

13. *Ibid.*, p. 198.

14. Dario Niccodemi, *Tempo passato* (Milan: Treves, 1929), pp. 82–8; for translation into English, see Bassnett and Lorch, *Pirandello in the Theatre*, pp. 59–61.

15. Personal communication, in conversation with Orazio Costa, 6 April 1998.

16. For Pirandello's relationship with Fascism, see Gian Franco Venè, *Pirandello fascista* (Venice: Marsilio Editori, 1981); Gaspare Giudice, 'Il fascismo' in *Luigi Pirandello* (Turin: Unione Tipografica-Unione Torinese, 1963), pp. 413–64; and Bassnett and Lorch, *Pirandello in the Theatre*, pp. 87–9.

17. Pirandello, *Lettere a Marta Abba*, p. 930.

18. See Roberto Campa's review in *Vivere settimanale* (5 December, 1946).

19. Personal communication, see note 15.

20. There is a little cache of photographs in the Civico Museo Biblioteca dell'Attore del Teatro Stabile di Genova, showing the young people trying on their costumes.

21. See note 15.

22. Arnaldo Frateili in *Il giornale della sera* (3 March 1949).

23. Roberto Alonge, 'Le messinscene dei *Sei personaggi in cerca d'autore*' in Enzo Lauretta (ed.), *Testo e messa in scena in Pirandello* (Rome: La Nuova Italia Scientifica, 1986), p. 74.

24. David L. Hirst, *Giorgio Strehler* (Cambridge University Press, 1993), p. 13.

25. *Ibid.*

26. *Ibid.*

27. Francesco Marchesi, 'Vorrei che fosse uno spettacolo magico, fantastico e vero nello stesso tempo e terribilmente umano' in Federica Mazzocchi and Alberto Bentoglio (eds.), *Giorgio Strehler e il suo teatro* (Rome: Bulzoni, 1997), pp. 158–61.

28. Giorgio Strehler (ed.), *1947–1958 Piccolo Teatro* (Milan: Moneta, 1958), p. 146.

29. *Ibid.*

30. *Ibid.*

31. See Duilio Morosini, 'I *Sei personaggi* di Pirandello hanno di nuovo sconcertato Parigi' in *L'Ora del Popolo* (4 April 1953).

32. One of the illustrations of Costa's 1948 production in the little cache of photographs in the Civico Museo Biblioteca dell'Attore del Teatro Stabile di Genova (see note 20) shows the Father holding his stepson.

33. For details concerning the formation of the Compagnia dei Giovani, see Antonio Audino, *La compagnia dei Giovani* (Florence: Editalia, 1995), pp. 13–16.

34. Guido Davico Bonino, *Romolo Valli, ritratto d'attore* (Milan: Il Saggiatore, 1983), pp. 126–7.

35. *Ibid.*, p. 165.

36. *Six Characters in Search of an Author* was followed by *The Rules of the Game* in 1965/6, *The Wives' Friend* (1968/9), *Right You Are! (If You Think So)* (1971/2) and *Henry IV* (1977/8); the company, with changes from its original formulation, was at this time the Compagnia di Prosa del Teatro Eliseo.

37. Davico Bonino, *Romolo Valli, ritratto d'attore*, p. 166.

38. *Ibid.*, p. 166. See also p. 212 for Valli's views on the actor as 'repository of memory'. 'Between the actor and the character as written by the author, there is a margin of creativity, which, on the whole is small, but it is in that gap, in that space between the character as written and the actor who has to interpret that character, that the wealth of memories and the capacity to recall them comes into play.'

39. *Ibid.*, p. 166.

40. *Ibid.*, p. 14.

41. *Ibid.*, p. 201.

42. *Ibid.*, p. 200.

43. For evidence of Pirandello's hopes for productions of his plays in Russia, see a letter he wrote to Marta Abba (26 May 1929) in Pirandello, *Lettere a Marta Abba*, p. 183.

44. Renzo Tian, 'Con La Compagnia dei Giovani per la prima volta in Russia', *Il Messaggero* (8 February 1963), quoted in Audino, *La Compagnia dei Giovani*, p. 73.

45. See Paolo Puppa, *Dalle parti di Pirandello* (Rome: Bulzoni, 1987), pp. 293–4. 'But he is not loved. He is admired as a paternal figure of authority, whose discourse effects tension, but does not attract consensus.'

46. Audino, *La Compagnia dei Giovani*, p. 78.

47. See the illustration in *ibid.*, p. 134.

48. Maurizio del Ministro, 'Critica di De Lullo' in *Pirandello: Scena personaggio film* (Rome: Bulzoni, 1980), p. 114.

49. This moment is very well caught in the video of the television version (see VideoRai VRB 2093).

50. See del Ministro, *Pirandello: Scena personaggio film*, p. 115.

51. Davico Bonino, *Romolo Valli, ritratto d'attore*, p. 167.

52. Earlier productions of distinction include Orazio Costa's productions of *Right You Are! (If You Think So)* in Rome (1952) and *Henry IV* in Milan (1962–3), and Luigi Squarzina's production of *Each in His Own Way* in Genoa (1961); see Firth, *Pirandello in Performance*, pp. 57–60; 68–70.

53. By Giuseppe Patroni Griffi, Massimo Castri, Mario Missiroli and Gian Carlo Sepe.

54. Roberto Tessari, 'Il sacrificio della donna ignuda' in Roberto Alonge and Roberto Tessari, *Immagini del teatro contemporaneo* (Naples: Guida Editore, 1977), pp. 183–4.

55. Roberto Tessari, quoted in Firth, *Pirandello in Performance*, pp. 87–8.

56. Firth, *Pirandello in Performance*, p. 88.

57. Roberto de Monticelli, quoted in Felicity Firth, *Pirandello in Performance*, p. 84.

58. Renzo Tian, 'Nel bunker del teatro i fantasmi: perplessi' in *Il Messaggero* (30 October 1980).

59. Giorgio Prosperi, 'Cobelli apocalittico con bomba e Requiem' in *Il Tempo* (30 October 1980).

60. Tommaso Chiaretti, 'Una notte sognando la morte' in *La Repubblica* (30 October 1980).

61. *Ibid.*
62. Firth, *Pirandello in Performance*, p. 97.
63. Guido Davico Bonino, 'Pirandello ha fascino anche con il "traditore" Cobelli' in *La Stampa* (9 December 1980).
64. Odoardo Bertani in *Avvenire* (2 November 1980).
65. *Ibid.*
66. Nico Garrone, 'Pirandello questo sconosciuto' in *La Repubblica* (7 October 1980); see also Firth, *Pirandello in performance*, p. 99.
67. Franco Zeffirelli in his introduction to the play in the theatre programme, p. 19.
68. *Ibid.*
69. Luigi Pirandello, 'Introduzione al teatro italiano' in Silvio d'Amico (ed.), *Storia del teatro italiano* (Milan: Bompiani, 1936), pp. 25–6.
70. Rita Franchetti was interviewed by Alessandro Tinterri on 27 April 1981; the tape is held in the Civico Museo Biblioteca dell'Attore del Teatro Stabile di Genoa. See Claudio Vicentini, *Pirandello: Il disagio del teatro* (Venice: Marsilio Editori, 1993), pp. 191–2.
71. Edward Williams and Emmanuela Tandello, 'Interview with Franco Zeffirelli', *The Yearbook of the Society for Pirandello Studies* 12 (1992), p. 78.
72. Franco Zeffirelli in his introduction to the play in the theatre programme, p. 19.
73. Elizabeth Schächter, '*Sei personaggi in cerca d'autore* in a new version by Franco Zeffirelli and Luigi Vanzi', *The Yearbook of the Society for Pirandello Studies* 12 (1992), p. 86.
74. See Enrico Salerno's statement in the theatre programme, p. 3.
75. See, for instance, Olga Ragusa, *Pirandello: An Approach to his Theatre* (Edinburgh University Press, 1980), pp. 150–1.
76. Firth, *Pirandello in Performance*, p. 91.
77. Personal interview (Rome, 4 April 1998).
78. *Ibid.*
79. *Ibid.*
80. *Ibid.*
81. Giovanni Raboni, in *Corriere della Sera* (12 November 1993).
82. See note 77.
83. Silvana Gaudio in *Il Tempo* (7 November 1993).

84. Renzo Tian in *Il Messaggero* (14 November 1993).
85. Franco Quadri in *La Repubblica* (12 November 1993).
86. *Ibid.*

8. Two English productions (1929 and 1963)

1. Nicholas de Jongh, *Politics, Prudery and Perversions: The Censoring of the English Stage 1901–1968* (London: Methuen, 2001), p. 68.
2. Letter from Barry Jackson to the Lord Chamberlain (13 July 1925), Lord Chamberlain's Files, British Library; letter from Philip Ridgeway to the Lord Chamberlain (14 June 1926), *ibid.*; Lord Chamberlain to Walter Peacock, writing on behalf of Barry Jackson, confirming that he had not granted a licence to present the play, *ibid.* The Lord Chamberlain had added by hand 'and gave him an interview in the following month'.
3. G. S. Street's Reader's Report, cited in Jongh, *Politics, Prudery and Perversions*, pp. 67–8; and other Readers' Reports dated 20 December 1924 (Lord Buckmaster) and 21 December 1924, Lord Chamberlain's Files, British Library.
4. Reader's Report (21 December 1924), *ibid.*
5. Lord Buckmaster's Reader's Report, *ibid.*
6. See chapter 6, p. 81, of this book. See also chapter 9, pp. 140–2, for the reinsertion of this passage in Bourseiller's production at the Comédie française in 1978.
7. De Jongh, *Politics, Prudery and Perversions*, p. 69.
8. For information concerning Guthrie's life at this time, see James Forsyth, *Tyrone Guthrie* (London: Hamish Hamilton, 1976), pp. 80–97.
9. See Kenneth Barrow, *Flora, An Appreciation of the Life and Work of Dame Flora Robson* (London: Heinemann, 1981), pp. 36–54, and Janet Dunbar, *Flora Robson* (London, Toronto, Wellington and Sydney: George G. Harrap & Co. Ltd, 1960), pp. 72–4.
10. Dunbar, *Flora Robson*, p. 91.
11. Forsyth, *Tyrone Guthrie*, p. 85.
12. Dunbar, *Flora Robson*, p. 89.
13. *Ibid.*
14. Raffaello Piccolo, 'The Festival Theatre. *Six Characters in Search of an Author*', *Cambridge Review* (18 October 1920), p. 42.

15. 'Festival Stage Puzzle. Pirandello's "Six Characters"', unidentified newspaper cutting lent to me by Felicity Firth.

16. Tyrone Guthrie, *A Life in the Theatre* (London: Hamish Hamilton, 1960), cited in Felicity Firth, 'English Actors and Pirandello: A Rag-bag of Gossip', *Pirandello Studies* 20 (2000), p. 36.

17. *The Guardian* (19 December 1979).

18. Dunbar, *Flora Robson*, p. 88.

19. *Ibid.*, p. 87.

20. Barrow, *Flora*, p. 68.

21. F. J. O., 'Miss Flora Robson's Success' from unidentified newspaper cutting lent to me by Felicity Firth.

22. Barrow, *Flora*, p. 68.

23. F. J. O., see note 21.

24. D. T. in *The Gownsman* (12 October 1929), p. 8.

25. Barrow, *Flora*, p. 68.

26. Script held in the Lord Chamberlain's Files, British Library. See also Luigi Pirandello, *Six Characters in Search of an Author*, transl. Paul Avila Mayer (New York: Studio Duplication Service, 1963).

27. Robert Kee, *Queen* (8 July 1963).

28. *Ibid.*

29. Pat Wallace, *The Tatler* (17 July 1963).

30. Kee, *Queen* (8 July 1963).

31. Gary O'Connor, *Ralph Richardson* (London, Sydney, Auckland and Toronto: Hodder and Stoughton, 1982), pp. 112–13.

32. W. J. Lambert, '*Six Characters in Search of an Author*', *The Sunday Times* (July 1963).

33. O'Connor, *Ralph Richardson*, p. 191.

34. Wallace, *The Tatler* (17 July 1963).

35. *The Times* (18 June 1963).

9. Becoming part of national theatre in France and England

1. Sylvie Chevalley, 'Pirandello à la Comédie française', *Comédie française* 71 (1978), p. 35.

2. Patrick Devaux, *La Comédie française* (Paris: Presses Universitaires de France, 1993), p. 86.

3. *Combat* (5 March 1952).
4. See the production script in the Comédie française archives. (The Comédie française keeps excellent records of its productions and is generous in allowing access to researchers.)
5. *Franc-Tireur* (8–9 March 1952).
6. *Combat* (5 March 1952).
7. See note 4.
8. *Ibid.*
9. Georges Neveux, *Arts* (14 March 1952).
10. Patrick Devaux, *La Comédie française*, p. 87.
11. See an undated and unattributed press cutting held with the theatre programme in the Société des Auteurs archives, Paris.
12. Jean Jacques Gautier, *Le Figaro* (12 March 1953).
13. Robert Kemp, *Le Monde* (12 March 1953).
14. Dominique Fernandez, 'Mettre en scène Pirandello', *Comédie française* 72 (1978), p. 12.
15. Dominique Fernandez has written a number of works on Italian literature, including *Le roman italien et la crise de la conscience* (1958) and *L'échec de Pavese* (1967).
16. Luigi Pirandello, *Six personnages en quête d'auteur*, French version by Benjamin Crémieux (Paris: Librairie Gallimard, 1927), p. 54.
17. Dominique Fernandez, 'Mettre en scène Pirandello', p. 12.
18. *Ibid.*
19. *Ibid.*
20. *Ibid.*
21. *Ibid.*, p. 10.
22. *Ibid.*
23. *Ibid.*, p. 11.
24. See note 4.
25. Elisabeth Roudinesco, *Jacques Lacan & Co., A History of Psychoanalysis in France, 1925–1985*, transl., with a Foreword, by Jeffrey Mehlman (London: Free Association Books, 1990).
26. See chapter 8, p. 125.
27. See Nicholas de Jongh, *Politics, Prudery and Perversions* (London: Methuen, 2001), pp. 67–8.
28. *Times Literary Supplement* (26 March 1925), p. 218.

29. *Saturday Sunday Monday* at the National Theatre; *Filumena* at the Lyric; *Ducking Out* first at the Greenwich Theatre, then the Duke of York's; *Accidental Death of an Anarchist* first at the Half Moon Theatre, then Wyndham's Theatre.

30. *Observer* (4 November 1973); *Punch* (14 November 1973).

31. *New Statesman* (November 1973). See also Stefania Taviano and Jennifer Lorch, 'Producing Pirandello in England', *Pirandello Studies* 20 (2000), pp. 18–30.

32. Martin Esslin, '*Filumena*', *Plays and Players* (January 1978), p. 79.

33. See Dario Fo, *Manuale minimo dell'attore* (Turin: Einaudi, 1987), pp. 250–1.

34. Barbara Godard, 'A Translator's Diary' in Sherry Simon (ed.), *Culture in Transit: Translation and the Changing Identities of Quebec Literature* (Montreal: Vehicule Press, 1995), p. 81.

35. Susan Bassnett, 'Pirandello and Translation', *Pirandello Studies*, 20 (2000), p. 16.

36. See Octavio Paz, 'Translation, Literature and Letters', transl. Irene del Corall, in Rainer Schulte and John Biguenet (eds.), *Theories of Translation: An Anthology of Essays from Dryden to Derrida* (Chicago and London: University of Chicago Press, 1992), pp. 152–63, quoted in Bassnett, 'Pirandello and Translation', p. 16.

37. Bassnett, 'Pirandello and Translation', p. 17.

38. Gwenda Pandolfi's text is in the National Theatre Archives.

39. Chris Peachment, 'In search of a stage', *The Times* (18 March 1987).

40. *Ibid.*

41. *Ibid.*

42. Nicholas Wright's adaptation of *Six Characters in Search of an Author*, p. 20. His adaptation was not published and is in the National Theatre Archives.

43. *Ibid*, p. 52.

44. *Ibid*, p. 62.

45. *Ibid*, p. 61.

46. Peachment, 'In search of a stage'; Mark Lawson, 'Middlebrow beater', *Independent* (17 March 1987).

47. John Elsom, *Plays International* (May 1987).

48. Michael Ratcliffe, *Observer* (22 March 1987).

49. John Peter, *Sunday Times* (22 March 1987).

50. Giulia Ajmone Arsan, 'Six Characters in Search of an Author', *The Yearbook of the British Pirandello Society* 7 (1987), p. 35.

51. Katharine Worth, 'Six Characters in Search of an Author', *ibid.*, p. 39.

52. Michael Coveney, 'Six Characters in Search of an Author/Olivier', *Financial Times* (19 March 1987).

10. Making *Six Characters* accessible: Robert Brustein and Richard Jones

1. Stefania Taviano and Jennifer Lorch, 'Producing Pirandello in England', *Pirandello Studies* 20 (2000), p. 25.

2. Robert Brustein won the George Nathan Award in 1962 for Outstanding Drama Critic of the USA.

3. Arthur Holmberg, 'The Art of Theater at Its Highest', *Harvard Magazine* (May–June 1986), p. 30.

4. *Ibid.*, pp. 29–30.

5. Robert Brustein, *The Theatre of Revolt* (London: Methuen 1965), pp. 285 and 316.

6. William Harris, 'Brustein confronts *Six Characters*', *New York Times* (10 July 1988), pp. 5–6.

7. 'So, the part was adapted to fit the company, as Shakespeare usually adapted his own plays to fit his company.' See Harris, 'Brustein confronts *Six Characters*', p. 6.

8. I have looked at two versions of Brustein's text. One relates to the 1984 North American tour and is held in the Harvard Theater Archives. The second is the published version: Luigi Pirandello, *Six Characters in Search of an Author*, in a new adaptation by Robert Brustein and the American Repertory Theatre Company (Chicago: Ivan R. Dee, 1998).

9. See 1984 text, p. 36 and Pirandello, *Six Characters in Search of an Author*, adapted by Brustein, p. 52.

10. Both Niccodemi and Pitoëff cast their respective company's backstage staff in their productions.

11. See Brustein's Introduction to Pirandello, *Six Characters in Search of an Author*, p. 4.

12. *Ibid.*, p. 8.

13. *Ibid.*, p. 5
14. *Ibid.*
15. *Boston Globe* (17 May 1984).
16. Brustein's Introduction to Pirandello, *Six Characters in Search of an Author*, p. 6.
17. 1984 Tour Production of Brustein's *Six Characters in Search of an Author*: Stage Manager's Reports in Harvard Theater Collection.
18. Vic is short for Victoria. For a fuller version of this section on Richard Jones's production, see Jennifer Lorch, *Six Characters Looking for an Author* at the Young Vic, 9 February 2001', *Pirandello Studies* 21 (2001), pp. 119–24.
19. Luigi Pirandello, *Six Characters Looking for an Author*, in a new version by David Harrower (London: Methuen, 2001).
20. Personal communication, in conversation with Richard Jones (16 March 2001).
21. English version by Joseph Machlis of Ruggiero Leoncavallo, *I pagliacci* (USA: G. Schirmer, 1964).
22. See Michael Billington, *Guardian* (16 February 2001).
23. See Taviano and Lorch, 'Producing Pirandello in England', pp. 18–30.
24. See note 20.
25. In conversation Richard Jones told me that he had wanted to have the Characters emerge from a great figure of Pirandello at the typewriter, but a limited budget had prohibited this.
26. See note 20.
27. I am indebted to Patricia West for the insight concerning the manifestations of sexual abuse in Leah Muller's acting.

11. Pushing at the frontiers of theatre: Klaus Michael Grüber and Anatoli Vasiliev

1. See Roberto Alonge, 'Teoria e tecnica della messinscena nella trilogia del teatro nel teatro' in Enzo Lauretta (ed.), *Trilogia del teatro nel teatro: Pirandello e il linguaggio della scena* (Agrigento: Edizioni Centro Nazionale Studi Pirandelliani, 2002), pp. 16–22, for a comparison between the German and Italian understanding of this play.

2. John London, 'Non German drama in the Third Reich' in John London (ed.), *Theatre under the Nazis* (Manchester University Press, 2000), p. 225.

3. *Ibid.*

4. *Ibid.*

5. The archives at the Pirandello Centre in the University of Munich carry details of productions from the early 1950s.

6. See Michael Patterson, *Peter Stein* (Cambridge University Press, 1981), pp. 102–3.

7. See Antonio Attisani (ed.), *Enciclopedia del teatro del '900* (Turin: Feltrinelli, 1980), pp. 221–2, and Don Rubin (ed.), *The World Encyclopedia of Contemporary Theatre: I Europe* (London: Routledge, 1994), p. 366.

8. Bernard Dort, 'Le geste latéral de Klaus Michael Grüber' in Georges Banu and Mark Blezinger (eds.), *Klaus Michael Grüber . . . Il faut que le théâtre passe à travers les larmes* (Paris: Editions du Regard, 1993), p. 25.

9. Angela Winkler, 'Etre simple et fier' in Banu and Blezinger, *Klaus Michael Grüber*, p. 93.

10. *Ibid.*, p. 93.

11. *Ibid.*, p. 94.

12. Franco Quadri, 'Repères pour un itinéraire' in Banu and Blezinger, *Klaus Michael Grüber*, p. 118.

13. Marcel Bozonnet, 'Pareil à un maître de chant' in Banu and Blezinger, *Klaus Michael Grüber*, pp. 80–1.

14. Guy Scarpetta, *Le festival d'Automne de Michel Guy* (Paris: Editions du Regard, 1992), p. 221.

15. Quadri, 'Repères pour un itinéraire' in Banu and Blezinger, *Klaus Michael Grüber*, p. 19.

16. See Georges Banu, 'La fatigue éclairée' in Banu and Blezinger, *Klaus Michael Grüber*, p. 51.

17. Winkler, 'Etre simple et fier' in Banu and Blezinger, *Klaus Michael Grüber*, p. 92.

18. See, for instance, Helmut Schödel, 'Sechs Personen finden einen Autor', *Die Zeit* (27 March 1981), and Roland H. Wiegenstein, 'Doppelte Versuchsanordnung', *Frankfurter Rundschau* (25 March 1981).

19. See Günther Grack, 'Theater als gespenstische Ansalt', *Tagesspiegel* (24 March 1981).

20. Titina Maselli, 'Etre aimé par le théâtre' in Banu and Blezinger, *Klaus Michael Grüber*, p. 141.

21. Schödel, 'Sechs Personen finden einen Autor'.

22. Irene Böhme, 'Lebindige Figuren ohne Leben', *Süddeutsche Zeitung* (23 March 1981).

23. Luc Bondy, 'C'est si dur créer l'illusion, A propos de *Six personnages en quête d'auteur*' in Banu and Blezinger, p. 183.

24. Schödel, 'Sechs Personen finden einen Autor'.

25. *Sender Freies Berlin* (22 March 1981).

26. Georg Hensel, 'Theater gegen das Theater', *Frankfurter Allgemeine Zeitung* (23 March 1981).

27. See Peter Szondi, ed. and transl. Michael Hays, *Theory of the Modern Drama* (Cambridge: Polity Press, 1987), p. 79.

28. Schödel, 'Sechs Personen finden einen Autor'.

29. *Ibid.*

30. Grack, 'Theater als gespenstische Anstalt'.

31. Schödel, 'Sechs Personen finden einen Autor'.

32. Wiegenstein, 'Doppelte Versuchsanordnung'.

33. Schödel, 'Sechs Personen finden einen Autor'.

34. Claudio Vicentini, *Pirandello: Il disagio del teatro* (Venice: Marsilio Editori, 1993), p. 128. See also John Willett, *The Theatre of the Weimar Republic* (New York and London: Holmes & Meier, 1988), chapters 4, 7 and 10.

35. Banu, 'La fatigue éclairée' in Banu and Blezinger, *Klaus Michael Grüber*, pp. 49–52.

36. *Sender Freies Berlin*.

37. Ellen Hammer, 'Vingt ans de confiance' in Banu and Blezinger, *Klaus Michael Grüber*, p. 230.

38. Wiegenstein, 'Doppelte Versuchsanordnung'.

39. Schödel, 'Sechs Personen finden einen Autor'; Böhme, 'Lebindige Figuren ohne Leben'; Bondy, 'C'est si dur créer l'illusion' in Banu and Blezinger, *Klaus Michael Grüber*, p. 184.

40. Banu, 'La fatigue éclairée' in Banu and Blezinger, *Klaus Michael Grüber*, pp. 51–2.

41. *Sender Freies Berlin.*

42. See chapter 2, p. 32 and note 5.

43. Victor Borovsky, 'Russian theatre in Russian context' in Robert Leach and Victor Borovsky (eds.), *A History of Russian Theatre* (Cambridge University Press, 1999), p. 14.

44. *Ibid.*, pp. 13–14.

45. Anatoly Smeliansky, *The Russian Theatre after Stalin* (Cambridge University Press, 1999), p. 144.

46. Anatoli Vassiliev, *Sept ou huit leçons de théâtre* (Paris: P.O.L. éditeur, 1999), p. 145.

47. Smeliansky, *The Russian Theatre after Stalin*, p. 191.

48. *Ibid.*, p. 193.

49. Birgit Beumers, 'The "thaw" and after' in Leach and Borovsky, *A History of Russian Theatre*, p. 380, and Smeliansky, *The Russian Theatre after Stalin*, p. 192. I should like to record my appreciation of Birgit Beumers's generosity in sharing her knowledge of Vasiliev's work and lending me relevant material.

50. Smeliansky, *The Russian Theatre after Stalin*, p. 193.

51. *Ibid.*, p. 193. See also Vassiliev, *Sept ou huit leçons de théâtre*, p. 139, where Vasiliev explains that for him the actor is an empty vessel.

52. Dick McCaw, transcript of Vasiliev's workshop held at the Scottish Academy of Music and Drama, Glasgow, October 1996, on Dostoyevsky's *The Meek One – Krotkaya*, day 2, p. 13. I am grateful to Dr Dick McCaw for sending me his transcriptions of the workshops conducted by Vasiliev in the UK. This transcript and the one of *The Gambler* (see note 70) are now held in the Library of the University of London, Royal Holloway.

53. Ruth Wyneken-Galibin, *Anatolij Wassiljew* (Frankfurt am Main: Fischer Taschenbuch Verlag, 1993), p. 84.

54. Vassiliev, *Sept ou huit leçons de théâtre*, p. 116.

55. McCaw, *The Meek One*, day 1, p. 10.

56. *Ibid.*, day 1, page 3.

57. Vasiliev used a term from chemistry to explain his idea, which the French translator rendered as '*le sas*', and explained in the glossary as 'cette chambre permettant le passage entre deux milieux de pression différente'. See Vassiliev, *Sept ou huit leçons de théâtre*, pp. 58 and 215.

58. McCaw, *The Meek One*, day 1, p. 10.
59. Luigi Pirandello, 'Illustrators, Actors and Translators' in Susan Bassnett and Jennifer Lorch (eds.), *Luigi Pirandello in the Theatre: A Documentary Record* (Chur: Harwood Academic Publishers, 1993), p. 28.
60. Wyneken-Galibin, *Anatolij Wassiljew*, p. 15.
61. Vassiliev, *Sept ou huit leçons de théâtre*, p. 127.
62. *Ibid.*, p. 25.
63. John Freedman, *Moscow Performances* (Amsterdam: Harwood Academic Publishers, 1997), p. 135.
64. Vassiliev, *Sept ou huit leçons de théâtre*, pp. 179 and 127.
65. *Ibid.*, pp. 162–3.
66. McCaw, *The Meek One*, day 2, p. 13.
67. *Ibid.*
68. *Ibid.*
69. *Ibid.*, p. 14.
70. Dick McCaw, transcript of Vasiliev's workshop held at the National Theatre Studio, London, November 1991, on Dostoyevsky's *The Gambler*, day 11, p. 2. See note 52.
71. Wyneken-Galibin, *Anatolij Wassiljew*, pp. 57–8.
72. *Ibid.*, pp. 112–13.
73. 'Gelächter am Abgrund: Vassiljev inszeniert Pirandellos "Sech Personen suchen einen Autor"', *Bühnenbunst* 1 (1988), p. 8.
74. Antonio Alessio, 'Pirandello riciclato: i "Sei personaggi" di Anatoli Vasiliev' in Enzo Lauretta (ed.), *Pirandello e il teatro* (Milan: Mursia, 1993), pp. 223–4.
75. *Ibid.*, p. 224.
76. Programme of *Summerfare, The International Performing Arts Festival of the State University of New York at Purchase*, 10 (1989), 'The Grand Finale July 7–August 6', p. 64.
77. Alessio, 'Pirandello riciclato: i "Sei personaggi di Anatoli Vasiliev', p. 227.

12. A brief look at *Six Characters* in other media

1. Antonio Alessio, *Pirandello pittore* (Agrigento: Edizioni del Centro Nazionale di Studi Pirandelliani, 1984).

2. For analyses in English of this novel, see Nina Davinci Nichols and Jana O'Keefe Bazzoni, *Pirandello & Film* (Lincoln and London: University of Nebraska Press, 1995), pp. 3–18, and Ann Hallamore Caesar, *Characters and Authors in Luigi Pirandello* (Oxford: Clarendon Press, 1998), pp. 219–30.

3. See Francesco Càllari, *Pirandello e il cinema* (Venice: Marsilio Editori, 1991), p. 10.

4. 'Every descriptive or narrative prop should be abolished on stage.' Luigi Pirandello in 'L'azione parlata' in *L'umorismo e altri saggi*, ed. Enrico Ghidenti (Florence: Giunti, 1994), p. 314. See also Susan Bassnett and Jennifer Lorch (eds.), *Luigi Pirandello in the Theatre: A Documentary Record* (Chur: Harwood Academic Publishers, 1993), p. 20.

5. See Davinci Nichols and O'Keefe Bazzoni, *Pirandello & Film*.

6. *Ibid.*, p. 86.

7. Càllari, *Pirandello e il cinema*, p. 126.

8. See Càllari's analysis of all the films connected with Pirandello's works in *ibid.*, pp. 284–435.

9. This televised version was transmitted by BBC2 on 12 December 1992.

10. There is a version on CD of the 1990 revival: New World 80454-2.

11. Olga Ragusa, *Pirandello: An Approach to His Theatre* (Edinburgh University Press, 1980), p. 151.

12. *New York Times* (19 February 1960). The opera was completed in 1956 and was performed by the New York City Opera in its 1958–9 and 1959–60 seasons.

Conclusion

1. See Ilona Fried, 'Exorcism: An Extraordinary Performance of *Six Characters in Search of an Author* in Hungary', *The Yearbook of the British Pirandello Society* 8 and 9 (1988–9), pp. 107–12.

2. Critics compared the Théâtre de la Ville to a factory and a hangar: Jean Dutourd summed it up as 'une pure horreur' (*France Soir*, 19 December 1968).

3. Nina Davinci Nichols and Jana O'Keefe Bazzoni, *Pirandello & Film* (Lincoln and London: University of Nebraska Press, 1995), p. 163.

4. *Ibid.*, p. 67.

5. *Ibid.*, pp. 169–70.

6. Richard Jones told me that he had put illustrations from Pitoëff's production on the walls of the dressing rooms, that he had some knowledge of Grüber's production, and that he knew of Bill Bryden's 1992 televised version for the BBC. He had not seen Vasiliev's production.

SELECT BIBLIOGRAPHY

Note: For reasons of space, newspaper reviews are cited only in the notes.

Aguirre d'Amico, M. L., *Vivere con Pirandello* (Milan: Mondadori, 1989).

Ajmone Arsan, Giulia, 'Six Characters in Search of an Author', *The Yearbook of the British Pirandello Society* 7 (1987), pp. 32–5.

Alessio, Antonio, *Pirandello pittore* (Agrigento: Edizioni del Centro Nazionale di Studi Pirandelliani, 1984).

Alessio, Antonio, 'Pirandello riciclato: i "Sei personaggi" di Anatoli Vasiliev' in Enzo Lauretta (ed.), *Pirandello e il teatro* (Milan: Mursia, 1993).

Alonge, Roberto, *Immagini del teatro contemporaneo* (Naples: Guida Editori, 1977).

Alonge, Roberto, 'Le messinscene dei *Sei personaggi in cerca d'autore*' in Enzo Lauretta (ed.), *Testo e messa in scena in Pirandello* (Rome: La Nuova Italia Scientifica, 1986), pp. 63–84.

Alonge, Roberto, 'Teoria e tecnica della messinscena nella trilogia del teatro nel teatro' in Enzo Lauretta (ed.), *Trilogia del teatro nel teatro: Pirandello e il linguaggio della scena* (Agrigento: Edizioni Centro Nazionale Studi Pirandelliani, 2002), pp. 13–26.

Alvaro, Corrado, *Cronache e scritti teatrali* (Rome: Abete, 1976).

Apollonio, Mario, *Prologo ai 'Sei personaggi'*, *Quaderni dell'Istituto di Studi pirandelliani* I (Rome: Bulzoni, 1973).

Artaud, Antonin, *Oeuvres complètes* II (Paris: Librairie Gallimard, 1961).

Attisani, Antonio (ed.), *Enciclopedia del teatro del '900* (Turin: Feltrinelli, 1980).

Audino, Antonio, *La compagnia dei Giovani* (Florence: Editalia, 1995).

Bandettini, Anna, Fabio Battistini, Marina de Stasi, Maria Grazia Gregori and Mario Sculatti, *Pirandello l'uomo lo scrittore il teatrante* (Milan: Mazzotta, 1987).

Banu, Georges and Mark Blezinger (eds.), *Klaus Michael Grüber . . . Il faut que le théâtre passe à travers les larmes* (Paris: Editions du Regard, 1993).

Barbina, Alfredo (ed.), 'Lettere d'amore da Luigi ad Antonietta', *Ariel* 3 (1986).

Barrow, Kenneth, *Flora, An Appreciation of the Life and Work of Dame Flora Robson* (London: William Heinemann, 1981).

Bassnett, Susan and Jennifer Lorch, *Luigi Pirandello in the Theatre: A Documentary Record* (Chur: Harwood Academic Publishers, 1993).

Bassnett, Susan, 'Pirandello and Translation', *Pirandello Studies* 20 (2000), pp. 9–17.

Beumers, Birgit, 'The "thaw" and after' in Robert Leach and Victor Borovsky (eds.), *A History of Russian Theatre* (Cambridge University Press, 1999).

Borovsky, Victor, 'Russian theatre in Russian context' in Robert Leach and Victor Borovsky (eds.), *A History of Russian Theatre* (Cambridge University Press, 1999).

Bradby, David, *Beckett: Waiting for Godot* (Cambridge University Press, 2001).

Braun, Edward, *The Director and the Stage* (London: Methuen, 1982).

Brustein, Robert, *The Theatre of Revolt* (London: Methuen, 1965).

Büdel, Oscar, 'Pirandello sulla scena tedesca' in Sandro d'Amico (ed.), *Pirandello ieri e oggi, Quaderni del Piccolo Teatro* 1 (1961), pp. 99–124.

Bürger, Peter, *Theory of the Avant-garde*, transl. M. Shaw (Minneapolis: University of Minnesota Press, 1984).

Caesar, Ann Hallamore, *Characters and Authors in Luigi Pirandello* (Oxford: Clarendon Press, 1998).

Càllari, Francesco, *Pirandello e il cinema* (Venice: Marsilio Editori, 1991).

Chevalley, Sylvie, 'Pirandello à la Comédie française', *Comédie française*, 71 (1978), pp. 35–7.

Colli, Giacomo, 'L'educazione teatrale di Orazio Costa' in Paola Quarenghi and Aida de Lellis (eds.), *Orazio Costa, pedagogia e didattica del teatro* (Rome: Università di Roma, 'La Sapienza', 1987–8).

Cometa, Michele, *Il teatro di Pirandello in Germania* (Palermo: Edizioni Novecento, 1986).

Corsinovi, G., '*Questa sera si recita a soggetto*': il testo. Tra progettazione vitalistica e partitura musicale' in Enzo Lauretta (ed.), *Testo e messa in scena in Pirandello* (Rome: La Nuova Italia Scientifica, 1986), pp. 105–32.

Corsinovi, G. 'Questa sera si recita a soggetto: Dalla "rappresentazione scenica" alla "creazione scenica"' in J. C. Barnes and S. Milioto (eds.), Le due trilogie pirandelliani (Palermo: Palumbo, 1992), pp. 63–70.

Costa, Orazio, 'La regia teatrale', Rivista italiana del dramma 3, 2 (1939), pp. 189–99.

Culler, Jonathan, Structuralist Poetics (London and Henley: Routledge & Kegan Paul, 1975).

D'Amico, Alessandro and Alessandro Tinterri, Pirandello capocomico (Palermo: Sellerio, 1987).

D'Amico, Silvio (ed.), Storia del teatro italiano (Milan: Bompiani, 1936).

D'Amico, Silvio, Cronache del teatro (Bari: Laterza, 1963).

Davico Bonino, Guido, Romolo Valli, ritratto d'attore (Milan: Il Saggiatore, 1983).

Davinci Nichols, Nina and Jana O'Keefe Bazzoni, Pirandello & Film (Lincoln and London: University of Nebraska Press, 1995).

De Grazia, Victoria, The Culture of Consent: Mass Organization of Leisure in Fascist Italy (Cambridge University Press, 1981).

De Jongh, Nicholas, Politics, Prudery and Perversions: The Censoring of the English Stage 1901–1968 (London: Methuen, 2001).

Del Ministro, Maurizio, Pirandello: Scena personaggio film (Rome: Bulzoni, 1980).

Devaux, Patrick, La Comédie française (Paris: Presses Universitaires de France, 1993).

Draper, Hal (transl.), The Complete Poems of Heinrich Heine (Boston: Suhrkramp/Insel, 1982).

Dunbar, Janet, Flora Robson (London, Toronto, Wellington and Sydney: George G. Harrap & Co. Ltd, 1960).

Fernandez, Dominique, 'Mettre en scène Pirandello', Comédie française 72 (1978), pp. 9–12.

Firth, Felicity (transl.), 'Six Characters in Search of an Author' in Luigi Pirandello, Collected Plays II (London and New York: John Calder and Riverrun Press, 1988), pp. 1–68.

Firth, Felicity, Pirandello in Performance (Cambridge and Alexandria, VA: Chadwyck-Healey, 1990).

Fo, Dario, Manuale minimo dell'attore (Turin: Einaudi, 1987).

Forsyth, James, Tyrone Guthrie (London: Hamish Hamilton, 1976).

Frabetti, Anna, 'Pirandello a Parigi. L'interpretazione del teatro pirandelliano in Francia nei primi anni venti', *Filologia critica* 24, 3 (September–December 1999), pp. 375–426.

Freedman, John, *Moscow Performances* (Amsterdam: Harwood Academic Publishers, 1997).

Fried, Ilona, 'Exorcism: An Extraordinary Performance of Six Characters in Search of an Author in Hungary', *The Yearbook of the British Pirandello Society* 8 and 9 (1988–9), pp. 107–12.

Gielgud, John, *Early Stages* (London: Macmillan & Co. Ltd, 1939).

Gielgud, John, *An Actor and His Time* (London: Sidgwick & Jackson, 1979).

Gillet, L., 'Deux pièces étrangères à Paris' in *Revue des Deux Mondes* (1 May 1923).

Giudice, Gaspare, *Pirandello* (Turin: Unione Tipografica-Unione Torinese, 1963).

Guthrie, Tyrone, *A Life in the Theatre* (London: Hamish Hamilton, 1960).

Hirst, David L., *Giorgio Strehler* (Cambridge University Press, 1993).

Holmberg, Arthur, 'The Art of Theater at Its Highest', *Harvard Magazine* (May–June 1986), pp. 24–31.

Hort, Jean, *La vie héroïque des Pitoëff* (Geneva: Pierre Cailler, 1966).

Hutchens, John, 'Spring Reckoning', *Theatre Arts Monthly* 16, 6 (1931).

Illiano, Antonio, 'The New York Premiere of Six Characters: A Note with Excerpts from Reviews', *Romance Notes* 13 (1971), pp. 18–25.

Jomaron, Jacqueline, *Georges Pitoëff, metteur en scène* (Lausanne: l'Age d'Homme, 1979).

Komisarjevsky, Theodore, *Myself and the Theatre* (London: William Heinemann Ltd, 1929).

Lamb, Stephen, 'Staging Change, Changing the Stage in the Weimar Republic', *Pirandello Studies* 19 (1999), pp. 30–40.

Lauretta, Enzo (ed.), *Testo e messa in scena in Pirandello* (Rome: La Nuova Italia Scientifica, 1986).

Leach, Robert and Victor Boronsky, *A History of Russian Theatre* (Cambridge University Press, 1999).

Leiter, Samuel, *Encyclopedia of the New York Stage 1920–1930* (Westport, CT, and London, England: Greenwood Press, 1985).

Lelièvre, Renée, *Le théâtre dramatique italien en France (1850–1940)* (Paris: Armand Colin, 1959).

Lenormand, H.-R., *Les Pitoëff, souvenirs* (Paris: Odette Lieutier, 1943).

Leoncavallo, Ruggiero, *I pagliacci*, transl. Joseph Machlis (USA.: G. Schirmer, 1964).

London, John (ed.), *Theatre under the Nazis* (Manchester University Press, 2000).

Lopez, Guido (ed.), *La 'cesta' di Ruggero Ruggeri* (Milan: De Carlo Editore, 1980).

Lopez, Sabatino, *Dal carteggio di Virgilio Talli* (Milan: Treves, 1931).

Lorch, Jennifer, 'The 1925 text of *Sei personaggi in cerca d'autore* and Pitoëff's production of 1923', *The Yearbook of the British Pirandello Society* 2 (1982), pp. 32–47.

Lorch, Jennifer, '*Six Characters Looking for an Author* at the Young Vic, 9 February 2001', *Pirandello Studies* 21 (2001), pp. 119–24.

Lorch, Jennifer, 'Pirandello for the new Italy: Orazio Costa's productions of *Sei personaggi in cerca d'autore*' in George Talbot and Pamela Williams (eds.), *Essays in Italian Literature and History in Honour of Doug Thompson* (Dublin: Four Courts Press Ltd, 2002).

Lorch, Jennifer, 'Brock Pemberton's Production of *Six Characters in Search of an Author*' in Simon Gilson, Katherine Keen and Brian Richardson (eds.), *Theatre, Opera and Performance in Italy from the Fifteenth Century to the Present: Essays in Honour of Richard Andrews* (Leeds: Society for Italian Studies, 2004).

McCarthy, Desmond, *Drama* (London and New York: 1948).

Mantle, Burns, *The Best Plays of 1922–1923 and the Year Book of the Drama in America* (New York: Dodd, Mead and Company, 1934).

Marinetti, F. T., *Teatro* II (Rome: Vito Bianco Editore, 1960).

Marshall, Norman, *The Other Theatre* (London: John Lehmann, 1947).

May, Frederick, 'Alfred Wareing and the Production of Pirandello in the West Riding', *The University of Leeds Review* (June 1966).

Mazzocchi, Federica and Alberto Bentoglio, *Giorgio Strehler e il suo teatro* (Rome: Bulzoni, 1997).

Møestrup, J., 'Le correzioni ai *Sei personaggi* e il Castelvetro di Pirandello', *Revue Romane* 2 (1967), pp. 121–35.

Nardelli, Federico Vittore, *Vita segreta di Pirandello* (Rome: Vito Bianco Editore, 1962).

Niccodemi, Dario, *Tempo passato* (Milan: Treves, 1929).

O'Connor, Gary, *Ralph Richardson* (London, Sydney, Auckland and Toronto: Hodder and Stoughton, 1982).

Patterson, Michael, *The Revolution in German Theatre, 1900–1933* (Boston, London and Henley: Routledge & Kegan Paul, 1981).

Perrelli, Franco, 'Colloqui con Orazio Costa', *Il castello di Elsinore* 38 (2000), pp. 127–34.

Pirandello, Luigi, *Three Plays* (London and Toronto: J. M. Dent & Sons Ltd, 1923.

Pirandello, Luigi, 'En confidence', *Le Temps* (20 July 1925).

Pirandello, Luigi, *Six personnages en quête d'auteur*, French version by Benjamin Crémieux (Paris: Librairie Gallimard, 1927).

Pirandello, Luigi (transl. Paul Avila Mayer), *Six Characters in Search of an Author* (New York: Studio Duplication Service, 1963).

Pirandello, Luigi, 'Discorso al Convegno "Volta" sul teatro drammatico' in *Saggi, Poesie, Scritti varii*, ed. Manlio Lo Vecchio-Musti (Milan: Mondadori, 1973), pp. 1036–42.

Pirandello, Luigi, *Saggi, Poesie, Scritti varii*, ed. Manlio Lo Vecchio-Musti (Milan: Mondadori, 1973).

Pirandello, Luigi, *Théâtre complet*, ed. Paul Renucci (Paris: Librairie Gallimard, 1977).

Pirandello, Luigi, *Epistolario familiare giovanile* , ed. Elio Providenti (Florence: Le Monnier, 1986).

Pirandello, Luigi, *Collected Plays* II (London and New York: John Calder and Riverrun Press, 1988).

Pirandello, Luigi, *Six Characters in Search of an Author*, new adaptation by Robert Brustein and the American Repertory Theater Company (Chicago: Ivan R. Dee, 1988).

Pirandello, Luigi, *Maschere nude* II, ed. Alessandro d'Amico (Milan: Mondadori, 1993).

Pirandello, Luigi, *Sei personaggi in cerca d'autore*, ed. Guido Davico Bonino (Turin: Einaudi, 1993).

Pirandello, Luigi, *Lettere giovanili da Palermo e da Roma*, ed. Elio Providenti (Rome: Bulzoni, 1994).

Pirandello, Luigi, *L'umorismo e altri saggi*, ed. Enrico Ghidenti (Florence: Giunti, 1994).

Pirandello, Luigi, *Lettere a Marta Abba*, ed. Benito Ortolani (Milan: Mondadori, 1995).

Pirandello, Luigi, *Six Characters Looking for an Author*, new version by David Harrower (London: Methuen, 2001).

Pirrotta, Nino and Povoledo, Elena, *Music and Theatre from Poliziano to Monteverdi*, transl. Karen Eales (Cambridge University Press, 1982).

Pitoëff, Georges, *Notre Théâtre*, textes et documents réunis par J. de Rigault (Paris: Librairie Bonaparte, 1949).

Puppa, Paolo, *Dalle parti di Pirandello* (Rome: Bulzoni, 1987).

Ragusa, Olga, *Pirandello: An Approach to His Theatre* (Edinburgh University Press, 1980).

Reinhardt, Max, *Ausgewählte Briefe, Reden, Schriften und Szenen aus Regiebüchern* (Vienna: Prochner Verlag, 1963).

Roudinesco, Elisabeth, *Jacques Lacan & Co., A History of Psychoanalysis in France, 1925–1985*, transl., with a Foreword, Jeffrey Mehlman (London: Free Association Books, 1990).

Rubin, Don (ed.), *The World Encyclopedia of Contemporary Theatre: I Europe* (London: Routledge, 1994).

Scarpetta, Guy, *Le festival d'Automne de Michel Guy* (Paris: Editions du Regard, 1992).

Schächter, Elizabeth, '*Sei personaggi in cerca d'autore* in a new version by Franco Zeffirelli and Luigi Vanzi', *The Yearbook of the Society for Pirandello Studies* 12 (1992), pp. 86–7.

Schulte, Rainer and John Biguenet (eds.), *Theories of Translation: An Anthology of Essays from Dryden to Derrida* (Chicago and London: University of Chicago Press, 1992).

Simon, Sherry (ed.), *Culture in Transit: Translation and the Changing Identities of Quebec Literature* (Montreal: Vehicule Press, 1995).

Slonim, Marc, *Russian Theatre: From the Empire to the Soviets* (London: Methuen, 1963).

Smeliansky, Anatoly, *The Russian Theatre after Stalin* (Cambridge University Press, 1999).

Strehler, Giorgio (ed.), *1947–1958 Piccolo Teatro* (Milan: Moneta, 1958).

Szondi, Peter, *Theory of the Modern Drama*, ed. and transl. Michael Hays (Cambridge: Polity Press, 1987).

Tamberlani, Carlo, *Pirandello 'nel teatro che c'era', Quaderni dell'Istituto di Studi pirandelliani* III (Rome: Bulzoni, 1982).

Taviani, Ferdinando, '"Sei personaggi": due interviste in una al primo padre', *Teatro e Storia* 7, 2 (1992).

Taviano, Stefania and Jennifer Lorch, 'Producing Pirandello in England', *Pirandello Studies* 20 (2000), pp. 18–30.

Tessari, Roberto, 'Il sacrificio della donna ignuda' in Roberto Alonge and Roberto Tessari, *Immagini del teatro contemporaneo* (Naples: Guida Editore, 1977).

Tinterri, Alessandro, 'Two Flights of Steps and a Stage Direction: Pirandello's Staging of *Six Characters in Search of an Author* in 1925', *The Yearbook of the British Pirandello Society* 3 (1983), pp. 33–7.

Vassiliev, Anatoli, *Sept ou huit leçons de théâtre* (Paris: P.O.L. éditeur, 1999).

Venè, Gian Franco, *Pirandello fascista* (Venice: Marsilio Editori, 1981).

Vicentini, Claudio, *Pirandello: Il disagio del teatro* (Venice: Marsilio Editori, 1993).

Willett, John, *The Theatre of the Weimar Republic* (New York and London: Holmes & Meier, 1988).

Williams, Edward and Emmanuela Tandello, 'Interview with Zeffirelli', *The Yearbook of the Society for Pirandello Studies* 12 (1992), pp. 79–81.

Worth, Katharine, 'Six Characters in Search of an Author', *The Yearbook of the British Pirandello Society* 7 (1987), pp. 36–44.

Wyneken-Galibin, Ruth, *Anatolij Wassiljew* (Frankfurt am Main: Fischer Taschenbuch Verlag, 1993).

Other materials

Lord Chamberlain's Files, British Library.

Dick McCaw transcripts in Library of University of London, Royal Holloway.

Video of Giorgio de Lullo's production: VideoRai VRB 2093.

Ms. of Georges Pitoëff's script for the 1923 performance in Paris.

CD of the 1990 revival of Hugo Weisgall's opera *Six Characters in Search of an Author*: New World 80454–2.

INDEX